Real Estate *and the* Financial Crisis

How Turmoil in the Capital Markets Is Restructuring Real Estate Finance

Anthony Downs

Urban Land Institute

Recommended bibliographic listing:
Downs, Anthony. *Real Estate and the Financial Crisis: How Turmoil in the Capital Markets Is Restructuring Real Estate Finance.* Washington, D.C.: Urban Land Institute, 2009.

Urban Land Institute
1025 Thomas Jefferson Street, N.W.
Washington, D.C. 20007-5201

ULI Catalog Number: C80
ISBN: 978-0-87420-119-2

10 9 8 7 6 5 4 3 2 1
Printed in the United States of America.

About the Urban Land Institute

The mission of the Urban Land Institute is to provide leadership in the responsible use of land and in creating and sustaining thriving communities worldwide. ULI is committed to

- Bringing together leaders from across the fields of real estate and land use policy to exchange best practices and serve community needs;
- Fostering collaboration within and beyond ULI's membership through mentoring, dialogue, and problem solving;
- Exploring issues of urbanization, conservation, regeneration, land use, capital formation, and sustainable development;
- Advancing land use policies and design practices that respect the uniqueness of both built and natural environments;
- Sharing knowledge through education, applied research, publishing, and electronic media; and
- Sustaining a diverse global network of local practice and advisory efforts that address current and future challenges.

Established in 1936, the Institute today has more than 38,000 members worldwide, representing the entire spectrum of the land use and development disciplines. ULI relies heavily on the experience of its members. It is through member involvement and information resources that ULI has been able to set standards of excellence in development practice. The Institute has long been recognized as one of the world's most respected and widely quoted sources of objective information on urban planning, growth, and development.

Project Staff

RACHELLE L. LEVITT
Executive Vice President, Global Information Group
Publisher

DEAN SCHWANKE
Senior Vice President, Publications and Awards

JAMES A. MULLIGAN
Managing Editor

LISE LINGO, PUBLICATIONS PROFESSIONALS LLC
Manuscript Editor

BETSY VANBUSKIRK
Creative Director

BYRON HOLLY
Senior Designer

CRAIG CHAPMAN
Director, Publishing Operations

About the Author

ANTHONY DOWNS IS A SENIOR FELLOW at the Brookings Institution in Washington, D.C., where he has been since 1977. He also was a visiting fellow at the Public Policy Institute of California in San Francisco from July 2004 until February 2005. Brookings is a private, nonprofit research organization specializing in public policy studies. The Public Policy Institute of California is a similar organization specializing in such studies about California. Before 1977, Downs for 18 years was a member and then chairman of Real Estate Research Corporation, a nationwide consulting firm advising private and public decision makers on real estate investment, housing policies, and urban affairs.

He has served as a consultant to many of the nation's largest corporations, to major developers, to dozens of government agencies at local, state, and national levels (including the Department of Housing and Urban Development and the White House), and to many private foundations. President Lyndon Johnson appointed him to the National Commission on Urban Problems in 1967, and HUD Secretary Jack Kemp appointed him to the Advisory Commission on Regulatory Barriers to Affordable Housing in 1989. He is a director or trustee of General Growth Properties and the NAACP Legal and Educational Defense Fund. He was also a past director of the MassMutual Life Insurance Company, Bedford Property Investors, the Urban Land Institute, Essex Property Trust, the National Housing Partnership Foundation, Penton Media Inc., and the Counselors of Real Estate.

Downs received a PhD in economics from Stanford University. He is the author or coauthor of 27 books and over 500 articles. His most famous books are *An Economic Theory of Democracy* (1957), translated into several languages, and *Inside Bureaucracy* (1967). Both are still in print. His most recent books are *Niagara of Capital: How Global Capital Has Transformed Housing and Real Estate Markets* (2007), published by the Urban Land Institute; *Still Stuck in Traffic* (2004) and *Growth Management and Affordable Housing: Do They Conflict?* (editor, 2004) from Brookings; *Costs of Sprawl 2000* (coauthor, 2002) from the Transit Cooperative Research Board; and *New Visions for Metropolitan America* (1994) from Brookings and the Lincoln Institute.

Downs is a frequent speaker on real estate economics, housing, transportation, smart growth, urban policies, and other topics. He has made over 1,000 speeches to hundreds of organizations of all types, and is well-known for using humor to enliven his subjects.

Preface

IRONICALLY, TODAY'S FINANCIAL CRISIS and acute shortage of credit result directly from the massive inflow of financial capital into U.S. real estate and other markets after the stock market crash of 2000, as described in my 2007 ULI book, *Niagara of Capital*. How such a torrent of money could lead to such a drought of lending and subsequent financial crisis is the subject of this book.

This book was very difficult to write. Since I began writing in May 2008, the economic situation has fluctuated dramatically, intensified by presidential primaries and the McCain and Obama campaigns. New terms such as *subprime, credit freeze,* and *toxic assets* entered the vernacular. Credit default swaps, monetizing debt, and mortgage-backed securities became hot topics. A new Niagara of names, abbreviations, initials, and acronyms flooded the news: IndyMac, Bear Stearns, Lehman Brothers, FDIC, AIG, TARP, the F-words (Fed, Fannie, and Freddie), and the B-words (bankruptcies, bonuses, bailouts), not to mention talk in triple-digit trillions. Defaults, foreclosures, layoffs, and rising unemployment hit closer and closer to home.

Plans were announced, policies were debated, Wall Street was vilified. With markets plummeting, who could predict what would happen next? As soon as I finished one chapter, cascading events made it obsolete or incomplete. So I would have to rewrite that chapter, revise others, and start new ones. I hope the velocity has by now slowed enough that what I have written will be relevant for a considerable time.

Having been active in ULI for decades gives me the advantage of many splendid friends who understand real estate and share their wisdom. Their integrity and stature inspire me. Their ideas and assistance have been invaluable in helping me grapple with the difficult issues facing our nation and the world. I am especially grateful to Peter Linneman, whose excellent suggestions stimulated my thinking; to Steve Wechsler, who knows more about real estate investment trusts than anyone; to Jim Griffin, a fellow economist with exceptional breadth of vision; to Buzz McCoy, whose leadership of ULI's real estate finance seminars is so valuable; to Ken Rosen, who foresaw trouble coming down the road before most others; and to Jack Rice, my longtime Minneapolis sponsor and friend.

The Urban Land Institute deserves credit for its willingness to publish controversial books on critical real estate issues, and for the outstanding quality of its professional staff. Dean Schwanke labored with me to shape the many concepts in this volume. I am also grateful to Lise Lingo, who edited my first drafts; Byron Holly, who did the layouts; and Jim Mulligan, who coordinated the production.

Finally, my appreciation goes to my wife, Darian. Her patience with my foibles, her readiness to give me good advice—which I often don't want to hear—and her loving care and consideration are central to my existence.

In all respects, I am a fortunate man.

ANTHONY DOWNS
McLean, Virginia
April 2009

Contents

One   **An Overview of the Financial Crisis**   **2**

Fundamental Factors Underlying the Financial Crisis   2
A Flood of Capital and Rising Real Estate Prices: 2000 through 2002   7
Rapid Credit Expansion and Increasing Risk: 2003 through 2005   15
Complex Securities and Lax Investment Practices: 2005 through Early 2007   19
Housing Slowdown and Growing Loan Defaults: 2006 to Mid-2007   23
Credit Crunch and Financial Crisis: Mid-2007 to 2009   26
Continuing Turmoil   30

Two   **The Financial Crisis and Housing Markets**   **32**

Why So Much Money Went into Housing Markets after 2000   32
The Cyclical Nature of U.S. Housing Production   34
Why What Happens in Housing Markets Greatly Affects the Entire Economy   37
The Housing and Credit Boom from 2000 through 2006   38
The Subprime Mortgage Phenomenon   41
How Subprime Mortgage Problems Caused the Real Estate Credit World to Freeze Up   45
Three Indices for Measuring Home Price Changes   48
An Error Committed by All Three Major Home Price Indices   50
What Has Happened to Home Prices?   53
Regional and Metropolitan-Area Variations in Home Prices and Their Rates of Change   56
What Has Happened to the Stock Prices of U.S. Homebuilders?   59
Some Broader Impacts of Changes in the Organization of Housing Mortgage Markets   60
Conclusion   61

Three   **Subprime Lending and Housing Foreclosures**   **62**

How Many Subprime Mortgages Are There?   62
Where Subprime Mortgage Loans Are Concentrated   63
The Nature of Foreclosures   64
How Foreclosures May Affect State and Local Governments   71
Other Adverse Impacts of Concentrated Foreclosures   72
Some Ameliorating Factors   75
Traumatic Period   75

Four   **The Financial Crisis and Commercial Property Markets**   **76**

Supply and Demand in Commercial Property Space Markets, 1989–2000   76
Effects of the Flood of Capital into Commercial Property Markets after 2000   77
Increasing Use of Financial Derivatives in Commercial Property Markets   82
Contagious Spread of Credit Uncertainty from Housing Markets   84
The Revised Viewpoints of Capital Suppliers on Commercial Property Markets   86
Property Owners' and Borrowers' Responses to Capital Suppliers' New Requirements   88
REIT Share Prices and Private Commercial Property Prices   88
The Decline in CMBS Activities and the Shortage of Lendable Funds in Commercial Property Markets   92
The Dearth of Public Policy Responses to Credit Problems in the Commercial Property Market   94
Unexpected Declines in Private Lenders' Willingness to Make Loans on Commercial Properties   95
In This Financial Standoff, Who Is Going to Blink First?   97

Five **The Basic Instability of U.S. Financial Markets**   **100**

The Expansion of the Financial Sector since 1950   100
Chronic Instability in the Financial Sector   101
Why Has the Financial Sector Been So Unstable?   103
The Inherent Tendency of Self-Interest to Generate Financial Exploitation   103
Minsky's Theory: Long Periods of Prosperity Motivate Investors to Become Overoptimistic and
  Use Too Much Leverage   107
The Complexity of Financial Innovations and the Tight Linkages of Financial Instruments   110
The Importance and Unpredictability of Random Events   111
Does Market Participant Behavior Make Predicting Downward Movements Impossible?   113
The Long-Term Cycle in American Politics   114
Linking the Financial Crisis to Globalization   116
Restricting the Behavior of Financial Firms through Reserve Requirements   118
Conclusion   120

Six **Public Policy Responses to the Financial Crisis**   **122**

The Role of the Federal Reserve in the Financial Crisis   123
Policy Responses to Burgeoning Home Foreclosures   130
Public Policy Responses by the Federal Reserve and Treasury Department   137
Restructuring Federal Financial Entities and Oversight   139

Seven **New Public Policies for Improving the Financial System**   **142**

Mortgage Lending and Securitization   142
Improving Mortgage Securitization   148
Financial Derivatives   149
Commercial Banks   151
Strategies to Address Bank Problems   155
A Shrinking Financial Sector   159
Redirecting Key Housing Policies   161
The Need for a Global Approach   163
Considering Financial Policy Options   164

Eight **Critical Near-Term Financial Questions and Scenarios**   **166**

Basic Problems: Savings, Consumption, and Deficits   166
Critical Economic and Financial Questions   169
Economic Stability   169
Housing Stabilization   172
Capital Market Stabilization   179
Four Scenarios   182

Nine **Long-Run Consequences of the Financial Crisis**   **186**

Impacts of Globalization on Capital Markets   186
Global Policies to Reduce International Financial Crises   187
Greater Financial Regulation   188
Impacts on the Residential Housing Sector   189
Impacts on the Commercial Property Sector   193
Changing Public and Private Roles in the American Economy   199
A New Financial Era   201

Real Estate *and the* Financial Crisis

An Overview of
the Financial Crisis

THE GREAT REAL ESTATE CREDIT CRUNCH and financial crisis of 2007–09 resulted from several quite different causes that interacted in surprising ways. The results of those interactions transformed a massive surplus of lendable funds that arose in real estate markets from 2000 to 2005 into an acute shortage of such funds in 2007 and after. That paradoxical outcome happened because the owners of those funds refused to keep investing them. Their refusal caused turmoil in the real estate and debt markets, freezing most transactions therein for well over a year. The chronological overview in this chapter summarizes what happened, when it happened, how it happened, and why. The implications of these events are dealt with in later chapters.

This overview consists of five sections that describe specific factors or actions that took place during a certain time period. The first section sets forth many fundamental factors underlying the initial massive flow of financial capital into real estate markets. These elements came into play during a decades-long period up to and including the stock market crash of 2000. The next four sections cover factors or actions during specific periods between that stock market crash, after which the initial flow of capital into real estate markets really surged, and early 2009, when the credit crunch and financial crisis was still in force. Most of these elements consisted of processes that took place over time, rather than single events that occurred on a given date. Hence, in most cases, several such elements overlapped in a single time period, occurred concurrently, or occurred in a slightly different order from how they are presented here. Nevertheless, grouping these elements into the specific time periods provides as clear a chronological description of what happened as can be created, given the overlapping and often ambiguous nature of the elements involved.

Fundamental Factors Underlying the Financial Crisis

Nine principal factors that occurred before and during 2000 set the stage for the credit crunch and financial crisis of 2007–09:

- The increasing speed and ease of financial transactions,
- An influx of low-wage workers into the labor markets,

- The growing U.S. trade deficit,
- A surge in available capital,
- Emerging nations' buildup of large currency reserves,
- A continuous rise in home prices,
- A radical reorganization of real estate lending,
- Tax advantages that favored costly homes, and
- A shift of funds into real estate.

Increasing Speed and Ease of Financial Transactions

Over several decades, major increases occurred in the speed and ease with which financial capital could be moved around the globe from one nation to another. This resulted from four advances:

- Technical improvements such as satellites, computers, and the Internet;
- The development of ways to securitize many real estate loans into large pools, divide those pools into tranches with different return and risk characteristics, and sell them to investors as bonds;
- The creation of new financial entities that were not carried on the balance sheets of major financial institutions and therefore were not inhibited by the extensive regulations that had been devised to control the behavior of banks and insurance companies; and
- The reduction of tariff and other barriers to the movement of money among nations.

Low-Wage Workers Entering Labor Markets

Also over several decades, millions of low-wage workers in China and India, as well as in eastern European and other developing nations, entered the world's industrial labor markets. These workers constituted a significant percentage increase—probably at least 20 percent and perhaps much more—in the global supply of trained industrial workers. That increase held industrial wages low throughout the world. Low wages in turn prevented manufacturing firms everywhere from raising prices, which checked inflationary price movements and even threatened deflationary pressures on some economies (such as that of Japan). The entry of China into the World Trade Organization in 2001 increased the influence of low-wage Chinese workers in world markets. So did the expiration of the Agreement on Textiles and Clothing on January 1, 2005, which greatly reduced the limits on Chinese production and export of clothing and textile goods.

Growing U.S. Trade Deficit

The American foreign trade deficit with the rest of the world increased sharply after 1997, flooding the world with U.S. dollars in payment for America's imports. Many firms and nations receiving those dollars tended to spend them in the United States for securities, goods, and services.

Surge in Available Capital

For many disparate reasons, a massive generation of financial capital emerged around the world after 2000, looking for some place to invest in, mainly outside the economies that generated most of that capital. The reasons for and effects of this surge in financial capital are examined in depth in my earlier book, *Niagara of Capital*, also published by the Urban Land Institute. This torrent of capital originated in seven sources:

- Rising oil prices, profits, and capital accumulation among oil-producing nations;
- The entry into capitalistic markets of thousands of newly competitive firms in Eastern Europe that had formerly been controlled by communist or Soviet-leaning governments;
- High profits among U.S. business firms, owing to technological improvements and competition from low-wage workers in Asia that kept U.S. wages low while the U.S. economy was booming;
- The "yen carry trade," in which entrepreneurs borrowed capital at depressed interest rates in Japan and invested it in higher-paying alternative uses elsewhere;
- Aging populations in Japan and Western Europe, which induced large-scale savings by pension funds to prepare for future liabilities when more workers would retire; and
- The desire of many profit-making firms in developed nations to shift capital out of their factories or offices into uses that were more profitable; and
- China's huge export trade to the United States, which generated large profits in dollars that China invested in U.S. Treasury securities and other American assets.

Many of these sources had much more financial capital to invest than they thought was wise to focus within their own economies, so they began seeking investments abroad.

Emerging Nations' Buildup of Large Currency Reserves

After the Asian credit crisis in 1997–98, several Asian nations that had suffered devastating recessions when they were suddenly forced to devalue their currencies decided to avoid that possibility in the future by building up huge foreign currency reserves. Some, like China, did this by holding the trading value of their own currencies below their true market value to encourage more net exports. Martin Wolf's excellent recent book, *Fixing Global Finance*, describes this process in detail. China did not suffer from a recession, but its leaders determined to avoid any in the future. As a result, China alone had a foreign currency reserve of $1.2 trillion by early 2007; Japan had $900 billion, and Taiwan, South Korea, and India had more than $200 billion each. Wolf also concluded that

> The [U.S.] current account deficit that absorbs (or offsets) the desired excess savings of the rest of the world will emerge naturally. But to achieve this, the level of domestic demand within the United States must exceed the level of output consistent with the internal balance by a large margin [as it did from 2000 to 2007].[1]

These reserves were an important part of the capital that enabled the United States to run large-scale balance-of-payments deficits by importing much more than it exported, and that helped drive up the prices of real properties around the world.

Continuously Rising Home Prices

From 1968, when the National Association of Realtors started recording median home prices, until 2006, the median sale price of existing single-family homes in current dollars, in the

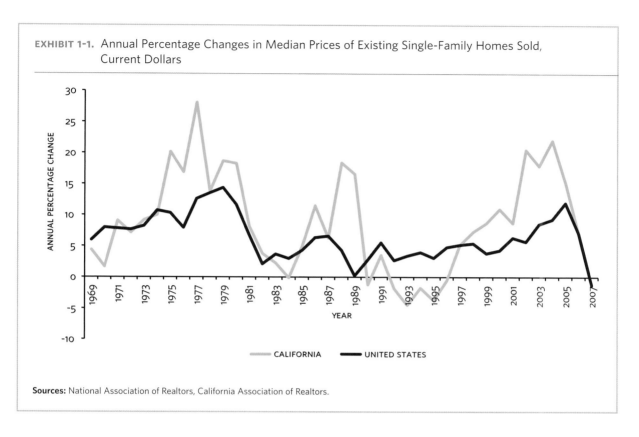

EXHIBIT 1-1. Annual Percentage Changes in Median Prices of Existing Single-Family Homes Sold, Current Dollars

Sources: National Association of Realtors, California Association of Realtors.

United States as a whole, rose continuously from year to year. This is shown in exhibit 1-1. Home prices did not rise uninterruptedly in all regions of the country during those 38 years. For example, median prices fell sharply in Texas in the late 1980s, when oil prices declined and most of the major banks in the state went bankrupt. Similarly, median prices of existing homes sold fell in California during that state's recession in the early 1990s. Nevertheless, the uninterrupted record of increasing home prices at the national level helped convince most American households, real estate agents, mortgage lenders, and homebuilders that housing prices would keep rising, no matter what. This conviction formed the foundation for a widespread belief that investing in homeownership would always be profitable and therefore superior to investing in stocks and bonds or other assets, even when home prices soared much faster than household incomes.

Radical Reorganization of Real Estate Lending

A radical reorganization occurred in the real estate lending processes used by commercial banks and many insurance companies after the major changes brought about by banking deregulation in the 1990s. Before this deregulation, most commercial banks and insurance companies had made mortgage loans against real properties, and each lending institution had held all mortgages it made until such loans matured or were repaid. They had done so in part because bank and savings and loan lenders were obliged to hold substantial financial reserves against such loans. But overbuilding in the 1980s caused the real estate earnings of commercial banks to decline sharply from 1989 through 1991 because so many borrowers defaulted on property loans and property values fell. To improve banks' profit prospects, Congress changed banking regulations in the Financial Services Modernization Act of 1999. This law allowed the creation of bank holding companies that were empowered to set up new, affiliated organizations that were not carried on the bank's balance sheets. Those new organizations were largely unregulated and thus could make loans without having to hold reserves against them. This change enabled banks to increase their profitability by charging large fees when their unregulated new divisions made real estate–related loans. This they did, packaging many such loans together in the form of securities similar to bonds, selling those securities to investors, and then using the funds thus raised to make another set of real estate loans and repeat the process.

Such loans were especially critical to the profits made by commercial banks after 2000. Intense competition among commercial banks and other mortgage lenders, arising from the huge supply of capital in real estate markets after the stock market crash, had driven interest rates to very low levels. Interest payments on their loans fell well below the earnings that commercial banks thought were essential to their prosperity; hence, they did not want to rely solely on interest payments for income. To become profitable again, they needed both to charge large fees for lending and to repeatedly lend, securitize, recover, and relend their capital over time, rather than holding all mortgages until repayment without recirculating the capital involved.

Thus, the process of real estate lending was transformed from making long-term investments and holding them over the long term to making very short-term investments and distributing them widely to longer-term holders. Banks rapidly unloaded their initial risks from making real estate loans onto any investors that bought those loans in securitized form. As some observers put it, real estate lending by banks was reconfigured from a storage business into a moving business. This radical change also greatly increased the amount of real estate lending that commercial banks could support from a given deposit base—hence it increased their leveraging of debt against their reserves. And it encouraged many capital suppliers who had been unwilling to make real estate loans to start doing so, because they thought the risks involved had been greatly reduced by securitization. That outcome further expanded the total supply of capital entering real estate markets looking for property to buy or lend against.

Tax Advantages Favoring Costly Homes

For decades, the federal government had been encouraging American households to buy homes by providing special tax advantages for homeownership, especially favoring the most costly homes. These benefits are all still in place. Homeowners can deduct their mortgage interest payments and property taxes from their taxable income and can shelter some capital gains from selling each home by rolling the funds over into another home. Profits of up to $250,000 ($500,000 for married couples) on the sale of a home are not taxed.

The deductibility of mortgage interest provides more tax benefit per dollar of interest paid for high-income homeowners than for middle- or low-income ones, thereby encouraging

EXHIBIT 1-2. Major Stock Index Value Changes, 1990–2002

	Dow Jones Industrials Index	S&P 500 Stock Index	NASDAQ Composite Index
Value on January 2, 1990	2,810	360	459
Value at peak in 2000	11,722	1,529	5,048
Value at low point, October 9, 2002	7,286	777	1,114
Percentage rise in value, 1990–peak	317.15	324.72	999.78
Percentage fall in value, peak–low point	-37.84	-49.18	-77.93

the purchase of expensive homes by relatively wealthy households. This bias of government policy favoring owning over renting has been reinforced by advertising, social pressures, and political pressures from the many industries that benefit from greater homeownership. All of them have vigorously promoted "the American dream" of owning one's own home. These groups included homebuilders, real estate agents, mortgage bankers, banks, savings and loan associations, furniture and houseware manufacturers, and even local governments that benefit from higher property taxes. As a result, in the 1990s and after, strong latent demand grew among many of the approximately one-third of American households who were then renters to buy their own homes when the opportunity arose.

Funds Shifting into Real Estate

The worldwide stock market crash in 2000 caused many investors with capital to avoid stocks and bonds and shift their funds into real estate. This was a crucial and immediate cause of the flood of money into real estate markets. All three major U.S. stock indices soared in the 1990s, peaked at different dates in 2000, and then plunged sharply when the Internet stock bubble burst. They kept falling until all reached their low points on October 9, 2002. The magnitudes of their value increases in the 1990s and their declines from 2000 to 2002 are set forth in exhibit 1-2.

A Flood of Capital and Rising Real Estate Prices: 2000 through 2002

The elements described in the preceding subsections initially generated the following major impacts on the world's financial markets, especially real estate markets, from 2000 through about 2002:

- A flood of liquidity in many economies;
- Reduced short-term interest rates;
- A massive flow of capital into real property markets;
- Intense competition among investors and lenders;
- A faster increase in the FTSE NAREIT (National Association of Real Estate Investment Trusts) index than in the major stock indices;

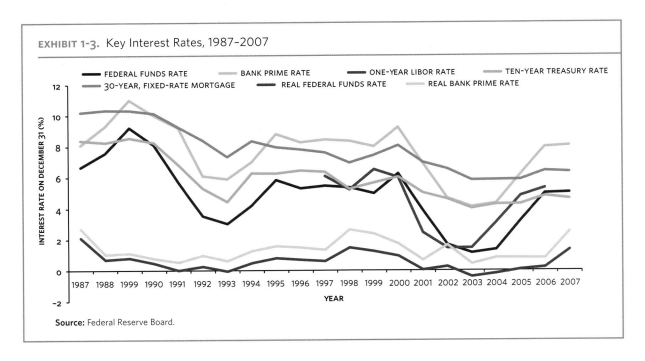

EXHIBIT 1-3. Key Interest Rates, 1987–2007

Legend: FEDERAL FUNDS RATE · BANK PRIME RATE · ONE-YEAR LIBOR RATE · TEN-YEAR TREASURY RATE · 30-YEAR, FIXED-RATE MORTGAGE · REAL FEDERAL FUNDS RATE · REAL BANK PRIME RATE

Y-axis: INTEREST RATE ON DECEMBER 31 (%)
X-axis: YEAR

Source: Federal Reserve Board.

■ A paradigm shift by institutional investors favoring real estate;

■ Sharp increases in real estate prices;

■ A disconnect between property ownership markets and space markets; and

■ A deterioration of underwriting standards.

These impacts are discussed in the following subsections.

Growing Liquidity

Immediately after the stock market crash of 2000, central banks in many developed and some developing nations decided to slash interest rates and flood their economies with more financial liquidity, in order to prevent recessions. These policies were reinforced by added fears of an economic downturn after the 9/11 attacks on the United States. Cutting interest rates and increasing liquidity both strongly enhanced the desirability of real properties as investments for investors and households alike. That happened because the profitability of real properties is greatest when interest rates are low and money can be borrowed easily. In many cases, real interest rates—nominal rates corrected for inflation—became negative.

Ironically, central banks around the world were able to cut interest rates and increase liquidity without causing sharp increases in general inflation. That was possible because the entry of millions of low-wage workers into the globe's industrial labor force kept worldwide manufacturing costs low, thereby checking inflation. Thus, the shifting of many manufacturing jobs from developed nations to low-wage developing nations actually contributed to rapidly rising property prices in world real estate markets when investors moved out of stocks and bonds. That in turn made homeowners in many developed nations like the United States—where homeowners make up about two-thirds of all households—much wealthier, at the very moment when their political leaders were complaining about losing jobs to low-wage foreigners.

Reduced Short-Term Interest Rates

The huge flow of capital from all over the world into real estate markets, plus the actions central banks took to cut interest rates, reduced short-term interest rates to very low levels. This drastically cut the cost of short-term debt and encouraged investors to borrow heavily in short-term markets and use the money so obtained to buy longer-term assets, such as real properties. The U.S. Federal Reserve Bank cut its federal funds rate (in nominal terms) from 6.24 percent in 2000 to 1.13 percent in 2003, as shown in exhibit 1-3. But the rate of inflation as measured by the Consumer Price Index averaged 3.38 percent in 2000 and 2.27 percent in 2003, averaging 2.37 percent from 2001 to 2007. Therefore, the real value—corrected for inflation—of the federal funds rate was very low from 2001 through 2006 and slightly negative in 2003 and 2004. The real bank prime rate was also quite low—under 1 percent from 2001 through 2006, except for 2002, when it was 1.65 percent.

Wharton School economist Peter Linneman said

Investors played the yield curve [by buying] long-term assets [with] short-term liabilities. As [short term] rates began to rise [in 2005 and 2006], they added leverage and moved even longer [in the terms of their assets] and more illiquid to get a bit more yield.[2]

The relevant yield curves are shown in exhibits 1-4 and 1-5, the first in nominal terms and the second with interest rates corrected for inflation—hence in real terms. In both exhibits, the

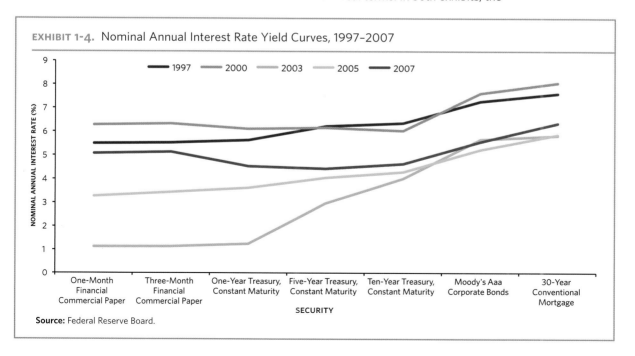

EXHIBIT 1-4. Nominal Annual Interest Rate Yield Curves, 1997–2007

Source: Federal Reserve Board.

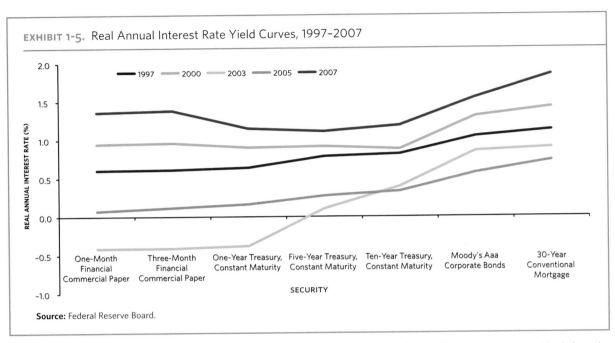

EXHIBIT 1-5. Real Annual Interest Rate Yield Curves, 1997–2007

Source: Federal Reserve Board.

yields are shown for securities of different maturities, with very short-term ones on the left and longer-term ones on the right. In exhibit 1-4, the 2000 yield curve is relatively flat, with all the Treasury securities having similar yields. But by 2003, rates on the shortest-term maturities had fallen much lower than rates on the long-term ones, thanks to the huge flow of capital into real estate (and other) markets and the Federal Reserve's policy of slashing the federal funds rate. This situation encouraged many investors to borrow short and lend long to capture the yield spread. But that left them vulnerable to increases in short-term rates that they could not pay for by matching rates on their long-term securities, which were locked in for longer periods. That is what happened in 2005 and 2007, when short-term rates were much closer to long-term rates. The same thing happened when rates are stated in real terms, as shown in exhibit 1-5.

A Massive Flow of Capital into Real Property Markets

A massive flood of financial capital from all around the world flowed into real property markets in the United States and other developed nations looking for desirable real properties in which to invest. This enormous capital flow created a huge imbalance of financial demand over property supply in real estate markets. Peter Linneman estimated the amount of financial capital flowing into U.S. commercial property markets as shown in exhibit 1-6. Even larger amounts flowed into residential markets, mainly through financing of mortgages used by homebuyers and households that refinanced their homes. One reason is that home mortgage rates declined sharply from 2000 to 2003: a 30-year, fixed-rate mortgage dropped from 8.21 percent to 5.97 percent, as shown in exhibit 1-7. The resulting explosion of mortgage lending can be seen in exhibit 1-8, which is based on data from the Mortgage Bankers Association. In 2003 alone, almost $4 trillion of such mortgages were originated.[3]

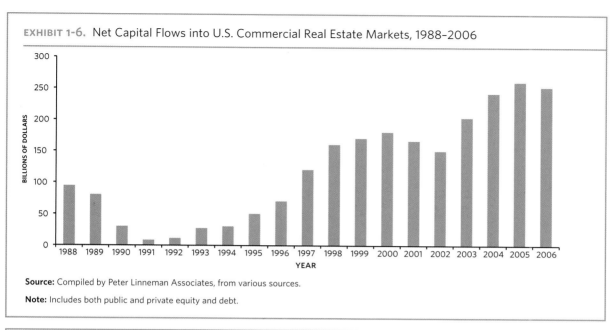

EXHIBIT 1-6. Net Capital Flows into U.S. Commercial Real Estate Markets, 1988–2006

Source: Compiled by Peter Linneman Associates, from various sources.

Note: Includes both public and private equity and debt.

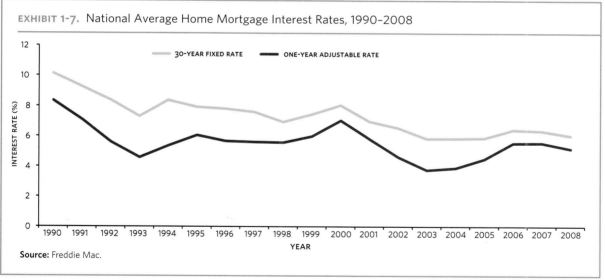

EXHIBIT 1-7. National Average Home Mortgage Interest Rates, 1990–2008

Source: Freddie Mac.

Intense Competition among Investors and Lenders

The amount of dollars and other currencies seeking to buy or lend against desirable real estate thus vastly outnumbered the profitable properties available. That caused intense competition among investors and lenders to acquire or lend against desirable real properties. It may seem incredible that an immense oversupply of capital funds from 2000 to 2006 was a major cause of the real estate credit crunch in 2007–09, which consisted of an acute shortage of lendable funds available to financial intermediaries (although there was a lot of capital, suppliers

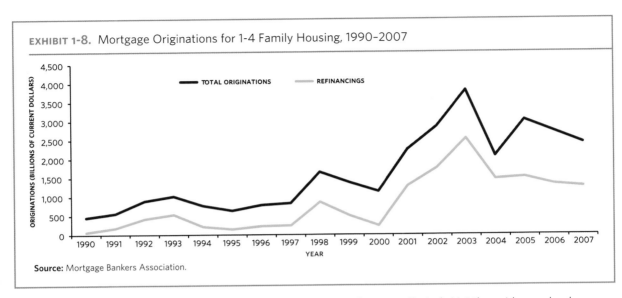

EXHIBIT 1-8. Mortgage Originations for 1-4 Family Housing, 1990-2007

Source: Mortgage Bankers Association.

were unwilling to make it available to financial intermediaries). Yet the evidence clearly supports that conclusion, as this book seeks to show.

A Rapid Increase in the FTSE NAREIT Index

Another result of the massive flow of money into real estate markets was that the equity real estate investment trusts (REIT) stock index of the National Association of REITs (that is, the FTSE NAREIT index) rose much faster than the three main stock indices from 2000 through February 2007. The FTSE NAREIT index had increased only 54.24 percent from 1990 through 2000—far less than the other stock indices. But then it kept on rising. From mid-2000 to October 9, 2002—when the other stock indices hit their low points—the FTSE NAREIT index rose 15.58 percent. It then continued rising much faster than the three main indices, which all began recovering on October 10. By February 7, 2007, when the FTSE NAREIT index hit a high point of 10,980.62, it had risen 298.19 percent above its July 2000 level. Yet on that same day, the Dow Jones Industrials index was only 8.1 percent above its highest level in 2000, the S&P 500 index was still 5.1 percent below its 2000 maximum, and the NASDAQ Composite index was 50.6 percent below its 2000 maximum. Thus, REIT stocks—a measure of real estate in general—greatly outperformed non-REIT stocks from 2000 to February 2007. This is shown in exhibit 1-9. However, it should also be noted that the FTSE NAREIT index is a total return index, including dividends, whereas the other indices in this chart are price indices that do not include dividends.

A Paradigm Shift Favoring Real Estate Investments

This change in the relative performance of real estate stocks versus all other stocks caused a worldwide paradigm shift among many institutional investment firms in favor of greater investment of their assets in real estate. Most such firms had previously avoided buying real properties because they had regarded commercial real estate as both being too illiquid and requiring too much specialized knowledge of local property markets to be appropriate

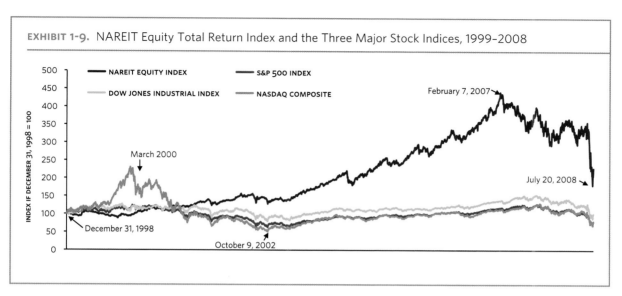

EXHIBIT 1-9. NAREIT Equity Total Return Index and the Three Major Stock Indices, 1999–2008

investments. But the collapse of stock prices worldwide in 2000—plus the far superior economic performance of real properties thereafter—caused many institutional investors to start regarding real estate as a separate asset class into which they ought to place a much larger share of their total capital. This change in investor opinion was strengthened by the wider use of securitized lending and REIT shares for investing in real properties, because both those instruments appeared to have high liquidity compared with owning properties directly. Owning real estate in some form seemed desirable both because it increased the diversity of portfolios and because although nearly all stocks were plunging in value and bonds were vulnerable to possible increases in inflation, real estate property values kept rising.

Sharp Increases in Real Estate Prices
Sharp increases in the market prices of all types of real properties, especially in housing markets, resulted from intense competition among investors seeking to buy or lend against such properties. When there are more buyers and lenders in a property market than owners and sellers, prices are inescapably driven upward by intense competition among the former to procure the latter. This happened in housing markets in nearly all major developed nations except Japan and Germany. For example, in Spain, the median price of single-family home units rose approximately 1,400 percent from 1980 to 2005, according to data compiled by *The Economist* magazine.

In the United States, that median price rose 51 percent in the ten years of the 1990s, then soared another 59.6 percent from 2000 to 2006, according to the National Association of Realtors. The big change in the annual rate of U.S. median price increases came after 2002. From 1996 through 2002, the median price in the United States rose an average of 5.07 percent per year. From 2003 to 2005, it rose an average of 9.90 percent per year. However, in California, the median price skyrocketed 130 percent in the same six years that the U.S. median gained 59.6 percent. Prices of all types of commercial properties also rose sharply, reflected in major declines in capitalization rates from about 1997 through 2006.

EXHIBIT 1-10. Median Home Price Changes in Four Metropolitan Areas with Minimal Growth Constraints and for the Nation, 1990–2006

Metropolitan Area	1990 Median Home Price ($ Thousands)	2000 Median Home Price ($ Thousands)	2006 Median Home Price ($ Thousands)	Gain, 1990–2000 (%)	Gain, 2000–2006 (%)
Charlotte	93.1	140.3	190.6	50.7	35.9
Dallas–Fort Worth	89.5	122.5	149.5	36.9	22.0
Atlanta	86.4	131.2	171.8	51.8	30.9
Houston	70.7	116.1	149.1	64.2	28.4
Entire United States	92.0	139.0	221.9	51.1	59.6

Source: National Association of Realtors.

U.S. home prices appeared to rise most in those metropolitan areas that had severe constraints on building more housing because of exclusionary local building regulations, especially along the West Coast. Metropolitan areas that had large supplies of open land nearby and few exclusionary zoning rules saw much smaller price increases, even if they had rapid population growth. This is shown in exhibit 1-10.

Disconnect between Investment and Space Markets

The rising prices of commercial properties caused by the flood of capital at first led to an economic disconnect concerning conditions in U.S. commercial real estate markets between property investment markets, where transactions and prices were booming, and space markets, where rising vacancies and falling rents prevailed. A general economic activity downturn occurred in the United States and elsewhere after the stock market crash in 2000. That slump was aggravated by the terrorist attacks in the United States on September 11, 2001. In all previous such downturns, falling demand for rental space caused distress in all aspects of the property markets. Property prices had almost always fallen along with rent levels and occupancy rates, because the profitability of operating most commercial real properties would decline. But in this downturn after 2000, intense competition among investors seeking real estate—because they were fleeing from stocks and bonds—drove commercial property prices up at the same time that the operating results of such properties were deteriorating. Fortunately for investors, the U.S. general economy recovered fairly rapidly after 2001. Hence conditions in space markets reflected rising rents and occupancy rates within two to three years after 2000. This restored consistency between conditions in property ownership markets and those in space markets.

A Deterioration of Underwriting Standards

The enormous oversupply of financial capital in U.S. and other real estate markets caused a deterioration of the underwriting standards used by lenders and buyers. This deterioration plus the widespread use of securitization led lenders and buyers to systematically underestimate the risks of all types of real estate investments. The prevailing underwriting standards worsened right after 2000 and remained weak and inadequate until well into 2006. This failure to take risks fully into account was a direct result of the intense competition among lenders and investors trying to buy or control real properties. Frantic bidding occurred among investors in commercial markets and homebuyers in residential markets to obtain the best-quality real properties. Their sense of urgency reduced both the amount of time available to perform due diligence on deals offered to them and their efforts to do so, but the pressure to put their capital to work persuaded many to invest anyway. That was one of the key ways in which the initial oversupply of available capital seeking to invest eventually led to a serious undersupply of capital suppliers willing to make investments.

A major contributor to the deteriorating underwriting standards was widespread securitization of real estate mortgage loans. Loans were repackaged into bond-like securities that were then given favorable ratings by major credit rating agencies. The complexity of these securities and the favorable ratings received by those in the highest-quality tranches (which were also the largest tranches, often more than 80 percent of each issue) caused many lenders and property buyers to assume that owning such securities posed little risk. In many cases, those who bought such securities had no clear idea of the many ingredients built into the securities by multiple layers of securitization, as in many collateralized debt obligations (CDOs).

Another cause of poor underwriting was a tendency to judge the profitability of investments by the initial spreads between the low interest rates on the short-term loans used to finance purchases of longer-term assets and the higher rates of return on those assets. Bonuses were often computed on the basis of those spreads, but such spreads were vulnerable to increases in the short-term rates on the funds borrowed—which occurred after the bonuses were awarded. Since the yields on long-term assets did not rise along with later increases in short-term rates, profits were decimated over the long run.[4]

Rapid Credit Expansion and Increasing Risk: 2003 through 2005

The fundamental causal elements described earlier then began to interact with their own first-round impacts. Together, they generated a second round of impacts on financial and real estate markets, occurring mainly from 2003 through 2005:

- Low returns, which pushed capital into riskier property investments;
- Unsustainable levels of home production;
- Millions of new homeowners entering the market;
- Record levels of new single-family home loans; and
- The Fed's reluctance to intervene in lending.

Low Returns Pushing Capital into Riskier Investments

Rising property prices and low interest rates generated low rates of immediate financial return from owning or lending against real estate, as expressed in declining capitalization rates linking property incomes to property prices. Those low yields pressured capital suppliers to seek property investments that would have above-average short-term yields—and therefore greater-than-normal riskiness. This pressure was most evident in single-family home markets,

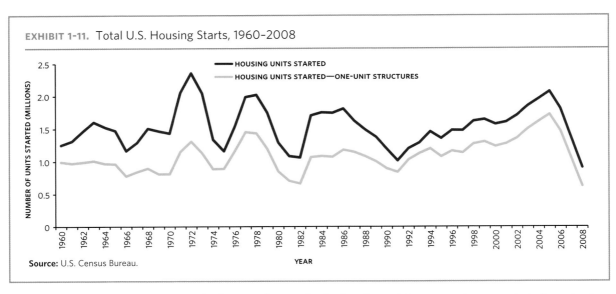

EXHIBIT 1-11. Total U.S. Housing Starts, 1960–2008

HOUSING UNITS STARTED
HOUSING UNITS STARTED—ONE-UNIT STRUCTURES

NUMBER OF UNITS STARTED (MILLIONS)

YEAR

Source: U.S. Census Bureau.

where mortgage brokers made use of subprime loans. Those were loans made to homebuying borrowers who had poor credit records or resources. From the viewpoint of investors in mortgage securities, the reduced ability of such borrowers to repay their loans was supposedly balanced by interest rates that were about three percentage points higher than those available on loans made to borrowers with normal credit resources. Thus, lenders who supported subprime loans could obtain higher apparent yields than were generated by more normal—and less risky—prime loans. Also, mortgage brokers earned higher fees from such loans than from more traditional prime loans.

Unsustainable Levels of Home Production

In order to capture the high immediate profits made possible by rising home prices, homebuilders that served booming housing markets raised their annual production of new units to levels that were unsustainable over time. They increased production levels by selling homes into what normally would have been future demand—especially in 2004 and 2005, when more than two million new homes were built each year (including manufactured homes). This forward selling soon undermined homebuilders' ability to maintain those high production levels. Moreover, the rate at which home prices rose each year soon slowed dramatically because markets were saturated and defaults among buyers who had poor credit ratings began to rise. In all four periods since 1945 in which new home production exceeded two million new units per year, new starts fell sharply in the next three to four years, dropping an average of 37 percent overall. Total housing starts from 1960 to 2008 are shown in exhibit 1-11.

Millions of New Homeowners

Rapid increases in home prices motivated millions of households to become homeowners because they saw their homeowning neighbors being enriched by large increases in the net equity in their homes. The households so motivated included

EXHIBIT 1-12. New and Existing Single-Family Homes Sold, 1996–2008

Year	Existing Homes Sold (Thousands)	New Homes Sold (Thousands)	Total Homes Sold (Thousands)
1996	4,196	757	4,953
1997	4,381	804	5,185
1998	4,970	886	5,856
1999	5,205	880	6,085
2000	5,152	877	6,029
2001	5,296	908	6,204
2002	5,561	973	6,534
2003	6,183	1,086	7,269
2004	6,784	1,203	7,987
2005	6,180	1,282	7,462
2006	5,677	1,051	6,728
2007	4,939	776	6,428
2008	4,350	483	4,833

Sources: U.S. Census Bureau, National Association of Realtors.

- Renters with good credit who wanted to achieve the American dream of homeownership,
- Renters with poor credit who had the same aspiration, and
- Speculators who hoped to make fast profits by purchasing homes with low downpayments and "flipping" them by reselling those homes quickly to others at higher prices.

As long as home prices kept rising and mortgage credit was readily available to these groups, their demand for buying both existing and new homes sustained both high levels of new home production and strong upward pressures on prices of both new and existing homes. As a result, the number of single-family homes sold each year expanded to record levels, peaking in 2004 at nearly 8 million units, as shown in exhibit 1-12 (which excludes manufactured housing units).

Record Levels of New Single-Family Home Loans

Mortgage lending on single-family homes—both new and existing—soared after 2000 to record levels, as shown in exhibit 1-8. The average annual amount of such originations rose from $790 billion during the seven years from 1991 through 1997 to $2.972 trillion in the five years from 2001 through 2005. That is a gain of 276 percent.

The initial profitability of subprime loans for both mortgage brokers and investors in mortgage-backed securities motivated brokers to pressure borrowers with poor credit into taking on such loans—in many cases even if they qualified for prime loans that had lower interest rates. Congressional pressure to make homeownership more widely available was also involved in the wider use of subprime mortgages. Mortgage brokers stimulated even greater use of subprime lending by adopting tactics that made it easier for potential homebuyers who had incomes previously thought too low to qualify for mortgages to think they could afford to buy homes, even when they really could not. These tactics included reducing downpayments to zero and not confirming borrowers' statements of their incomes, as well as others described in chapter 2.

All such loosened credit terms were motivated by the higher upfront profitability of subprime loans, despite their increased risk of default. Both brokers and capital suppliers tended to ignore that greater risk because, until 2006, housing prices were rising fast enough to add to the market values of the homes involved. This dual pressure to make more subprime loans—from mortgage brokers (motivated by higher fees) and from investors (motivated by higher interest rates)—increased the share of subprime loans in all mortgage lending, especially after 2001.

Data from the Mortgage Bankers Association on 1-4 family mortgage loans and data from Credit Suisse on subprime lending show the shares of subprime loans listed in exhibit 1-13. Similar increases in the riskiness of mortgage loans occurred in many commercial property markets too. Competitive pressure to put capital to work motivated many lenders to accept fewer and weaker covenants in their loans and to perform less due diligence on the properties involved. Commercial banks were supposedly protected from such increased riskiness by making loans to unregulated subsidiaries that were not included on their books. As a result, many commercial banks permitted those subsidiaries or related firms to assume the initial risks of loans that the banks themselves would never have made directly.

The Fed's Reluctance to Regulate Subprime Lending Practices

Edward Gramlich, a member of the Federal Reserve Board, reported to Chairman Alan Greenspan in 2000 and again in 2002 that subprime mortgage lending often involved fraudulent and misleading actions by mortgage bankers. He requested that the Fed do something to remedy

---

EXHIBIT 1-13. Share of Subprime Loans Compared to All Loans Made Annually, 1993–2005

Year	Total 1-4 Family Mortgages ($ Billion)	Total Subprime Mortgages Made ($ Billion)	Share of All Such Mortgages That Were Subprime (%)
1993	1,020	35	3.43
1994	769	65	8.45
1995	640	97	15.16
1996	785	125	15.92
1997	833	150	18.01
1998	1,656	160	9.66
1999	1,379	138	10.01
2000	1,139	173	15.19
2001	2,243	213	9.50
2002	2,854	332	11.63
2003	3,812	530	13.90
2004	2,073	665	32.08
2005	3,027	640	21.14

Sources: Mortgage Bankers Association and Credit Suisse.

these practices, but Greenspan rejected this suggestion. Greenspan decided instead not to intervene in the relatively unregulated practices being used by many mortgage brokers operating firms that were not on the books of major commercial banks. His decision was based on his basic distrust of nearly all forms of government regulation over financial markets, as stated in his book *The Age of Turbulence*, in which he wrote, "The benefit of more government regulation eludes me."[5] Later in the same chapter, he wrote, "An area in which more rather than less government involvement is needed, in my judgment, is the rooting out of fraud."[6] However, he did not follow his own advice in response to Gramlich's request for precisely such involvement. Greenspan's decision allowed many mortgage bankers engaged in subprime lending to continue with fraudulent or at least misleading lending practices in making subprime loans.

Complex Securities and Lax Investment Practices: 2005 through Early 2007

After the fundamental elements described earlier had the first- and second-round impacts just stated, all those factors began to interact with each other. Together, they generated a third round of impacts on financial and real estate markets, occurring mainly from 2002 until early 2007, as set forth below. Some of these impacts began during the second round of impacts but continued through at least 2005:

- High rates of refinancing for consumption;
- Expansion of lending beyond reserves;
- The rise of complex securitized instruments;
- Lack of regulation of complex securities; and
- Further expansion of homebuilding and homebuying.

High Rates of Home Refinancing

Many households who owned homes before home prices soared refinanced their initial mortgages and took capital out to use in spending for all types of consumption unrelated to those homes. The dollar value of mortgage originations that consisted of refinancings soared from 47 percent of annual originations from 1991 through 2000 to 65 percent from 2001 through 2004. In 2003, mortgage originations equaled more than $4 trillion, of which 72 percent were refinancings. This capital extraction process kept American consumption spending high and overall gross domestic product growing until after 2006.

Expansion of Lending beyond Reserves

Commercial banks increased their mortgage lending activities by financing their own off–balance sheet mortgage-brokerage subsidiaries, as well as unrelated mortgage brokers which originated mortgage loans directly to households. Then the banks securitized those mortgage loans. Those brokers sold the mortgages that they had originated back to the banks, which packaged them as securities, divided the securities into tranches with different repayment and risk characteristics, and then sold those securities to investors around the world. The banks then used the proceeds from such sales to fund additional loans to mortgage brokers, which gave rise to another round of securitization. This process enabled banks to increase the total volume of their mortgage lending far beyond what their deposits or reserves directly supported. Thus, banks shifted from their traditional roles as "originate and hold" suppliers of capital based on bank deposits to "originate and distribute" circulators of capital based on recycling money that was ultimately provided by investors in securitized loans.

Banks were motivated to undertake this rather complex process by two factors. One was the low interest rates then prevailing on mortgages. Banks thought these rates needed to be supplemented by charging fees and expanding their total lending. The other was the ability to shift direct responsibility for making mortgage loans to brokers that were not on the banks' balance sheets. Many of those brokers used the funds supplied by banks to make high-risk loans that the banks themselves would not have considered proper. Because most banks were not making such high-risk loans themselves, many remained ignorant of the level of risk in the loans they were ultimately financing, or at least ignored such loans.

The Rise of Complex Securitized Instruments

Commercial and investment banks and mortgage conduits began to package home mortgage loans into relatively complex, securitized instruments in order to promote greater overall sales of mortgage loans to investors all over the globe. These instruments included CDOs, SIVs (structured investment vehicles), and CBOs (collateralized bond obligations). CDOs were unregulated and did not require filing information with the Securities and Exchange Commission or abiding by its rules. SIVs were set up by many commercial banks as nonbank subsidiaries in which the banks could carry out activities not permitted to them as commercial banks and keep those activities off their books. Such SIVs often raised money from very-short-term commercial paper, which they then used to originate longer-term investments like mortgages. It was that strategy of borrowing short and lending long that crushed the savings and loan business in the 1980s and early 1990s.

In many cases, these securitized instruments contained several types of mortgages originated in different locations and sometimes even nonmortgage debts, such as those from credit cards. Some CDOs even included in their portfolios parts of other, smaller CDOs, as well as mortgage-backed securities and credit card debt. To offset the resulting complexities of such instruments, firms that issued them sought high ratings from the established credit rating agencies. The result was that many investors did not really understand all the securitized instruments they were buying and relied mainly on favorable credit ratings as the only due diligence they used in making such investments. In many cases, some subprime mortgage loans were included within these complex instruments, and those buying such instruments were not fully aware of the extent to which their future income streams depended in part on subprime borrowers making their payments on time.

Lack of Regulation of Complex Securities

Financial innovators on Wall Street and elsewhere invented many new financial derivatives that were designed to offset the potential risks of buying such complex and nontransparent securities. Enormous quantities of these derivatives were manufactured and sold; yet these instruments remained almost totally free from government regulation. One of the most widely used was the credit default swap, or CDS. In a CDS, one party who might own securitized or other bonds would purchase what amounted to insurance against the default of those securities from another party, which was paid monthly to provide such a guarantee. However, neither party had to own the securities involved or have any direct connection with the owner. As a result, the total amount of CDSs became larger than the total amount of securities thus insured. For example, in 2008, the notional total amount of CDS securities outstanding exceeded $62 trillion, even though

- The total value of all stocks on all U.S. stock markets combined was about $21 trillion,
- The total value of all bonds throughout the world was about $61 trillion,
- The total value of all stocks on all world stock markets in May 2008 was about $57.5 trillion, and
- The total value of the U.S. gross domestic product in 2008 was about $14 trillion.

A trade organization concerning financial derivatives that are traded over the counter, rather than in organized exchanges, came into existence in Switzerland—the International Association of Swaps and Derivatives. It tried to impose some uniformity of terms and definitions on users of those derivatives. But the issuers were essentially unregulated and not required to report their over-the-counter transactions to any centralized regulators.

Peter Linneman regards the huge volume of CDSs as a sign of arrogance among financial market operators. He claims, "The confidence in CDSs was a perfect example of 'the end of history' arrogance of financial markets. A simple lesson was forgotten: any guarantee is only as good as the guarantor."[7]

Further Expansion of Homebuilding and Buying

Accelerating increases in home prices and commercial property prices in most parts of the nation from 2002 through 2005 stimulated further expansion of homebuilding, home purchases by former renters, home purchases by speculators interested only in flipping the units they bought, and greater investing in commercial real properties by institutional and other investors around the world. Median prices of single-family homes sold throughout the United States rose by annual averages of 4.07 percent from 1992 through 2000 and 8.34 percent from 2001 through 2005—twice as fast in the latter years. In California, home prices actually declined during six years in the 1990s, averaging a gain of only 2.2 percent from 1992 through 2000. But then home prices in the state shot up an average of 16.87 percent per year from 2001 through 2005.

These large increases in home prices lured millions of households into stretching their resources in order to own a home. Those homebuyers included many households who had barely enough resources to qualify even for the relaxed credit standards of subprime mortgage loans. Because investor yields—like capitalization rates—were unusually low during this period, thanks to rising prices for all types of property, investors all over the world were eager to take advantage of the ostensibly high yields from subprime mortgages. This tendency was furthered when the presence of such mortgages within CDOs and other complex loan instruments was not obvious to their buyers.

Another group of investors who rushed into housing markets consisted of speculators seeking to profit from rapid home price increases by quickly flipping homes that they had purchased with small downpayments. Although many homebuilders tried to avoid selling to such speculators, the shares of home and condominium sales to speculators reached amazing levels in a few hot housing markets. Data on certain metropolitan area markets show the percentage of total mortgages made for home purchase that were used either for second homes or by investors who were speculators. Most of the metropolitan areas that had high percentages of loans in that category are located in retirement or resort regions, such as much of Florida. Therefore, it is to be expected that they would have relatively high percentages of second-home purchases. But in many metropolitan areas, the percentage of loans in that dual category rose sharply in 2004, 2005, and 2006. Presumably, that sudden increase was caused by speculators buying individual homes for flipping. Exhibit 1-14 shows a few of the metropolitan areas concerned, their average percentages in this category from 1999 to 2002, their averages from 2003 through 2006, and the difference between those averages—which are presumed to be mainly speculative purchases. Fort Myers stands out in this table as a leading area for such speculation. Overall data for Boston, Milwaukee, and the entire United States are shown as benchmarks that were not greatly influenced by speculation.

In some condominium markets, especially in south Florida, the percentages of buyers who were intending to flip their units were even higher than this exhibit shows. Driving from the Miami Airport into downtown Miami early in 2007, I counted 32 cranes working on constructing high-rise condominium projects, to say nothing of the many more high-rise buildings already

EXHIBIT 1-14. Speculation Indicators: Share of Mortgages Made for Homes Sold to Nonoccupiers, in the Nation and in 15 Metropolitan Areas, 1999–2006

Metropolitan Area	Average Percentage of Mortgages Sold, 1999–2002	Average Percentage of Mortgages Sold, 2003–06	Percentage Point Increase, a Strong Indicator of Increased Speculation and Flipping
United States	8.35	14.8	6.4
Boston	8.30	8.93	0.63
Milwaukee	7.04	8.10	1.06
Sacramento	13.60	17.90	4.30
Riverside–San Bernardino	15.66	20.50	4.83
Fresno	15.69	21.55	5.86
Phoenix-Mesa	16.21	33.40	6.19
Tampa–St. Petersburg	18.03	24.28	6.25
Boise City	14.63	21.83	7.20
West Palm Beach	21.61	29.68	8.05
Sarasota	26.85	35.05	8.20
Daytona Beach	26.26	35.20	8.94
Naples	38.66	48.53	9.76
Tucson	10.88	22.63	11.75
Myrtle Beach	47.99	59.98	11.99
Fort Myers	23.23	42.63	19.40

EXHIBIT 1-15. Annual Median Home Price Changes by Region, 2000–07

	2000–01	2001–02	2002–03	2003–04	2004–05	2005–06	2006–07
United States (%)	6.3	7.0	7.5	8.3	12.2	1.3	-1.8
Northeast (%)	5.1	12.1	15.9	15.5	10.7	-0.5	2.6
Midwest (%)	5.3	4.5	3.9	5.4	11.1	-2.1	-2.1
South (%)	7.1	7.2	6.7	7.2	5.4	1.4	-2.6
West (%)	6.3	10.7	8.7	13.5	17.7	3.0	-2.3
Total Number of Metropolitan Areas	125	131	142	148	153	150	150
Metropolitan Areas Declining	2	11	4	7	4	36	60
Share Declining (%)	1.6	8.4	2.8	4.7	2.6	24.0	40.0

Source: National Association of Realtors.

completed there. At night, almost no lights shone in many of these enormous residential buildings. The unusually high fraction of all homebuyers from 2003 through 2006 who were short-term investors rather than owner-occupants was an indicator of potential problems to come.

Housing Slowdown and Growing Loan Defaults: 2006 to Mid-2007

The effects of the previous rounds produced a slowdown that consisted of
- Decelerating home price increases,
- Increasing subprime loan defaults,
- Slower home sales, and
- Illiquidity and lack of transparency.

Decelerating Rates of Home Price Increases

The year-to-year rate of increase of home prices accelerated until about the third quarter of 2005 and then gradually declined. By mid-2006, it was clear that the rate of home price increase was slowing sharply. This change is evident from exhibit 1-15, which shows year-to-year median home price changes for metropolitan areas in various regions, compiled by the National Association of Realtors. The median prices of existing homes sold rose steadily from 2000 through 2005, even accelerating from 2003 through 2005. But the rate of such increases definitely slowed from 2005 to 2007. The percentage of metropolitan areas showing year-to-year annual declines in median home prices rose from 1.6 percent in 2001 to 24 percent in 2006 and then to 40 percent in 2007. This slowdown in home price increases began to undermine the belief that home prices would continue rising indefinitely. It was becoming clear that three groups—homebuilders creating new units for sale, plus many owners of existing homes putting them on the market to take advantage of very high prices, plus

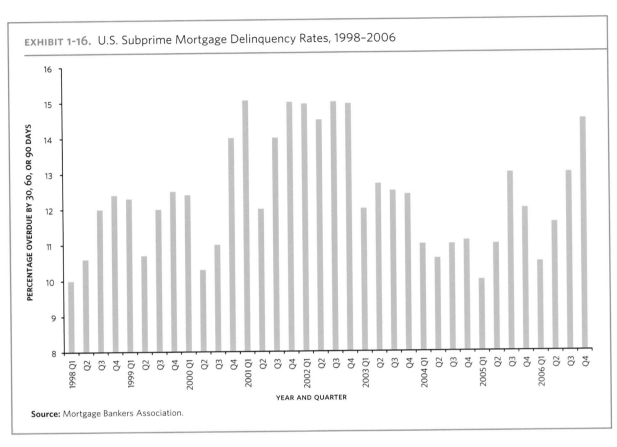

EXHIBIT 1-16. U.S. Subprime Mortgage Delinquency Rates, 1998–2006

PERCENTAGE OVERDUE BY 30, 60, OR 90 DAYS

YEAR AND QUARTER

Source: Mortgage Bankers Association.

"flippers" selling homes they had just purchased—were saturating housing markets across the nation, thus gradually undermining price performances in those markets.

Increasing Defaults by Subprime Borrowers

The slowing of home price increases, plus the upward resetting of interest rates on many subprime mortgages, thereby increasing their monthly payments, began to make it more difficult for many subprime borrowers to make those monthly payments. Those changes also put pressure to default on those buyers who were trying to flip homes because they could not resell at higher prices and had to pay higher interest costs if they retained ownership. Hence default rates on subprime mortgage loans began to rise again after coming down from the previous peak in 2001. Slower increases in housing prices undermined the belief among many subprime mortgage borrowers that paying off their mortgages would be made easier by rising home prices. They had expected higher prices to increase their equity in their homes, perhaps even enabling them to refinance their mortgages and withdraw cash while retaining the same or lower monthly payments.

Data for 309 metropolitan areas reported by the Federal Reserve Bank of San Francisco show that the faster home prices had risen from 2004 to 2006, the lower the delinquency rate among subprime borrowers in 2006.[8] In addition, because many subprime mortgages called for upward resets of their monthly payments after an initial period of low "teaser" interest rates, it became more difficult for such borrowers to continue making those payments on time. According to the weekly report *UBS Mortgage Strategist*, the number of subprime 2/28 and 3/27 subprime loans coming due for upward resets was only about 13,000 in 2004 but rose to 20,000 in 2005, 35,000 in 2006, 42,500 in 2007, and 44,000 in 2008.[9]

The percentage of delinquent subprime mortgages (overdue by 30, 60, or 90 days or more) began to rise again in 2005, after declining from a peak in 2001 and 2002 (owing to slumping general economic conditions then), as shown in exhibit 1-16. Such delinquency percentages had fallen from a peak of just over 15 percent to a low of 10 percent in the first quarter of 2005. However, this exhibit is somewhat misleading for two reasons: the lowest level shown is 8.0 percent rather than zero, and there were many more subprime mortgages in 2006 than in 2002. That means the number of subprime delinquencies was considerably higher in 2006 than in 2002, even though the percentage of loans that were delinquent was somewhat lower. As a result, owners of securities that contained some subprime mortgages became much more aware of their mortgage delinquency problems in 2005 and 2006 than such owners had been earlier, even though the percentages of delinquencies in 2005 and 2006 were somewhat lower than earlier.

Slowing Sales of All Homes

Sales of both existing and newly built homes in the United States slowed in 2006 and also in 2007, below their levels in 2004 and 2005. As shown in exhibit 1-12, existing home sales fell from a high of 6.784 million in 2004 to 5.652 million in 2007, a drop of 16.7 percent; whereas sales of newly built homes dropped from 1.282 million in 2005 to 776,000 in 2007, or by 39.4 percent. The stock values of major American homebuilders plummeted as a result. From mid-2005 to October 2008, the stocks of four major homebuilders declined more than 80 percent.

Illiquidity and Lack of Transparency

Slowdowns in both sales of homes and increases in home prices began to undermine the ability of mortgage bankers to convince potential buyers to purchase homes with the assumption that future increases in prices would ease their ability to pay their mortgage debts. Slowing home prices also killed the home-flipper market. As a result, originations of new home mortgages fell by 28.4 percent from their high point of $3.812 trillion in 2003 to $2.736 trillion 2006, and by 36.5 percent to $2.422 trillion in 2007.[10] The Mortgage Bankers Association estimated that total mortgage originations of all types fell by 28.4 percent from their high point of $3.812 trillion in 2003 to $2.726 trillion in 2006, and by 36.5 percent to $2.422 trillion in 2007.[11]

When the prices of key assets—including homes, many stocks, and mortgage-backed securities—began to decline, investors who had borrowed short-term funds to invest in long-term assets found that those assets were often too illiquid to sell readily at a profit. Potential buyers were not willing to pay the prices investors needed in order to make profits. Yet many investors had short-term liabilities that were rolling over and needed to be repaid. This situation was made more common by the lack of transparency of both the assets the investors had bought and the liabilities they had incurred. Such assets included CDOs, subprime loans or securities backed by such loans, homes purchased by flippers, and CDSs. Similarly nontransparent liabilities included SIVs, off–balance sheet subsidiary debts, and auction-based securities. Many borrowers failed to meet calls for debt payments that were triggered by mark-to-market requirements when there were no functioning markets for the liabilities involved; hence no clear market prices could be established—other than zero. The resulting overall lack of transparency in financial markets caused more and more lenders and borrowers to lose any confidence that they could reliably determine who was solvent and who was not—and therefore who could repay future loans and who could not. Ironically, financial transparency had virtually vanished despite all the accounting reforms passed by Congress in the Sarbanes-Oxley Act after the Enron financial scandals in 2001. The ensuing lack of confidence was a central factor leading to a freezing of credit transactions and availability, as discussed further below.

Credit Crunch and Financial Crisis: Mid-2007 to 2009

The credit crunch arrived in full because of
- Spreading subprime loan defaults,
- Profit losses and loan writeoffs by banks,
- A standoff between capital suppliers and property owners,
- An almost total credit freeze, and
- A cascade of federal attempts to loosen credit.

Spreading Effects of Subprime Defaults

Defaults on subprime mortgages began showing up all over the world as parts of CDOs and other sophisticated securitized instruments, although many of the owners of those instruments did not know that they had purchased interests in such mortgages. Commercial banks in both Europe and Asia had encouraged many of their investor customers to buy securities that those banks had created from many sources, including subprime loans to American homebuyers. Such securities appealed to those investors because of their relatively high interest rates and the favorable quality ratings they had received from major U.S. credit rating agencies. But when subprime mortgage defaults accelerated in the United States, many of the securities containing those mortgages failed to make the payments they had promised to investors.

Significant Profit Losses for Banks

Commercial and investment banks that had issued many securities based in part on subprime mortgages found themselves still holding a lot of those securities for three reasons:
- Their warehouses were full of unsold securities when investors stopped buying more because of rising defaults,
- They were holding some pieces for yield and to get deals done, and
- They came under pressure to take back some of those securities or assume responsibility for the liabilities arising from subprime defaults.

This began to cause significant profit losses among such banks. The European and Asian investors who had accepted the recommendations of their local banks to purchase such securities complained strongly. This caused those banks both to take back some of these securities and to fail to sell additional such securities, thereby having to bear the costs of the security defaults themselves. Both Credit Suisse and HSBC suffered sizable losses in this manner in 2007. In the United States, many banks began to suffer serious losses for the same reasons. These changes in conditions caused many commercial and investment banks to suffer significant losses in profit and income, starting in 2007 and continuing into 2008.

Capital Suppliers and Property Owners at Loggerheads

A critical result of all the losses, bankruptcies, writedowns, and other travails suffered by commercial and investment banks, other mortgage lenders and brokers, mortgage-backed security holders, and by real estate investors generally, was a sudden threefold realization by major owners of capital:

- They had not made sufficient allowances for the possible risks of the real estate loans and purchases they had been making for several years—including not only subprime loans but all types of real estate loans and purchases.
- Therefore they should start demanding higher rates of return and better terms on their capital than they had been receiving.
- They were extremely uncertain about what real estate securities—and other risky securities— and even real properties were worth in a market plagued by huge losses and problems.

These three realizations caused those capital owners to stop investing in real estate securities of all types and even in real properties directly until they could be sure that they were getting higher yields than they had been receiving. But such certainty was unavailable for two reasons. First, the owners of real properties and of real estate securities who wanted to sell them were initially unwilling to lower their prices enough to provide investors with significantly higher yields, because that would mean accepting much lower prices than they had become accustomed to. Second, neither the potential investors nor the property and security owners could be certain about what those properties and securities were going to be worth after the market settled down.

This divergence of yield objectives on both sides of the market, with no clear view of how these roiling markets would eventually settle down, caused a deep freeze on transactions in real estate markets of all types. Credit became unavailable because neither the capital suppliers—who wanted higher yields—nor the property owners—who did not want to accept higher capitalization rates—were willing to budge. People on both sides were unwilling to make deals at prices that might prove wrong or seem stupid when things finally settled down. The investors did not want to accept what they now thought were inadequate yields, and the owners did not want to sell at what they now thought were losses. People on both sides were fearful of looking foolish and incompetent if they accepted yields that eventually proved to be too low for investors or too high for owners. So the rate of transactions fell to almost zero and stayed there. Moreover, financial executives had strong incentives to forestall taking losses and recapitalizing, which they would have to do when carrying out transactions.

Credit Freeze

As a result of this "standoff at the I.O.U. corral," credit markets almost disappeared and the number of credit-based transactions hit record lows. This credit crunch really took hold in the last quarter of 2007 and extended into 2009. Some examples of this stunning credit freeze:

- In the commercial mortgage-backed securities market, the volume of deals was about $235 billion in 2007, or an average of $19.8 billion per month. In 2008 total deals for the year equaled only $12.2 billion, including virtually none in the latter half of the year.
- The overnight commercial paper market virtually disappeared, preventing security issuers from operating if they had relied on such short-term rollover instruments to support mortgages or other forms of longer-term credit that they were issuing. This also affected the firms that had been insuring tax-free bond issues for state and local governments with very short-term loans.
- Commercial banks that had made large loans to private equity firms to finance big acquisitions found themselves unable to sell the securitized paper they created after the fact to fund those loans to their usual investment clients. Those clients were demanding much higher yields than the banks had built into their original loans to the private equity firms. So these commercial banks could either sell such securities at a big loss and then be able to keep lending, or they could sit on the securities and have very little capital left to lend.
- Investors that were willing to gamble on the higher yields from subprime mortgages almost disappeared after too many such mortgages had suffered from defaults.
- Investors who had been gobbling up complex securitized instruments like CDOs and SIVs because of their relatively high yields became so wary of possible hidden problems that such instruments became very difficult to sell at almost any price.
- Firms of all types that had been using extremely high leverage rates to increase their ostensible profit margins found it almost impossible to continue borrowing with such high leverages without paying vastly greater interest rates, if even then. This situation slashed the potential profitability of such firms and even put many of them out of business.
- Investors became so wary of normal commercial transactions that they parked huge sums of their capital in safe-seeming U.S. Treasury securities and money market funds, driving yields on those instruments to near-record lows.

One London real estate attorney told me in May 2008 that his legal practice, which had consisted almost entirely of real estate transactions, had not seen a single transaction since fall 2007. So the credit crunch affected many people who were not themselves real estate operators but were closely linked to the industry.

A Cascade of Federal Responses

Lending markets were experiencing a virtual meltdown, not only concerning housing and other real estate but also concerning the provision of credit to all other businesses. This threatened to bring the entire U.S. economy to a halt. In response, the federal government made several dramatic moves to shore up the financial sector:

- It seized the government-sponsored enterprises Fannie Mae and Freddie Mac, fired their chief executives, and guaranteed that all their securities would be backed by the federal government.

- It refused to provide funds to prevent the investment banking house Lehman Brothers from going into bankruptcy, which it shortly did.

- It seized control of the nation's largest insurance company—AIG, provided it with $125 billion with which to stay in business, and controlled a majority of AIG's stock. It fired the top executives and replaced them with its own appointees, but it did not fully nationalize AIG.

- It opened up its lending window to provide credit to other financial institutions in dire need of funds to stay in business.

- Then Treasury Secretary Henry Paulson and Federal Reserve Chairman Ben Bernanke proposed a massive program of buying up so-called bad assets from banks and investment banks with federal funds. The goal was to get those assets off the books of major lenders, replace them with usable cash, and free lenders to start supplying credit again to the U.S. economy. The estimated overall gross outlay was $700 billion, to be paid for by enlarging the U.S. national debt. This proposal required action by Congress, which President George W. Bush promoted in a nationally broadcast speech in September 2008. The proposal set off an intense legislative effort by both houses of Congress to get something done before members recessed to participate in the national election in November. On September 29, the "bailout bill" was voted on by the House of Representatives and defeated, 228–205; the Dow Jones Industrial Average fell 777 points.

- On October 1, the Senate passed an expanded version of the same bill by a vote of 74 to 25. This version contained $107 billion in earmarks mostly unrelated to the financial crisis but added to persuade many Senate and House members to support the bill.

- Two days later, on October 3, the House of Representatives passed the same bill that the Senate had supported, this time by a vote of 263–171. The president immediately signed the bill into law. The Dow Jones Industrial Average fell anyway, but by a much smaller amount than on September 29.

- On October 13, the U.S. Treasury convened a meeting of nine of the nation's largest banks and announced that it would spend $125 billion to buy preferred stock and warrants in all those banks to shore up their capital. These infusions would amount to an average increase of 20 percent in the total capital of the nine banks. Treasury Secretary Paulson demanded that all nine banks agree to accept such capital infusions immediately, and they all did. He also announced that another $125 billion in such capital infusions would be made available to other smaller banks in the near future. The preferred stock would pay a dividend rate of 5 percent, rising to 9 percent after five years. The government would give up half of its warrants if the banks got private capital infusions matching the public investment before 2010. This second major federal approach to attacking the credit crunch followed a policy that the Bank of England had already suggested and carried out.

- On October 29, the Federal Reserve Board lowered its target for the federal funds rate to 1 percent, the lowest since 2003.

- Despite the credit squeeze, investors were still making about $5 billion in transactions of REIT stocks every day on the New York Stock Exchange, according to NAREIT. On November 25, the Federal Reserve and the Treasury announced $800 billion in new lending programs to help consumers and mortgage borrowers. These programs were designed to free up more private lending and put downward pressure on interest rates for households. Up to $600 billion of that was to be used to purchase debt issued by Fannie Mae, Freddie Mac, Ginnie Mae, and Federal Home Loan Banks ($100 billion) or debt tied to mortgages issued by Fannie Mae, Freddie Mac, and Ginnie Mae ($500 billion). Another $200 billion was to be used to support credit for consumers and small businesses.

- According to *The New York Times* of November 26, 2008, the federal government has advanced or promised to advance a total of $7.7 trillion to aid banks and other firms in difficulty. That included $3.1 trillion to insure against private defaults, of which $97 billion had already been spent; $3.0 trillion to invest in private banks and other companies, of which $649 billion had already been spent; and $1.7 trillion to lend to large financial institutions, of which $617 billion had already been spent. Thus, $1.363 trillion of federal funds had already been spent to shore up the financial sector of the economy and ameliorate the likely recession.[12]

At the time of this writing, new plans were being formulated and implemented by the Obama administration that were expected to add many new twists to this already complex federal response.

Continuing Turmoil

The credit freeze and financial crisis of 2007–09 are not over by far as this book is being completed in early 2009. As of this time, there are only a few signs that major changes are easing credit availability in real estate or other lending markets, the stock market is gyrating wildly in a mostly downward direction, and new policy responses are being introduced by the Obama administration. Possible future scenarios and policy options are addressed in chapters 6 to 9 of this book.

NOTES

1. Martin Wolf, *Fixing Global Finance* (Baltimore: Johns Hopkins University Press, 2008), pages 91 and 99.
2. Peter Linneman, personal note to the author, 2008.
3. Exhibit 1-9, showing 1-4 family home mortgage originations, has slightly different figures, which were based on a study of home mortgage originations made by the Federal Reserve Bank. However, both charts indicate roughly similar massive flows of capital into residential financing.
4. I am indebted to Peter Linneman of the Wharton School for pointing out this factor and for many other insightful contributions he made in critiquing the original draft.
5. Alan Greenspan, *The Age of Turbulence* (New York: Penguin Books, 2007), page 372.
6. *Ibid.*, page 375.
7. Peter Linneman, private note commenting on the initial draft.
8. Mark Doms, Frederick Furlong, and John Krainer, "House Prices and Subprime Mortgage Delinquencies," http://economistsview.typepad.com/economistsview/2007/06/frbsf_house_pri.html.
9. Data from *UBS Mortgage Strategist* reported in a briefing by Doug Duncan of the Mortgage Bankers Association on May 22, 2006.

10. These estimates from the Mortgage Bankers Association are somewhat lower than similar estimates made by Alan Greenspan and James Kennedy of the Federal Reserve Bank that I used in exhibit 1-9.
11. *Ibid.*
12. Stephanie Rosenbloom, "Treasury and the Fed Unveil Plans for Lending," *The New York Times*, November 25, 2008, pages A1 and A24.

The Financial Crisis and Housing Markets

THE FINANCIAL CRISIS OF 2007–09 began in U.S. housing markets and had its greatest impacts on those markets. This chapter explores why housing played such a crucial role in the origin and development of the credit crunch and ensuing crisis.

Why So Much Money Went into Housing Markets after 2000

My earlier book, *Niagara of Capital*, pointed out that housing markets in many parts of the world had been dramatically affected by massive inflows of financial capital that began in about 1997 and were especially strong after the stock market crash in 2000. Many major factors caused the worldwide flow of capital into real estate markets generally to hit housing markets first and with the greatest force, especially within the United States. Most of these factors were discussed in chapter 1; a few more are briefly mentioned below.

When the stock market crashed in 2000, real estate offered the most promising form of investment for most of the funds that were fleeing stocks and bonds and for the massive accumulations of excess savings from all over the world that were looking for somewhere to invest. Real estate properties had performed rather poorly from 1990 to 1993–95 because of the property market crash of 1990. But then real estate began to produce quite significant profits, which after 2000 made real estate seem much more attractive than stocks or bonds.

Moreover, housing was the most widely distributed form of real estate property in the world. It was available for investment in every nation, whether developed or developing. Also, owning a home was the only form of real estate investment that was relatively available to all households with reasonable incomes and that most households sought. Housing was also seen as a liquid investment with little downside, because home prices in the United States as a whole had risen steadily for more than 30 consecutive years. So the demand for housing was more widely distributed than the demand for any other type of real estate. In the United States in particular, the American dream of success had long included ownership of one's own home. Moreover, the federal government had vigorously advocated increasing homeownership

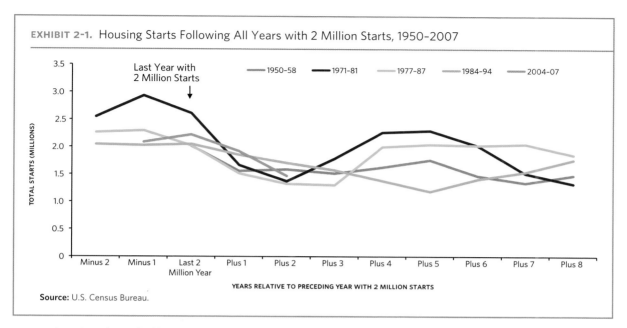

EXHIBIT 2-1. Housing Starts Following All Years with 2 Million Starts, 1950–2007

Source: U.S. Census Bureau.

among American households as a national goal and supported that goal by providing large-scale tax benefits to homeowners.

Innovations in the financing of home purchases also expanded the supply of credit available to potential homebuyers and investors. Greater use of mortgage securitization by banks and mortgage lenders opened up more sources of financial capital to support housing markets. Congressional deregulation of banking in the late 1990s permitted U.S. commercial banks to engage in more sophisticated types of mortgage lending and to lend more capital relative to their own reserves than ever before. Subprime residential lending became especially attractive to

- Investors, because of the high rates of interest charged to borrowers with poor credit;
- Mortgage brokers, because of the greater fees they were able to charge and the ease of selling higher-yielding products; and
- Commercial banks, because they could recirculate funds used to support subprime mortgages.

In addition, the Federal Reserve Board had less control over what investors of capital did in U.S. real estate markets than in the past. That occurred because so much of the capital involved came from abroad—that is, from investors who did not come under Federal Reserve Board jurisdiction.

In response to these conditions, U.S. homebuilders followed their usual procedure of building new homes as fast as they could in every year, regardless of the negative impacts that unusually high annual sales levels would have on housing demand in the following years. That led them to produce more than two million new units per year in both 2004 and 2005, generally overbuilding housing markets nationwide. That is shown in exhibit 2-1. But builders' previous negative experience with overbuilding in boom years did not stop them from doing it again.

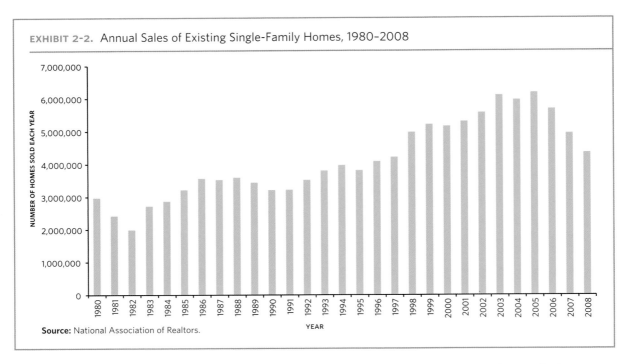

EXHIBIT 2-2. Annual Sales of Existing Single-Family Homes, 1980–2008

Source: National Association of Realtors.

For all these reasons, financial capital flooded into U.S. housing markets and others around the world, especially after 2000. This inflow financed very high levels of new housing construction and sales of existing homes. This was shown earlier in exhibit 1-8.[1] Mortgages could be originated only if capital was available. Thus, mortgage originations for single-family homes in the United States (excluding manufactured homes) soared from an average of $791 billion per year from 1991 through 1997, to averages of $1.257 trillion per year from 1998 through 2000 and $2.971 trillion per year from 2001 through 2005. Housing starts also rose sharply, as shown earlier, in exhibit 1-11. From 1990 through 1997, total new units (including manufactured homes) started each year averaged 1.503 million; from 1998 through 2002, the average was 1.893 million; from 2003 through 2006, it was 1.935 million. Sales of existing single-family homes (excluding manufactured homes) remained below four million per year until 1994, but rose to five million by 1998, and then to about six million in 2003, 2004, and 2005. This is shown in exhibit 2-2. Most of those sales were financed by the mortgage originations described above. In short, there was a strong housing production and sales boom from about 1997 to 2005, all financed by the massive flow of financial capital into housing all over the world.

The Cyclical Nature of U.S. Housing Production

The charts cited above show that sales of existing homes rose fairly steadily over the entire period from 1984 through 2005, but that the production of new homes definitely occurred in cyclical movements. From 1960 through 2007, there were six cyclical production peaks (1963, 1972, 1978,

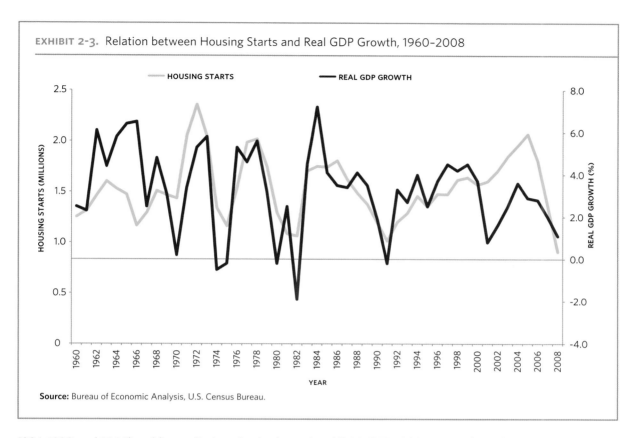

EXHIBIT 2-3. Relation between Housing Starts and Real GDP Growth, 1960–2008

Source: Bureau of Economic Analysis, U.S. Census Bureau.

1986, 1998, and 2005) and five cyclical production low points (1966, 1975, 1982, 1991, and 2001). The low points in 1975, 1982, and 1991 all occurred during years of negative real gross domestic product (GDP) growth—that is, economic recessions. Regarding the other two low-point years, 2001 saw only 0.75 percent GDP growth and 1966 saw 6.52 percent GDP growth.

At first glance, the cyclicality of housing production seems rather closely related to the movements of real GDP. When real GDP was moving up, housing production rose (except in 1966); when real GDP fell to negative levels, housing production hit the bottom of a cycle. These movements can be seen in exhibit 2-3. However, for the entire period from 1960 through 2007, the statistical correlation between annual percentage changes in housing starts and in real GDP is a relatively low 0.3420. One reason: real GDP nosedived before and then after the stock market crash in 2000, but housing starts remained quite high as money flooded into housing markets. The correlations between housing starts and 30-year fixed-rate mortgage rates, the federal funds rate, and the annual percentage changes in consumer prices are all negative.

The cyclicality of housing production in the past was partly related to attempts by the Federal Reserve Board to influence the speed of U.S. economic growth. The Fed raised interest rates when inflation got too high in order to cut housing production and reduce inflationary pressures (near GDP high points). The Fed cut interest rates to stimulate housing production so as to help end recessions (near GDP low points). The direction of the Fed's intentions

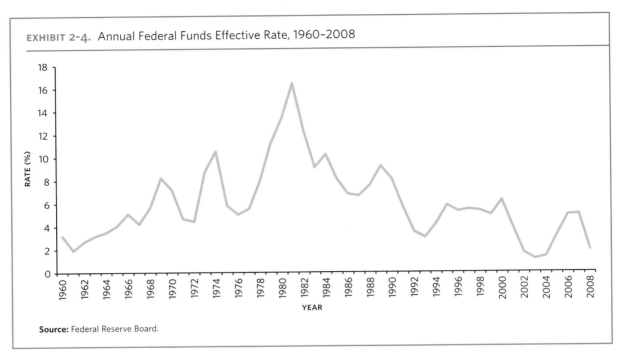

EXHIBIT 2-4. Annual Federal Funds Effective Rate, 1960–2008

Source: Federal Reserve Board.

regarding interest rates can be deduced from how it has altered the federal funds rate for short-term interbank borrowing. This is shown in exhibit 2-4. The Fed raised the federal funds rate when it wanted general interest rates to rise. The chart shows that this occurred in six periods from 1960 through 2007. In five other periods, the Fed cut the federal funds rate.

However, in the period from 2000 to mid-2007, the Fed's ability to influence housing starts by changing the federal funds rate was weakened by a large increase in the number and variety of capital sources that were willing to put money into U.S. housing. In the 1960s through the early 1990s—before the massive inflow of money—Fed policies could directly influence the amount of lending done by savings and loans and U.S. banks, then the main suppliers of housing credit—thereby controlling how much financial capital was available to potential homebuyers. But after the collapse of the savings and loan industry, the deregulation of commercial banks, and the massive inflows of capital from abroad in the 2000s, the Fed's control over the capital flowing into the housing industry was greatly reduced. Conduits for channeling funds from capital sources all over the world into U.S. housing markets sprang up or expanded after the stock market crash of 2000. These conduits included

- Commercial banks that operated under deregulation passed by Congress in 1999;
- Mortgage brokers that packaged many home loans into mortgage-backed securities that were then sold directly to U.S, and overseas investors through both U.S. and foreign banks and investment banks;
- Hedge funds that bought and resold subprime securities;
- U.S. investment banks that both supplied capital funds to mortgage brokers and securitized the resulting pools of home mortgages; and

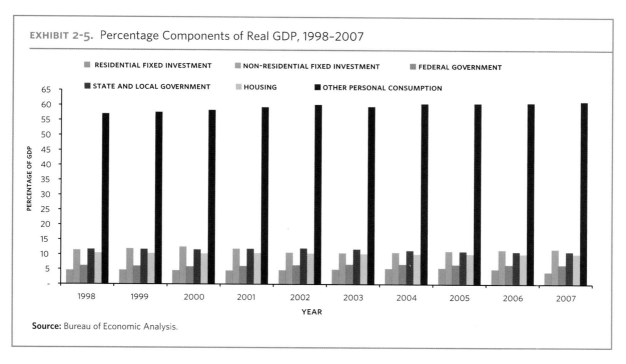

EXHIBIT 2-5. Percentage Components of Real GDP, 1998–2007

■ RESIDENTIAL FIXED INVESTMENT   ■ NON-RESIDENTIAL FIXED INVESTMENT   ■ FEDERAL GOVERNMENT
■ STATE AND LOCAL GOVERNMENT   ■ HOUSING   ■ OTHER PERSONAL CONSUMPTION

PERCENTAGE OF GDP

YEAR

Source: Bureau of Economic Analysis.

■ Fannie Mae and Freddie Mac, which facilitated securitization of mortgages made by U.S. banks and mortgage brokers.

All that activity laid the groundwork for the huge overbuilding that occurred in American housing markets during the 2000s.

Why What Happens in Housing Markets Greatly Affects the Entire Economy

The adverse impacts of the decline in housing production after 2005 and the subprime mortgage defaults of 2006–09 on the U.S. economy may seem out of proportion relative to the size of the housing sector. After all, housing is only one of many sizable segments of the U.S. economy, as shown in exhibit 2-5. That exhibit shows what percentage of GDP is formed by each of several major activities in the economy. Housing construction (residential fixed investment) averaged 4.78 percent of GDP in the time period shown. It is the smallest of all the bars in the exhibit, less than half the size of nonresidential fixed construction. But housing expenditures by households, which are part of personal consumption, are more than twice as large as housing construction and not far below state and local government spending. So, fixed residential investment and housing expenditures together are about 15 percent of real GDP. True, all those relatively small figures are dwarfed by "other personal consumption," which runs close to 60 percent of real GDP. But housing construction and consumption are certainly not trivial parts of the U.S. economy.

Moreover, the financing of housing is another large-scale activity in the U.S. economy. It is carried out by banks, savings and loans, insurance companies, investment banks, mortgage brokers, real estate agents, and many other actors. The financial sector includes real estate plus finance and insurance. Together, they made up 20.5 percent of GDP in 2005. Real estate was 60 percent of the combined activities. In fact, the financial sector was the single largest sector in the economy, surpassing manufacturing, transportation, and retail. Of course, financial activities cover many things besides financing housing. But in years when the homebuilding industry produces more than two million new housing units, housing finance is extremely important within the financial sector.

Thus, although housing construction is a relatively small segment of the U.S. economy, when housing expenditures by households and the financing of housing are taken into account, housing becomes much more important in the overall picture. Furthermore, personal consumption spending—other than on housing directly—includes such elements as furniture, rugs, home decorations, home insurance, and the services of gardeners, plumbers, decorators, and the like.

Finally, the housing industry has long been used by the Federal Reserve Board as a crucial lever in the Fed's attempts to speed up or slow down overall economic activity, as noted above. This use of housing as an accelerator or decelerator of overall economic activity has been reduced since the mid-1990s by the deregulation of the banking industry and the huge inflow of foreign money into American real estate markets. But the Fed still regards the health and level of activity in the housing industry as vital to the nation's economic welfare—as its recent reaction to the financial crisis has shown.

This longtime importance of the housing industry to the nation's overall economic activity was reinforced recently by the immense flow of financial capital into American real estate after the stock market crash of 2000. After all, in American society, homes are ubiquitous, capital intensive, crucial for every household's welfare, a central investment for every household, and closely related to how household members identify themselves socially. For all these reasons, what has happened to housing since 2000 has been a key factor influencing the overall health of the American economy. It has been far more important than the relatively small housing construction industry itself. That is why the financial crisis that started in housing markets has been exercising such immense influence on the overall health of the American economy.

The Housing and Credit Boom from 2000 through 2006

From 1996 through 2006, the homebuilding industry experienced a tremendous boom in new construction and sales, partly because mortgage credit boomed too. In those 11 years, builders created an average of 1.9 million new homes per year (including manufactured homes), for a total of 21.4 million new dwelling units. Surprisingly, that was not a record; more than 21.4 million new units had been built during consecutive 11-year periods ending in eight of the nine years from 1972 through 1981. Nevertheless, the housing boom in the 2000s was the climax of one of the longest sustained high-level housing production periods in U.S. history. It had begun with recovery from the near-recession year of 1991 and continued through 2006—15 years of strong prosperity in most housing markets. Ironically, California—home of the nation's most expensive housing—had a housing slump in the early 1990s because its economy suffered from a regional recession. But rising production in the rest of the nation

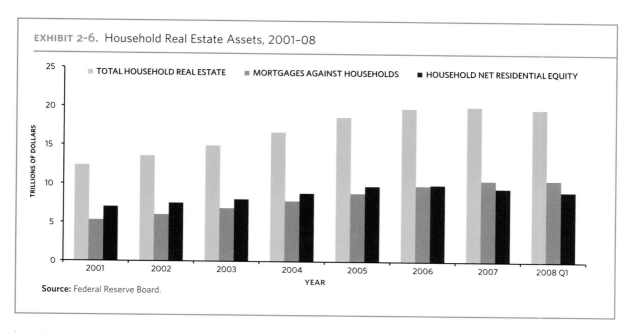

EXHIBIT 2-6. Household Real Estate Assets, 2001–08

■ TOTAL HOUSEHOLD REAL ESTATE   ■ MORTGAGES AGAINST HOUSEHOLDS   ■ HOUSEHOLD NET RESIDENTIAL EQUITY

TRILLIONS OF DOLLARS

YEAR

Source: Federal Reserve Board.

kept the housing boom accelerating elsewhere. After about 1997, California's large immigrant population helped state housing markets recover their former high sales rates.

Housing credit also boomed in this period, thereby enabling the housing production boom to occur. Exhibit 2-6 shows the total value of housing real estate owned by U.S. households at the end of each year from 2001 to 2007 and in the first quarter of 2008, as well as the mortgages and home equity loans owed against those homes and the net equity of owners. The gross value of homes owned rose from $12.8 trillion in 2001 to $19.7 trillion in the first quarter of 2008, up 53.9 percent. But both mortgage debt and home equity loans rose by even larger percentages in the same period, causing homeowners' net equity to increase by only 29.1 percent, from $7.05 trillion to $9.11 trillion. That happened both because homeowners took out larger mortgages in relation to home values as time passed and because so many homeowners were taking equity out of their homes and using the funds for all types of consumption. Another aspect of the credit boom was that employment in the mortgage lending and mortgage brokerage businesses (SIC code 616) exploded—to 338,000 persons in 2001 and even more in 2005 and 2006, according to the Bureau of Labor Statistics. No wonder more than $1 trillion worth of residential mortgage-backed securities were sold to investors in the United States and abroad in both 2005 and 2006.

The national median price of homes sold in this period, as measured by the National Association of Realtors (NAR), rose continuously—from $99,700 in 1992 to $221,000 in 2006. That was an increase of 121.7 percent in 14 years or an average of 8.7 percent per year (equal to a compound annual growth rate of 5.85 percent over 14 years). In California, the median price remained almost unchanged from 1992 through 1998 but then soared from $200,000 in 1998 to $560,578 in 2006. That was a gain of 180.3 percent in eight years, or 22.5 percent per year on average (13.75

percent if compounded annually). These large price increases should be kept in mind when pondering the significance of later price declines both in the country as a whole and in California.

The double boom in the number of new units built and the prices of both new and existing units had several important impacts, which are described in detail in my earlier book, *Niagara of Capital*. These impacts are set forth below.

Relatively rapid increases in home prices motivated many households who were renting to try to buy a home so that they could enjoy the capital gains that appeared inherent in homeownership. These aspirants included many who had relatively low incomes. Rapid increases in home prices also motivated many homeowners to refinance their homes with new mortgages, especially because interest rates were falling in this period, particularly after 2000. From 2001 through 2006, well over half of all mortgages financed involved such refinancing.

Refinancing enabled many households to buy larger and costlier homes without incurring any larger monthly payments or to take cash out from the refinancing and use it to pay for other types of consumption expenditures. Banks began promoting home equity loans to help owners do just that. As a result, massive refinancing of homes stimulated sizable increases in consumer spending on many types of goods and services unrelated to homeowning.

Mortgage bankers wanted to expand the universe of households eligible to become homeowners, so they promoted subprime mortgages for households with poor credit ratings. Subprime mortgages had the advantage to brokers and lenders of charging interest rates about three percentage points higher than prime mortgages, after initially low "teaser" rates reset. That made them especially attractive to both mortgage brokers and investors who bought the securitized paper that was created by packaging subprime mortgages together, as well as to the banks that provided the funding for the mortgage brokers and often did such securitizing.

The combination of eager potential homebuyers wanting to get on the home-value escalator and eager mortgage brokers trying to expand the most profitable part of their business created a very strong tendency in both groups to make unwise deals. Potential homebuyers lied about their incomes to become eligible for a mortgage. Overeager mortgage brokers adopted terms for subprime mortgages that unrealistically qualified many households as buyers who really could not afford to pay. They did this by

- Reducing downpayment requirements (often to zero).
- Accepting undocumented statements of borrower incomes from the borrowers themselves.
- Using initially low "teaser" interest rates that would later be raised sharply.
- Making interest-only loans for many initial years.
- Sometimes increasing loan amounts to exceed the market values of the homes involved.
- Using negative amortization loans, in which monthly payments were too low to cover the ongoing costs of amortizing the principal, so the uncovered principal amount was added to the total principal owed each month.
- Persuading borrowers who made low downpayments to avoid paying for mortgage insurance by taking out a second mortgage on top of the first one, to cover their downpayments.
- Abandoning the traditional practice of taking out escrow accounts to hold a piece of each monthly payment that was destined to pay local property taxes—which were rising along with housing prices. This reduced the monthly payment for subprime mortgages but shifted

the onus of paying local real estate taxes directly to the borrowers, who often failed to set aside money for that purpose.

■ Disguising in complex closing documents the fact that initial payments would soon increase sharply.

Many of these arrangements enabled low-income households to qualify to purchase homes when they really could not afford to do so.

Investors were motivated to purchase securities that were based in part on subprime mortgages because those mortgages paid much higher rates of interest than prime mortgages (after the initial rate resets). That made securities based on such mortgages seem very attractive in an economic situation of generally low interest rates. Moreover, investors were assured by those selling such securities that they were safe because they had been rated by established credit rating agencies.

Many people who bought homes during these boom years were speculators hoping to resell the homes soon at higher prices than they paid for them, without occupying the homes themselves. In some markets, especially markets for high-rise condominium homes, as many as 40 percent of all homebuyers were such speculators. These "flippers" contributed significantly to the boom in new housing production and to even faster increases in housing prices than would otherwise have occurred. They also provided an element of insecurity in housing markets, because they were not permanent home users.

All these developments generated an almost frenzied atmosphere in homebuying in many "hot" markets, characterized by fast-rising prices and fast-dealing mortgage brokers. Potential buyers had to wait in lines to see homes they might buy. Some builders auctioned off homes or used lotteries to determine who would have the privilege of buying new homes that were being built.

The Subprime Mortgage Phenomenon

As the housing boom continued, the use of subprime mortgages escalated rapidly, along with all other forms of financing. As former Federal Reserve Board member Edward Gramlich said in a speech to financial sector experts on August 31, 2007:

> In the early '90s, there were no subprime mortgages, but then a number of forces combined to lead to incredible growth. From essentially zero in 1993, subprime mortgage originations grew to $625 billion by 2005, one-fifth of total mortgage originations in that year, a whopping 26 percent annual rate of increase over the whole period. The growth was largely focused on racial and ethnic minorities and lower-income households who could not get prime mortgage credit. Something like 12 million new homeowners were created over this period, largely first-time homebuyers, largely racial and ethnic minorities, largely lower-income households. America's overall homeownership rate rose from 64 to 69 percent.[2]

Exhibit 2-7 shows that such mortgages increased greatly in total volume after 2002. Originations rose to a peak of $665 billion in 2005, declining slightly to $640 billion in 2006.

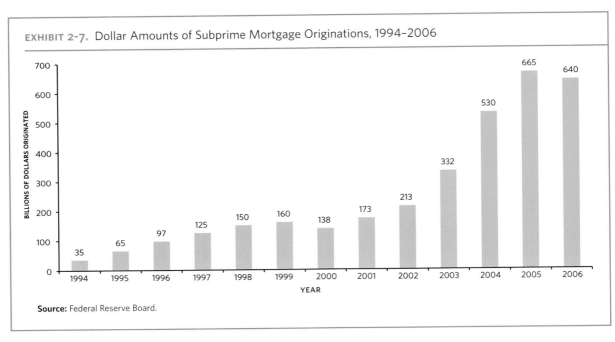

EXHIBIT 2-7. Dollar Amounts of Subprime Mortgage Originations, 1994–2006

Source: Federal Reserve Board.

These data are based on a study done for the Federal Reserve Bank by its chairman, Alan Greenspan, and an associate. However, the share of subprime lending in total mortgage lending did not rise nearly as much as the absolute volume of subprime mortgages that were made annually, mainly because all mortgage lending was expanding at unprecedented rates during this housing boom. The percentage shares of subprime loans in all outstanding mortgage loans are shown in exhibit 2-8. It was not until 2004 and 2005 that subprime loans reached or slightly exceeded one-fifth of all mortgage loans that had been made since 1994.

The Federal Reserve Board has created charts showing the number of subprime mortgages in effect, by state, as of February 2008.[3] It identifies 3.201 million subprime mortgages in effect in the United States. (The Mortgage Bankers Association estimated that there were 5.426 million subprime loans outstanding in the second quarter of 2008.) Their balances amounted to $576.585 billion, or an average loan balance of $180,101. The total home mortgage liabilities of households and nonprofit organizations in the first quarter of 2008 were $10.6 trillion, so subprime loans constituted about 5.4 percent of all household mortgage debt.[4] The average interest rate on subprime loans was 8.72 percent. About 11.73 percent of all subprime loans were interest-only. Less than 1 percent of homes carrying subprime mortgages were not owner occupied.

In the nation as a whole, 52.6 percent of subprime loans had had at least one late payment in the preceding 12 months, 8.6 percent of subprime loans had payments overdue by 90 days or more, and 9.6 percent were in foreclosure. Exhibit 2-9 shows those states that had the highest and lowest percentages of subprime loans with a payment 90 days or more past due and of subprime loans in foreclosure. Western states seem to have had less exposure to subprime problems than others.

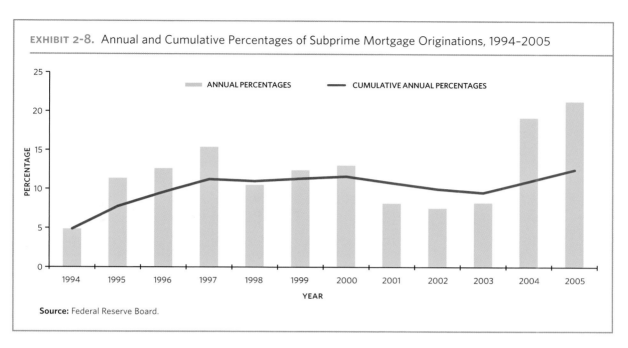

EXHIBIT 2-8. Annual and Cumulative Percentages of Subprime Mortgage Originations, 1994–2005

Source: Federal Reserve Board.

According to the Federal Reserve, 64.2 percent of all subprime loans then were adjustable-rate mortgages (ARMs). Among those subprime ARMs, 36.8 percent had already had their interest rates reset for the first time, 39.1 percent would have rates reset within 12 months from February 2008, 15.3 percent would be reset in 12 to 24 months from that date, and 5.0 percent would be reset in more than 24 months. Thus, by February 2009, 75.9 percent of subprime ARMs would have had the first resets of their interest rates. Total foreclosures and serious delinquencies had already appeared in 18.2 percent of all subprime mortgages (including fixed-rate mortgages) as of February 2008. Yet just over one-third of the ARMs, or 23.6 percent of all subprime mortgages (including both ARMs and fixed-rate), had had their interest rates reset by that time. This meant that delinquencies and foreclosures were surely going to rise in the future, as more ARM interest rates were reset. That outcome is especially likely because the U.S. economy is in a deepening recession. The Federal Reserve reported that subprime defaults had already reached 19.5 percent by October 2007, including 8 percent that were in foreclosure. The percentage of subprime loans in delinquency was actually higher in 2001 and 2002 than it was in 2006. But because the numbers of subprime loans originated in 2001 and 2002 were much smaller than the numbers originated from 2004 to 2006, the absolute numbers of subprime delinquencies were larger in these latter years.

Another category of loans below prime quality consists of Alt-A loans. The people obtaining such loans have poorer credit ratings than those getting prime loans but somewhat better credit ratings than those taking out subprime loans. The average FICO score (credit score) for subprime loans was 617, whereas for Alt-A loans it was 701. As of February 2008, there were 2.34 million Alt-A loans outstanding in the United States, or 73 percent of the number of subprime loans outstanding. The total of Alt-A mortgage loans was $679.6 billion, or an average

EXHIBIT 2-9. States with the Highest and Lowest Shares of Subprime Mortages in 2005

Share of Subprime Loans with Payments 90+ Days Past Due (%)		Share of Subprime Loans in Foreclosure (%)	
Mississippi	13.6	Florida	15.8
Tennessee	13.0	Wisconsin	13.9
Alabama	12.1	Maine	13.5
Georgia	11.9	New Jersey	13.4
Michigan	10.2	Ohio	12.7
Missouri	10.4	California	12.5
Washington, D.C.	10.3	New York	12.5
Maryland	10.0	Illinois	12.3
North Dakota	4.9	Wyoming	3.4
Montana	5.0	Tennessee	3.6
New Mexico	5.2	Alabama	3.9
Hawaii	5.2	Texas	4.2
Alaska	5.2	Arkansas	4.4
Wyoming	5.3	Alaska	4.6
Oregon	5.3	Utah	4.6
Idaho	5.7	Missouri	4.8

Source: Federal Reserve Board.

balance of $290,756. That was 61 percent larger than the average balance among subprime loans. (Thus, subprime and Alt-A loans together constituted about 11.85 percent of all household mortgage loan liabilities in the first quarter of 2008.) The average interest rate on Alt-A loans was 6.89 percent, 21 percent lower than the average for subprime loans (8.72 percent).

Among properties bought with Alt-A loans, 27.8 percent were not owner occupied—much higher than among properties bought with subprime loans. The loans were held mainly by speculators or other investors. Also, 28.06 percent were interest-only loans, more than double the percentage for subprime loans. The share of Alt-A mortgages with at least one late payment in the past 12 months was 22.1 percent, versus 52.1 percent among all subprime loans. The shares of Alt-A loans with payments overdue by 90 or more days or in foreclosure were 2.8 and 3.8 percent respectively—much lower than for subprime loans. Altogether, people who took out Alt-A loans seemed to do much better at repaying them on time than those who took out subprime mortgages.

However, it should be pointed out that among the 5.38 million borrowers who had used either Alt-A or subprime loans, the majority were making their monthly payments on time and had not defaulted as of October 2008. Thus, from the viewpoint of society as a whole, both subprime and Alt-A loans had achieved at least one of their ostensible objectives: making homeownership more widely available to households that have relatively poor credit ratings. It is most likely that many people not paying on their subprime mortgages were speculators who used their loans to flip homes for a profit but were unable to sell them at a profit—so they defaulted.

Many experts have predicted that default rates on subprime mortgages, in particular, will rise in the future when the interest rates on such loans are reset to much higher levels. As of February 2008, 23.7 percent of a sample containing all subprime loans outstanding had already had their interest rates reset, 39.2 percent would be reset in the next 12 months, and 15.3 percent would be reset in 12 to 24 months. Even so, it is quite likely that more than half of all subprime borrowers will be able to keep making enough payments on their loans to avoid foreclosure, as will a much higher fraction of Alt-A borrowers. True, default rates on subprime loans will probably rise to much higher levels than have been experienced on mortgage loans of all types in the past. Yet if considerably more than half of such borrowers manage to keep their homes, that would be a notable achievement—though it would come at a high psychological and economic cost to those who failed and were foreclosed. It should also be noted that in 2005, according to the American Housing Survey, 33.1 percent of America's 74.9 million homeowning households did not have any mortgages of any kind on their homes.

How Subprime Mortgage Problems Caused the Real Estate Credit World to Freeze Up

By late 2006, rising defaults on subprime mortgages began appearing in mortgage-backed securities that had been distributed to many investors, both within and outside the United States. Many holders of these securities—especially those outside the United States—had not realized until then that their securities were notably dependent on returns from American subprime borrowers. These investors had purchased mortgage-backed securities containing many types of real estate loans or had purchased CDOs, a generalized form of asset-backed security. CDOs often contained securitized paper from many types of loans or other assets, including mortgage-backed securities from commercial properties, prime borrowers, subprime borrowers, and credit card debt. The sellers of CDOs were often commercial banks or investment banks that had obtained favorable credit ratings for the largest tranches in those securities. Some CDOs had requirements to be marked to market, which would require writedowns if notable defaults occurred in many of the basic asset loans on which those CDOs were built.

Investors were attracted to these complex securitized investments in part because the interest rates built into subprime loans were considerably higher than those found in prime residential loans. Hence the yields of CDOs that contained subprime loans could be significantly higher than those of most other fixed-income investments then available in debt markets. Many investors attracted by those higher yields, which were strongly promoted by the providers of such securities, were assured by those providers that this paper was economically sound because it had received favorable ratings from well-known credit rating agencies.

When unexpectedly high levels of default began appearing in such securities, many of the firms promoting and selling them were surprised. They found themselves under pressure to take back some of the defaulting securities or had to absorb the losses resulting from defaults that occurred before they could sell their securities to final holders. When investment banks that had been buying such loans and packaging them in CDOs or other vehicles began to sustain large losses, investors who had bought other securities from those investment banks began to be alarmed. Those investors realized that they had not done adequate due diligence about the nature of what they were buying before committing large sums to such purchases. From the perspective of pure free enterprise, they deserved to suffer losses or be wiped out if they were heavily leveraged because of their own incompetence in making investments carelessly.

Since the massive flood of capital into real estate markets after 2000, the underwriting of real estate security investments of all types and of direct purchases of real estate had become grossly inadequate. Competition among capital suppliers for a limited stock of high-quality properties or real estate securities became intense, as noted in chapter 1. The result was a decline in the quality of underwriting of all types of real estate investments. Banks and other investors were putting up money without carefully investigating the quality or riskiness of what they were buying. If these investors demanded more time for careful underwriting, they would lose out on many deals to other, less prudent investors. In many cases, investors relied entirely on the credit ratings put on security issues by reputable credit rating agencies. But those agencies also often failed to carry out appropriate underwriting.

Another major factor was that housing prices in many U.S. metropolitan markets stopped rising when homebuilders flooded new construction markets with more than two million units in 2004 and 2005. In addition, some homeowners decided to try cashing in on high prices by putting their homes on the market, even though they did not really need to move. Finally, rising prices up through 2005 had created a whole new world of speculative buyers. Nearly all gambled on quickly flipping homes they bought with low downpayments to buyers paying much higher prices. So the inventory of homes for sale shot up beyond the capacity of homebuyers to absorb. The NAR reported that the inventory of existing single-family homes for sale each year averaged 1.696 million during the 1990s, rose to 2.302 million from 2000 to 2005, and then hit 3.712 million in 2006–07, exceeding 4.0 million in eight months of 2007.[5] As a result, home prices slowed, stopped rising, or even fell somewhat—as discussed later in this chapter.

One result has been what *The Mortgage Lender* calls an "implosion" of mortgage firms. Many of the mortgage-related firms that sprang up like mushrooms from 2000 to 2005 have disappeared; others may eventually emerge from bankruptcy. *The Mortgage Lender* listed 264 mortgage-related firms that imploded between late 2006 and July 1, 2008.[6] Overseas, many major banks have also suffered heavy losses from mortgage-related investments.

By August 2007, alarms concerning mortgage-backed securities of all types were spreading rapidly all over the globe. Moreover, the realization by investors in mortgage-related securities that they had not done thorough enough underwriting spread to investors in all types of real estate properties, from huge office buildings to individual homes. This created an enormous degree of uncertainty about what real estate–related investments—whether securities or properties—were actually worth.

Moreover, many commercial banks that had been big players in real estate markets suffered losses great enough to make them decide that they did not want to play there any more. The balance sheets of the largest U.S. commercial banks were already loaded with real estate loans, many of which were in trouble. Hence many banks decided that they did not want to make any more real estate loans of any kind. The share of all U.S. commercial bank assets consisting of real estate and home equity loans is shown in exhibit 2-10. This share hovered at just over 15 percent from 1973 through 1984. It then rose to just over 25 percent from 1991 to 1999. But then it soared to 37.6 percent in 2006. The *Wall Street Journal* reported on July 2, 2008, that

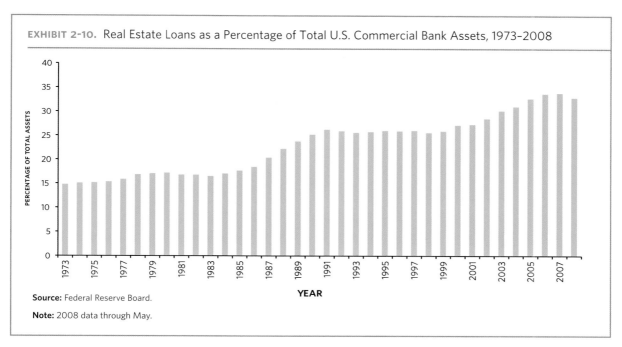

EXHIBIT 2-10. Real Estate Loans as a Percentage of Total U.S. Commercial Bank Assets, 1973–2008

Source: Federal Reserve Board.

Note: 2008 data through May.

delinquency rates on construction loans made by banks alone had risen to 13 percent for loans on condominium projects and 10.8 percent on loans for single-family home projects. As a result, many banks stopped making construction loans and were reluctant to make any real estate loans. If most banks were to largely withdraw from providing real estate credit, property markets would be in for a rough time for years to come.

By mid-2008, the only certainties remaining were as follows:

- Capital suppliers decided they had been undercompensated for the amount of risks they had been taking. Therefore, in the future they would have to
  - Do more thorough due diligence when considering any investments;
  - Charge higher rates of return from future investments, which for lenders means higher interest rates;
  - Include more equity and more stringent covenants in any loans they considered; and
  - Wait until the true value of real properties was clearer before investing more in them.
- Many commercial banks and investment banks were overloaded with real estate and real estate securities, so they decided to avoid more real estate and concentrate on rebuilding capital and serving other types of clients; and
- Conversely, property owners were not convinced that they should accept lower prices for their properties or pay higher interest rates for any money they borrowed to improve or buy properties.

In short, there was a standoff in real property transaction markets, both for buying or selling properties and for making real estate loans. Capital suppliers wanted higher returns and therefore higher interest rates and more covenants. If they got those changes, that would reduce the market values of the properties involved. But owners did not want to sacrifice any of the large market value increases they had achieved from 2000 to early 2007. This impasse was in essence the great real estate financial crisis of 2007–09. So the number of real estate transactions—including both sales and loans—collapsed to a tiny handful compared with the number before 2007. For example, in 2007, commercial mortgage-backed securities (CMBSs) had accounted for about $235 billion in transactions. In the entire first quarter of 2008, only one CMBS deal was completed. Through June 2008, only $12.1 billion had been issued, according to *Commercial Mortgage Alert.* That was 91 percent less than in the same period in 2007. A deep freeze settled over real estate markets of all types, not just housing markets.

Three Indices for Measuring Home Price Changes

One highly controversial variable of great importance to the financial crisis is how much U.S. housing prices have declined since reaching a peak in 2005 or 2006. This variable is controversial because several measures of price changes are used by different observers of housing markets, with significantly varying results. Moreover, none of the three major home price indices distinguishes between the sale prices of foreclosed homes and the sale prices of non-distressed homes, as discussed further below.

Three main statistical series measure what happens to housing prices in the U.S. market: the Case-Shiller index; the Office of Federal Housing Enterprise Oversight (OFHEO) index, which has recently been renamed the Federal Housing Finance Agency (FHFA) index; and the NAR Home Price Series.

The Case-Shiller index is frequently quoted by the *Wall Street Journal* and many other newspapers; hence it has great influence on what legislators, regulators, and even many homeowners believe is happening to U.S. home prices. This index is based upon repeat sales of the same properties over time, with data taken from 20 U.S. metropolitan areas. Data begin in March 1987 for 14 areas and at somewhat later dates for the remaining six. The metropolitan areas involved are listed in exhibit 2-11. The index values are calculated by setting the home price prevailing in each area on January 1, 2000, as equal to an index value of 100; all other data are linked to that base value.

The Case-Shiller index covers only 20 metropolitan areas out of the more than 350 in the United States; the index includes three cities in the Northeast, four in the Midwest, five in the South, and eight in the West. These cities include 18 of the 24 most populous metropolitan areas (based on 2003 population data). But that leaves out the Philadelphia, Houston, and Riverside–San Bernardino metropolitan areas, which are ranked fourth, eighth, and 13th in the top 20 by population. The 20 areas included in the index contained a total population of 99.2 million, or 34.1 percent of the nation's 290.79 million residents in 2003. They include eight of the areas with the highest housing prices in the nation (San Francisco, San Diego, Los Angeles, Miami, New York, Boston, Washington, and Portland, Oregon) and only two areas with relatively low housing prices and declining population (Detroit and Cleveland).

The FHFA home price index also measures average price changes in repeat sales of the same detached single-family homes. The database consists of pairs of transactions involving mort-

EXHIBIT 2-11. Metropolitan Areas Included in the Case-Shiller Housing Price Index

Metropolitan Area	Coverage Starting Date	Region	2008 Home Price Change
Cleveland	January 1987	Midwest	-6.1
Chicago	January 1987	Midwest	-14.3
Minneapolis	January 1989	Midwest	-18.4
Detroit	January 1991	Midwest	-21.7
Boston	January 1987	Northeast	-7.0
New York	January 1987	Northeast	-9.2
Washington, DC	January 1987	Northeast	-19.2
Dallas	January 1900	South	-4.3
Charlotte	January 1987	South	-7.2
Atlanta	January 1991	South	-12.1
Tampa	January 1987	South	-22.0
Miami	January 1987	South	-28.8
Denver	January 1987	West	-4.0
Portland, OR	January 1987	West	-13.1
Seattle	January 1990	West	-13.4
San Diego	January 1987	West	-24.8
Los Angeles	January 1987	West	-26.4
San Francisco	January 1987	West	-31.2
Las Vegas	January 1987	West	-33.0
Phoenix	January 1989	West	-34.0

Source: S&P/Case-Shiller Home Price Indices.

gages financed by either Fannie Mae or Freddie Mac, both known as Federal Housing Enterprise agencies. The index begins in 1975; its results are issued quarterly, but reports of price changes are also made every month by the FHFA. The sample of transactions is quite large, but it excludes attached and multiunit properties, properties financed by government-insured loans, and properties with loans that exceed the loan limits of Fannie Mae and Freddie Mac.

The NAR reports on the median prices of all single-family homes sold in 156 U.S. metropolitan areas, including all 20 in the Case-Shiller index. The reports come from Realtor offices in all 50 states and focus on detached single-family homes. The median sale prices of homes sold each month are reported, then compiled and published each quarter. Unlike the Case-Shiller and FHFA indices, which are both based on paired sales of the same homes over time, the NAR price estimates do not take account of different mixtures of homes, in terms of sizes and quality, sold in each period; they only compare what is sold with what was sold in previous periods. Therefore, they are not comparing the same types of homes sold in each month or quarter, which certainly influences the value of the reports. However, because the NAR uses median prices instead of average prices, which are always higher, this possible source of distortion is largely offset. (Also, the two other indices that use paired sales of the same homes do not account for quality upgrades made to those homes in the period between sales, though they do try to compensate statistically for the length of time between paired sales.) In addition, the metropolitan areas studied are not nearly as concentrated on the largest and most expensive areas in the nation, as in the Case-Shiller index. Because the NAR measure includes data from far more metropolitan areas, it reports a greater diversity of home price movements.

I calculated the percentage of all the metropolitan areas reporting median home prices to the NAR that had declining home prices year to year for each year from 2000 through 2008. This percentage was never zero even in the boom year of 2003. But it began rising notably in 2006, reaching 77 percent in 2008. This meant that about one-fourth of the 149 metropolitan areas were still showing increases in home prices in mid-2008. In contrast, the Case-Shiller index showed that all of the 20 areas from which it drew data were experiencing falling home prices in May 2008, compared with one year earlier.

The *Statistical Abstract of the United States: 2008* contains a Census Bureau table (table 26) that lists 171 metropolitan areas as having 2004 populations of 250,000 or more. Of those, 117 are included in the NAR database. The remaining 54 in the NAR database presumably have 2004 populations smaller than 250,000. Thus, the NAR database contains 7.8 times as many metropolitan areas as the Case-Shiller database. The total population of the 117 metropolitan areas in the NAR database that are listed in the Census table is 192.447 million, or 65.45 percent of the U.S. population in 2004. If the populations of the other 54 metropolitan areas in the NAR database were added in, the total population in the NAR database would surely be more than double that in the Case-Shiller database.

An Error Committed by All Three Major Home Price Indices

All three indices also commit an important error: not distinguishing between what is happening to the prices of foreclosed homes and what is happening to the prices of "normal" homes—that is, homes whose sellers are not experiencing financial difficulties related to their housing. In troubled times, foreclosed homes are almost always sold at a significant discount from their assessed values or from the prices that their original owners paid for them. That occurs because the lenders who foreclosed those homes want to get their capital out as fast as possible so they can use it elsewhere—before the vacant houses deteriorate. Hence they typically sell such homes at bargain prices. Usually, foreclosed homes sell at discounts from their initial value of 20 to 35 percent. In contrast, in troubled times, even "normal" homes may sell at a discount to their original purchase prices but not by nearly as big a cut in prices as foreclosed homes.

As the number of housing foreclosure filings in a state or community rises—and it rose to about three million per year nationwide in 2008—the share of all homes being sold that consist of foreclosed homes also rises, though it is almost always less than half of all foreclosure filings. This means that the share of homes being sold at heavily discounted prices—often well below their "true market values"—in the entire set of housing sales rises too. In prosperous times, such as 2003 and 2004, most home foreclosures occurred because some well-off family overpurchased a home and very few homes were foreclosed. Therefore, in those times foreclosed homes sold at almost the same prices as they would have otherwise. As a result, the average prices of both foreclosed and "normal" home sales were very similar. Hence for a home price index not to distinguish between these two types of sale did not seriously affect that index's accuracy at measuring home price levels.

But when many foreclosures are taking place because low-income homeowners cannot make their mortgage payments, two things happen. First, foreclosure sales become a much larger share of all home sales each month or year than in prosperous times. Second, because such foreclosures occur mainly among relatively lower-income households, the share of relatively low-cost homes in total homes sold rises significantly, compared with more normal times. Moreover, those lower-cost homes are sold at large discounts to their original prices. Both these changes cause the average or median prices of all homes being sold to decline relative to when only "normal" homes are being sold without heavy pressure from lenders. The resulting sharp decline in average sale prices may reflect these shifts in the composition of what is being sold more than actual declines in the market value of the more normal homes that are not being sold under duress.

Yet people who read in the media about what is happening to home prices may not distinguish between price declines caused by a change in the mix of housing being sold and those caused by a fall in the value of all homes. This misperception may cause many nondistressed owners of homes to believe their homes are worth far less than is really the case. That belief in turn might encourage some to think their homes are "underwater"—that is, have a market value smaller than the amount of the mortgage remaining on them—when that is not true at all.

These ideas can be seen clearly in California housing markets. The California Association of Realtors reported in September 2008 that the median price of homes sold in August statewide fell 40.5 percent below what it had been in August 2007. However, that certainly does not mean that the market value of the average California home not suffering from foreclosure had fallen 40.5 percent in the preceding year. The mix of homes sold in the state in August 2007 was far different from that in August 2008, as the California Association of Realtors clearly pointed out in its September newsletter. For one thing, the share of relatively low-priced homes sold (in California, that means homes priced below $500,000) was only 40 percent in 2007, but rose to 72 percent in 2008. In contrast, the share of homes sold for between $500,000 and $1 million dropped from 45 percent in August 2007 to 21 percent in August 2008.

Moreover, the share of home sales caused by foreclosure or other financial distress rose sharply in 2007 and 2008, compared with earlier periods, as shown in exhibit 2-12. In all of 2007, real estate–owned (REO) sales—that is, foreclosure sales—constituted 8.3 percent of all sales, whereas in May 2008, they constituted 38.6 percent of all sales, according to data from DataQuick. They were surely a higher percentage than that by December 2008.

Exhibit 2-13 shows how the prices of these two types of sale diverged from each other after about February 2007. From August 2005 through February 2007, the average REO and non-REO prices of California home sales reported by counties were almost identical. That undoubtedly occurred because the relatively small numbers of REOs were not caused by poor households defaulting but by households that were not poor being unable to make their mortgage payments. Hence their homes were sold at nearly "normal" market prices. But after that, and especially after both types of prices peaked in June 2007, the prices of REO sales fell much more than the prices of non-REO (normal) sales. By May 2008, non-REO sales

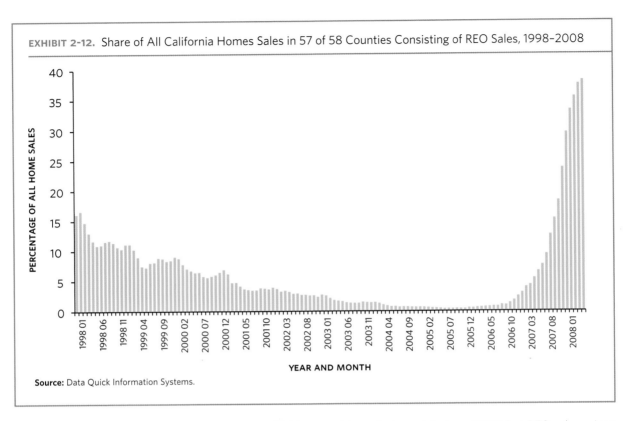

EXHIBIT 2-12. Share of All California Homes Sales in 57 of 58 Counties Consisting of REO Sales, 1998–2008

Source: Data Quick Information Systems.

prices had fallen an average of 16.1 percent from their peak in June 2007, but REO sales prices had declined by 28.2 percent—75 percent more. Thus, homes sold by owners experienced a much smaller decline in prices than homes sold by lenders following foreclosures. The only exception occurred in neighborhoods where many foreclosed homes were also for sale, so the prices obtainable by sellers who were not suffering from foreclosure were often dragged down by the presence of many foreclosed homes nearby.

This difference in price declines is crucial in how homeowners view the true market values of their homes. If they are normal sellers not under financial duress, they are likely to experience a much smaller decline in home prices than if they are foreclosed—except for nondistressed households whose homes are in the lower-priced brackets or in specific neighborhoods were many other homes are being foreclosed. In that case, they may become "infected" by the lower prices of foreclosed homes in the vicinity. Yet the media do not make this distinction in any quantified manner, although the California Association of Realtors does discuss it in its monthly sales reports.

Foreclosure filings and sales in 2008 were heavily concentrated in eight states. These states had the highest concentration of foreclosure activity, as indicated by the lowest number of resident households for each foreclosure filing in 2008. They were Nevada, California, Arizona, Florida, Colorado, Georgia, Michigan, and Ohio. Together they accounted for 61.7 percent of all foreclosure filings and 86.3 percent of all foreclosure sales likely to occur

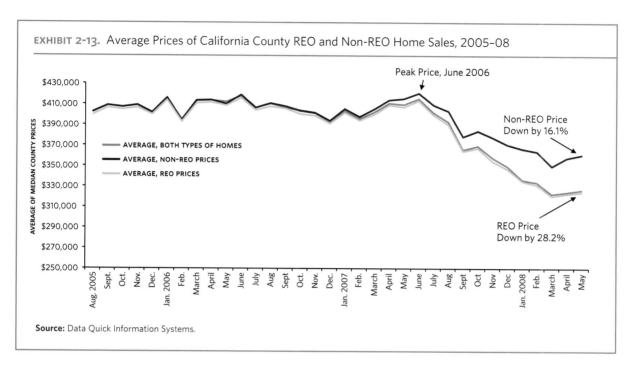

EXHIBIT 2-13. Average Prices of California County REO and Non-REO Home Sales, 2005–08

Source: Data Quick Information Systems.

in 2008. Yet all eight states combined contained only 32.2 percent of all U.S. households (based on 2006 data). In the top five of those eight states, average foreclosure sales prices were substantially higher than the national average for the first four months of 2008, which was $163,470. Thus California has one of the highest ratios of foreclosures to its total housing stock in the nation, exceeded only by Nevada. So this ability to quantify the difference between home price declines for normal sellers and those for distressed sellers is critical to Californians, but it is not as crucial in many other states with much lower foreclosure rates. Yet it would clearly be in the best interest of the nation, and especially of residents in those few states with the most foreclosures, for publishers of home price data and commentators on the housing market to distinguish clearly, and in quantitative terms, between these two fundamentally different types of home sales. I believe the federal government should pressure the private producers of housing price indices to make such distinctions in their normal reporting, so as to more clearly represent actual market conditions.

What Has Happened to Home Prices?

Abstract discussion of the relative merits of these three indices is not as meaningful as actually comparing what they report about home prices over time. The Case-Shiller index reports monthly price measures and quarterly data; the FHFA uses quarterly measures; and the NAR reports are both monthly and quarterly. Since they all use different base measures, I have adopted the Case-Shiller approach of setting the price in the first quarter of 2000 equal to 100 and revising the numerical values of all other time periods from that base. The results

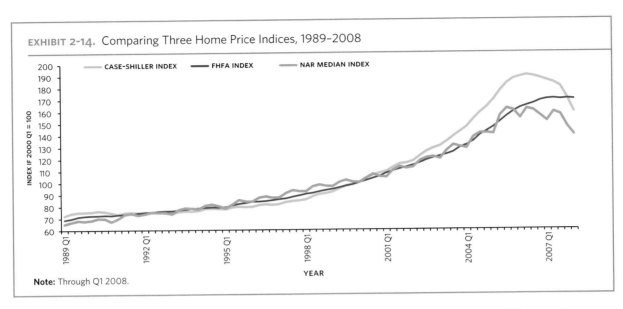

EXHIBIT 2-14. Comparing Three Home Price Indices, 1989–2008

Legend: CASE-SHILLER INDEX — FHFA INDEX — NAR MEDIAN INDEX

Y-axis: INDEX IF 2000 Q1 = 100

X-axis: YEAR (1989 Q1, 1992 Q1, 1995 Q1, 1998 Q1, 2001 Q1, 2004 Q1, 2007 Q1)

Note: Through Q1 2008.

for the entire country for the period from January 1989 through February 2008 are shown in exhibit 2-14, which is based on quarterly prices.

This exhibit shows that all three indices report very similar home prices before 2000, but the Case-Shiller index reports much higher home price increases from 2000 to their peaks in June and July 2006. From a base of 100 in the first quarter of 2000, the Case-Shiller index rose to its peak value in July 2006 of 189.93, a gain of 89.9 percent. In contrast, the NAR measure of median prices peaked at an index value of 169.88 in the second quarter of 2006, showing gains of about 70 percent. The high of 169.9 for the NAR measure was 10.5 percent below the high in the Case-Shiller index. The high reached by the FHFA index in the second quarter of 2007 was 169.9—almost identical to the peak of the NAR index.

The most striking thing about these divergences is that they have greatly influenced subsequent reports about how much housing prices have declined in the United States. The Case-Shiller index shows a steep decline in home prices by June 2008 of 18.2 percent from their peak in July 2006. In contrast, by the end of the second quarter of 2008, the FHFA index had declined by only 0.87 percent from its high and the NAR index had fallen 13.5 percent from its high. Economist Robert Shiller, one of the authors of the Case-Shiller index, has been widely quoted as saying that U.S. housing prices would fall, or perhaps had already fallen, by 20 percent—which is not far from what his data showed at the end of the second quarter of 2008.

In my opinion, the Case-Shiller index has overestimated both the rise in home prices since 2000 and their decline since 2005–06. The major reason for this outcome is the index's very small sample of metropolitan areas, compared with the much broader samples of the other two indices. Not only is the Case-Shiller index based on data from only 20 areas, but those areas have experienced much higher home price increases than most of the nation. This can be seen from the home price data for 14 metropolitan areas from the Case-Shiller index with median prices above the national median price, as reported by the more conservative NAR index for 2007, set forth in exhibit 2-15.

EXHIBIT 2-15. Home Price Increases in the 14 Case-Shiller Metropolitan Areas with Median Prices above the National Average, Using NAR Price Data

Metropolitan Area	Median Price 2007 ($)	Rank by Price	Percentage Rise, 1979–2007	Percentage Rise, 2000–07
San Francisco	805,400	2	208	77
Los Angeles	589,200	5	174	172
San Diego	588,700	6	223	119
New York	540,300	7	166	110
Washington, D.C.	430,800	12	204	79
Boston	395.600	13	136	43
Seattle	386,900	14	290	95
Miami	365,500	19	325	157
Las Vegas	297,700	25	247	116
Portland	295,200	26	327	76
Chicago	276,600	31	178	73
Phoenix	257,400	39	226	91
Denver	245,000	41	187	25
Minneapolis	225,000	51	158	49
U.S.	217,800	54	130	47

Source: National Association of Realtors.

All of the 14 metropolitan areas in the exhibit—70 percent of all the areas in the Case-Shiller index—have home prices and rates of price increase that are far above average from 1979 to 2007. They include seven of the most costly areas for home prices in the nation. This lineup creates a substantial upward bias concerning both price levels and past rates of price increases in the United States. That bias has caused the Case-Shiller index to provide misleading estimates of national home price increases—and declines—since 2000. In addition, the large metropolitan areas included in the Case-Shiller index contain many large neighborhoods where subprime loans—and foreclosures on them—are concentrated. The prices of foreclosed homes that are being sold now are lower than the prices of owner-occupied single-family homes, and this biases the Case-Shiller index toward larger price declines in 2008 and onward than are typical of the nation as a whole. Yet the *Wall Street Journal* and many other influential news sources quote Case-Shiller data without making such distinctions, rather than citing the two more conservative price indices, which I believe are more accurate and more relevant to national policies.

As noted above, the Case-Shiller index indicates a much larger increase in home prices from the base of 100 in 2000 to its peak than do either of the other two indices. It indicates an 89.9 percent gain, versus 61.9 percent for the NAR index and 69.4 percent for the FHFA Index. As a result, when prices started to fall, the Case-Shiller index indicated a much steeper and larger decline from its peak to mid-2008 than did the other two indices. Yet by the end of the second quarter of 2008, both the Case-Shiller and the FHFA indices show similar levels of home prices, compared with their levels in 2000. The Case-Shiller index was at 155.32 versus 168.4 for the FHFA index. The NAR index was lower, at 146.9.

Although all three indices are not terribly far apart at the end of the second quarter of 2008, the fact that the Case-Shiller index indicates a much larger and steeper decline in home prices than the other two indices is important. The steeper decline of the Case-Shiller index, which is widely quoted in the media, implies that prices may continue to fall rapidly in the future. In contrast, the less precipitous declines of the other two indices imply a slower rate of future price decline. What people believe about how fast home prices are likely to fall in the future is significant. That belief may influence the number of homeowners who go into default because they believe they have negative equity (that is, their homes have lower market values than the remaining amounts they owe on their mortgages). If homeowners believe home prices will continue to decline rapidly, they may be more willing to walk away from such situations than if they believe home prices are almost leveling off and may even start rising in the not too distant future. Thus, whichever of these indices is most widely believed to be accurate may have a significant effect on how many defaults and foreclosures take place. If the media continue to emphasize the Case-Shiller index, that might in itself accelerate the number of mortgage defaults and foreclosures that actually occur, compared with what would happen if they emphasized either of the other two indices.

Regional and Metropolitan-Area Variations in Home Prices and Their Rates of Change

Home prices vary tremendously across the nation from one state or metropolitan area to another. In fact, of all the expenditures that households make for daily survival, the cost of their housing is surely the one that differs most from place to place. Among the over 150 metropolitan areas in which home prices are tracked by the NAR, the San Jose area in California, which includes Silicon Valley and many expensive suburbs that surround it, has the highest median price. That price peaked at $865,000 in the second quarter of 2007 and had fallen to $780,000 in the first quarter of 2008, a decline of 9.8 percent. At the other end of the price scale, the Youngstown, Ohio, metropolitan area had the lowest median price. It peaked at $91,000 in the third quarter of 2004 but had fallen to $67,000 in the first quarter of 2008, a drop of 26.4 percent. Thus, in the first quarter of 2008, buying a home was 11.64 times as costly in San Jose as in Youngstown. But losses to homeowners in percentage terms were much greater in Youngstown than in San Jose.

Exhibit 2-16 shows the 30 highest-price and lowest-price metropolitan areas in the NAR's records as of 2006, the year when prices peaked in most regions. Sixteen of the 30 most expensive housing areas were located on or near the West Coast (eight) or the East Coast (eight). Five of the most costly six were in California; six of the top 30 were in the New York City area. At the other end of the scale, 17 of the least expensive 30 were in the Midwest, eight were in the Northeast, and five in the South; none were in the West.

The degree to which home prices have increased—and more recently, decreased—over time has varied just as much as their levels. To illustrate this fact, I ranked the median home prices in 132 metropolitan areas tracked by the NAR in descending order of their maximum quarterly prices from 2000 to 2008. In most metropolitan areas, home prices peaked sometime in 2006. I then divided the 132 areas into quintiles based on their maximum prices—that is, groups that

EXHIBIT 2-16. Metropolitan Areas with the Highest and Lowest Median Home Prices in 2006

Rank	Highest Median Prices	Median Price (Thousands of 2006 Dollars)	Rank	Lowest Median Prices	Median Price (Thousands of 2006 Dollars)
1	San Jose–Sunnyvale–Santa Clara, CA	775.0	1	Youngstown–Warren-Boardman, OH-PA	81.5
2	San Francisco–Oakland-Fremont, CA	752.8	2	Decatur, IL	85.4
3	Anaheim–Santa Ana–Irvine, CA	709.0	3	Elmira, NY	86.8
4	Honolulu, HI	630.0	4	South Bend-Mishawaka, IN	92.7
5	San Diego–Carlsbad–San Marcos, CA	601.8	5	Cumberland, MD-WV	95.7
6	Los Angeles–Long Beach–Santa Ana, CA	584.8	6	Binghamton, NY	96.9
7	New York–Wayne–White Plains, NY-NJ	539.4	7	Buffalo–Niagara Falls, NY	97.9
8	NY: Nassau-Suffolk, NY	474.7	8	Fort Wayne, IN	99.7
9	Bridgeport-Stamford-Norwalk, CT	473.7	9	Erie, PA	101.3
10	New York–Northern New Jersey–Long Island, NY-NJ-PA	469.3	10	Springfield, IL	105.4
11	Newark-Union, NJ-PA	433.0	11	Topeka, KS	106.1
12	Washington-Arlington-Alexandria, DC-VA-MD-WV	431.0	12	Waterloo–Cedar Falls, IA	108.9
13	Boston-Cambridge-Quincy, MA-NH**	402.2	13	Canton-Massillon, OH	109.3
14	Riverside–San Bernardino-Ontario, CA	400.7	14	Toledo, OH	110.0
15	Barnstable Town, MA	389.5	15	Beaumont–Port Arthur, TX	112.7
16	Edison, NJ	387.7	16	Peoria, IL	112.7
17	Sacramento-Arden-Arcade-Roseville, CA	374.5	17	Akron, OH	114.6
18	Miami–Fort Lauderdale–Miami Beach, FL	371.2	18	Rochester, NY	114.8
19	Boulder, CO	366.4	19	Amarillo, TX	114.9
20	Seattle-Tacoma-Bellevue, WA	361.2	20	Wichita, KS	114.9
21	Reno-Sparks, NV	347.2	21	Pittsburgh, PA	116.1
22	Sarasota-Bradenton-Venice, FL	334.3	22	Dayton, OH	116.7
23	Las Vegas–Paradise, NV	317.4	23	Syracuse, NY	116.8
24	Providence–New Bedford–Fall River, RI-MA	289.6	24	Indianapolis, IN	119.3
25	Trenton-Ewing, NJ	289.6	25	Rockford, IL	119.3
26	New Haven-Milford, CT	287.7	26	Charleston, WV	119.4
27	Worcester, MA	281.7	27	Davenport-Moline-Rock Island, IA-IL	119.7
28	Portland-Vancouver-Beaverton, OR-WA	280.8	28	Springfield, MO	124.8
29	Baltimore-Towson, MD	279.9	29	Oklahoma City, OK	125.0
30	Chicago-Naperville-Joliet, IL	273.5	30	Spartanburg, SC	126.7

Source: National Association of Realtors.

each contain about one-fifth of the total metropolitan areas involved. (There was some deviation in the exact number in each quintile because of insufficient home price data for some metropolitan areas.) Then I computed average values for a group of key variables for the metropolitan areas in each quintile. I also created a graph showing how home prices had moved from 1997 to their maximum price and then down to their price in the first quarter of 2008. (I used the first quarter rather than the second because prices were actually higher in the second quarter, and I wanted to test how far prices had fallen.) It appears in exhibit 2-18, which uses a price index: the NAR median home price in each area for 1997 was set to equal 100, and the maximum price and 2008 price were measured by the same index. That allows the reader to see immediately by what percentage prices had gone up and then down for each quintile of metropolitan areas. Thus, among the one-fifth of these areas with the highest maximum prices, the average median price rose from $153,800 in 1997 to $450,260 at the maximum, and then fell to $366,230 in the first quarter of 2008. As the exhibit shows, that was an increase from an index value of 100 to an index value of 292 from 1997 to the maximum, and then a fall to an index value of 238 in the first quarter of 2008. So the average price went up 192 index points—or 192 percent—and then fell by 54 index points. The average price in the first quarter of 2008 was still 138 percent above the price in 1997, and the fall in price was only 28 percent as great as the price gain from 1997 to the maximum point.

Review of the quintile analysis described above leads to the following conclusions:

■ Metropolitan areas that started out in 1997 with the highest prices also had the biggest price increases until 2006; those with the lowest initial prices had the smallest price increases.

■ The areas with the highest price increases on average had populations five times as large (2.654 million) as the areas with the least price increases (526,000), with the quintiles in between showing that average price gains increased directly with average metropolitan area size.

■ In terms of absolute dollars, the areas with the highest maximum prices had the biggest declines from their maximum prices to June 2008, and the areas with the smallest maximum prices had the smallest declines. But when those price declines are seen as percentages of the maximum prices, all five quintiles had very similar average declines.

■ When price declines are computed as percentages of the average gain in price, the areas in the quintile with the lowest maximum price fared worst, because their average price losses offset more than 40 percent of the gain that they had previously received. In contrast, for the highest-priced areas, the price declines offset an average of only one-fourth of their price gains up to the maximum.

■ Eighteen of the metropolitan areas in the highest-priced quintile were coastal. The number of coastal areas declined directly with the price quintiles, with only two in the fourth-lowest quintile and none in the lowest-priced quintile. Twenty-one of the 25 metropolitan areas in the lowest-priced quintile were in the Midwest; only one in the highest-priced quintile was in the Midwest (Chicago, ranked last in that quintile).

■ Whether considering the period from 1997 to 2008 or the period from 2000 to 2008, the following conclusions apply:
  • Home prices in all quintiles in June 2008 were still well above home prices in either 1997 or 2000.
  • The biggest net gains in home prices from either 1997 or 2000 to 2008 in absolute and relative terms occurred in the highest-priced quintile, and the least net gains occurred in the lowest-priced quintile.
  • Unless home prices decline in the future at an accelerating rate, it does not seem likely that they will ultimately fall as much as they have risen since either 1997 or 2000.

Three general conclusions can be drawn from all this information: Before changing locations, a potential homebuyer should check out housing costs, because they vary from one place to another more than any other cost of living. The least expensive housing is found inland, far from any of the three coasts (Atlantic, Pacific, and Gulf of Mexico) and not in the West. Designing any uniformly applicable national public policies on housing is made extremely difficult by the immense variations in home prices and their rates of change across the nation.

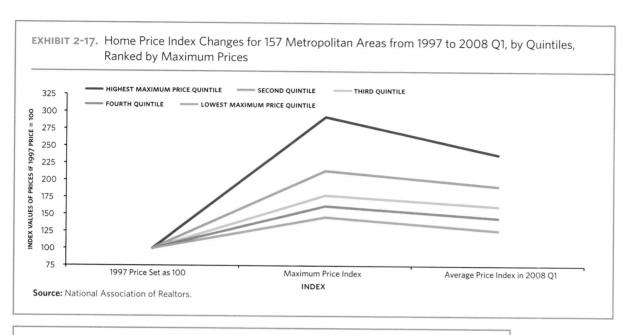

EXHIBIT 2-17. Home Price Index Changes for 157 Metropolitan Areas from 1997 to 2008 Q1, by Quintiles, Ranked by Maximum Prices

HIGHEST MAXIMUM PRICE QUINTILE — SECOND QUINTILE — THIRD QUINTILE — FOURTH QUINTILE — LOWEST MAXIMUM PRICE QUINTILE

INDEX VALUES OF PRICES IF 1997 PRICE = 100

1997 Price Set as 100 — Maximum Price Index — Average Price Index in 2008 Q1

INDEX

Source: National Association of Realtors.

EXHIBIT 2-18. Declines in Stock Prices of Four Major U.S. Homebuilder Firms, 2005–08

Name of Homebuilder	Stock Price, Mid-2005 ($)	Stock Price, Oct. 2008 ($)	Decline (%)
Centex Homes	70.67	8.78	–88.00
KB Homes	82.47	12.96	–84.29
D.H. Horton	41.46	6.77	–83.67
Pulte Homes	43.10	8.50	–80.28
S&P 500 Stock Index	1,245.04	877.00	–29.66

What Has Happened to the Stock Prices of U.S. Homebuilders?

Clear evidence of the radical change in real estate market conditions has been provided by what has happened to the stock prices of four major U.S. homebuilding firms. Exhibit 2-18 shows the change in their per-share stock prices from their recent peaks in mid-2005 to October 2008, compared with the decline of the S&P 500 over the same time period. These stock price changes hugely reduced the capitalized market values of all four homebuilders, drastically cutting the capital they have available or can borrow to keep building new homes.

The stocks of both Fannie Mae and Freddie Mac also fell dramatically as a result of fears that their losses on mortgages would exceed their capital reserves. By August 25, 2008, Fannie Mae's stock had fallen to $5.19 per share and Freddie Mac's to $3.20 per share. Those were declines of 92.4 percent and 95.04 percent, respectively, from one year earlier. Subsequently, the Treasury and Federal Reserve Board seized ownership of both these government-sponsored enterprises, thereby rendering their stocks of no value, while providing the financial resources to prevent them from getting into fatal trouble.

Some Broader Impacts of Changes in the Organization of Housing Mortgage Markets

The International Monetary Fund (IMF) devoted its April 2008 issue of *World Economic Outlook* to the subject of housing and the business cycle. Its analysts concluded that changes in mortgage finance since the 1980s have profoundly affected the relationship between a nation's housing markets and its overall economic growth or decline. The deregulation of banks and other financial institutions, plus a flood of money into real estate markets after 2000, greatly increased the impact of mortgage financing practices upon the business cycles in several developed nations.

In particular, much easier mortgage financing arrangements, supported by massive amounts of financial capital flowing into real estate, put a strong upward pressure on the market prices of homes, as noted earlier. This in turn led many homeowning households to refinance their mortgages and withdraw capital from the escalating equities they had accumulated in their homes. They then spent that capital on other types of consumption. Thus, prosperity in housing markets, accompanied by rising home prices and homeowner equities, helped stimulate overall economic growth in these nations. This was particularly significant in the nations that experienced the largest increases in housing prices—Ireland, the Netherlands, and the United Kingdom—even more than it was in the United States.

As a result, the overall economies in these nations were vulnerable to negative impacts on their growth rates from any major shocks in their housing markets. One reason is that homeowning households in nations with highly flexible mortgage markets tend to borrow more against their homes. As a result, those households develop higher loan-to-value ratios concerning their housing—which means more financial leverage—than do households in nations with more traditional mortgage financing arrangements. But, as discussed more in detail in chapter 5, higher leverage financing—whether for households or for businesses—creates greater vulnerability to critical conditions if some shock makes credit harder to obtain, as has clearly happened in the current financial crisis. Therefore, the IMF authors concluded that

> The housing sector may have become a more important source of economic volatility over the past two decades than previously. . . . The role of the housing market in providing collateral for loans reinforces the links between the housing sector and the wider economy. . . . Countries with a more flexible system of housing finance tend to experience stronger spillovers from the housing sector.[7]

This change was not universal among developed nations because several did not greatly deregulate or otherwise alter their mortgage markets in the 1990s and 2000s. But in those nations that did greatly alter their mortgage systems, including the United States, it may be advisable in the future for the authorities who set monetary policies to pay more attention to major swings in the prices of assets like stocks and homes. Such asset-price swings can have large impacts on the overall growth rates and economic cycles in those nations.

Conclusion

The great real estate credit crunch and financial crisis of 2007–09 represents the most serious adverse event in U.S. housing markets since the Great Depression of the 1930s. However, that financial crisis was preceded by six years of the largest run-ups in American history in home prices, homeownership, and using homes to finance equity withdrawals that supported consumption in general. Ironically, the credit crunch was fundamentally caused by a force exactly opposite to that crunch: a massive influx of financial capital into housing and other real estate markets the world over after the stock market crash in 2000. The negative results that ultimately sprang from that oversupply of capital were still operating when this book was being finalized in early 2009.

However, a key question remains unanswered. After the savings and loan crisis in the 1980s, the nation's housing finance system—and indeed the commercial real estate finance system—was rebuilt upon securitization. But the financial crisis has revealed some key drawbacks in securitization that have not yet been overcome; nor are there any clear ideas about how to overcome them. On what kind of financial arrangements can the future home finance system be built? That question has yet to be answered.

NOTES

1. Data from Alan Greenspan and James Kennedy, "Estimates of Home Mortgage Originations, Repayments, and Debt on 1-4 Family Residences," Federal Reserve Board, Washington, D.C., 2005.
2. Edward Gramlich also wrote a book on subprime mortgages: Edward M. Gramlich, *Subprime Mortgages: America's Latest Boom and Bust* (Washington, D.C.: Urban Institute Press, 2007).
3. Federal Reserve Board, "State Level Sub-Prime Loan Characteristics, February 2008." Statistics calculated on first-lien and active loans, including REO.
4. Data from the Federal Reserve Board's "Flow of Funds Report" for June 5, 2008, table L.100, page 62. This computation assumes that nonprofit organizations held a trivial amount of the home mortgage liabilities of both households and nonprofit organizations.
5. Data on unsold inventories of existing homes taken from many monthly issues of National Association of Realtors, "Real Estate Outlook: Market Trends and Insights," tables on existing single-family home sales.
6. The Mortgage Lender Implode-O-Meter, http://ml-implode.com/index.html#lists.
7. Roberto Cardarelli, Deniz Igan, and Alessandro Rebucci, "The Changing Housing Cycle and the Implications for Monetary Policy," chapter 3 in *World Economic Outlook* (Washington, D.C.: International Monetary Fund, April 2008), pages 14 and 15.

Chapter Three

Subprime Lending and Housing Foreclosures

THE PRECEDING CHAPTER BEGAN AN ANALYSIS of subprime lending because of its central role in how changes in lending conditions have affected housing markets. This chapter further explores the impacts of subprime lending and of the housing foreclosures that subprime defaults triggered.

How Many Subprime Mortgages Are There?

As chapter 2 pointed out, the Federal Reserve Board estimated that 3.201 million subprime mortgages were in effect in the United States as of February 2008. They had a total face value of $576.585 billion, which was 3.25 percent of the total amount of mortgages outstanding ($14.733 trillion in the first quarter of 2008). However, the MBA estimated that 5.426 million subprime loans were outstanding in the second quarter of 2008. The MBA does not estimate the dollar amount of subprime mortgages. In view of this disparity between two reputable authorities, it is not easy to determine exactly how many subprime loans in fact exist in the country.

The MBA further estimates that subprime mortgages make up about 12 percent of the 45.22 million mortgages of all types outstanding in the first quarter of 2008 and that subprime loans are about evenly divided between fixed-rate and adjustable-rate forms. In contrast, the Federal Reserve Board says that 62.4 percent of all subprime loans were adjustable-rate mortgages. The rate of foreclosure among subprime loans is estimated by the Federal Reserve to be 9.6 percent and by the MBA to be 4.20 percent, mainly concentrated among adjustable-rate versions of subprime loans (for which the foreclosure rate is 6.57 percent of outstanding loans).

To sum up as best as can be done, there are a lot of subprime mortgages, but they constitute less than 10 percent of all home mortgage loans by number and even less by dollar value. At least half are adjustable-rate mortgages, and that type makes up most of such loans that are in foreclosure. The foreclosure rate on subprime mortgages—especially adjustable-rate ones—is much higher than foreclosure rates on prime mortgages or Federal Housing Agency mortgages, which are all under 2 percent, with fixed-rate versions under 1 percent. That should be close enough to place the whole subprime situation in context reasonably well.

How much might be lost through subprime loan defaults? The maximum total number of subprime loans estimated by the MBA is 5.426 million. If the average subprime loan balance is $180,126, as estimated by the Federal Reserve, then the total value of outstanding subprime loans as of 2008 would be $977.4 billion. If 20 percent of those loans default overall (a much higher default rate than reported by either the MBA or the Federal Reserve), that would be a total value of $195.5 billion. If half of the defaulting amount were eventually recovered by resale, the total loss would be $97.7 billion. That is clearly a large amount, but it is much smaller than the amounts at stake often described by the media.

Where Subprime Mortgage Loans Are Concentrated

Subprime home loans are not scattered evenly across the country but are concentrated in certain types of neighborhoods. Chris Mayer and Karen Pence of the Federal Reserve Board wrote a detailed analysis of where subprime loans have been concentrated in the United States and what types of people were most likely to be associated with such loans.[1] From their thorough study of subprime loans made in 2005, they arrived at the following conclusions:

- Metropolitan areas where subprime loans were relatively high percentages of all home mortgage originations were of several types:
  - Areas where home prices had risen rapidly and populations were growing rapidly. In such areas, both total mortgage originations and subprime mortgage originations were higher than average in relation to the total supplies of housing. However, metropolitan areas in the Northeast, where home prices had risen rapidly but populations had not grown similarly, had below-average shares of subprime mortgage originations.
  - Economically depressed and slow-growing areas where total mortgage originations were low because of low prosperity, but the share of subprime borrowers was high because there were more low-income households needing special access to funds to buy homes. The states of Michigan and Ohio exemplify such areas.
  - Areas with relatively high proportions of African-American or Hispanic residents. In general, subprime lending was much more concentrated in such areas and within neighborhoods all over the nation that have high fractions of these minority residents, partly because they have lower incomes than whites and Asians, on average, and may have more difficulty getting prime loans.
- Memphis, Miami, Detroit, and three smaller cities in California are among the metropolitan areas that had the highest percentages of subprime mortgage originations among all home mortgage originations in 2005 (see exhibit 3-1).
- Within metropolitan areas, subprime loans were concentrated in low-income, inner-city areas where percentages of African-Americans and Hispanics were high, as well as in outlying areas where new housing construction was concentrated.
- Nevada, Arizona, California, and Florida had the highest percentages of subprime mortgage originations measured against the total number of existing housing units in the state; Pennsylvania, Alabama, and Louisiana had the lowest percentage (see exhibit 3-2).

EXHIBIT 3-1. Metropolitan Areas with High Percentages of Subprime Home Mortgages in 2005	
Year	Subprime Home Mortgages as Share of All Home Mortgage Originations (%)
Memphis, TN	34
Bakersfield, CA	34
Visalia, CA	32
Fresno, CA	31
Detroit, MI	29
Miami, FL	29
Houston, TX	28
Riverside, CA	28
Jackson, MS	27
Las Vegas, NV	27
McAllen, TX	27
Cleveland, OH	27
San Antonio, TX	26
Stockton, CA	28
Orlando, FL	25
Cape Coral, FL	24
Jacksonville, FL	24
Milwaukee, WI	24

Source: Federal Reserve Board.

- Subprime loans are also concentrated in areas where credit for low-income households is difficult to obtain, such as ZIP code areas where most residents have low credit rating scores and counties that have high unemployment rates.
- Except in the Midwest and Northeast, subprime lending was strong in areas that had experienced rapid home price appreciation and high levels of new housing construction since 2000. Subprime lending may have helped accelerate the housing boom that took place in such areas.

The Nature of Foreclosures

A foreclosure consists of a series of legal steps that a person or firm who has lent mortgage money to a home purchaser must undertake in order to reclaim the home involved if the borrower fails to make payments on the loan. Foreclosing is a long and detailed process containing five distinct stages, from a notice of delinquency to property being repossessed by the foreclosing party (usually a bank). The initial step is to file a foreclosure request. A later step is to gain legal control of the property (which is then called real estate–owned, or REO). The final step is to sell the property to a new owner.

EXHIBIT 3-2. States with the Highest and Lowest Shares of Subprime Mortages in 2005

Highest States	Subprime Mortgages as Share of All Housing Units (%)	Lowest States	Subprime Mortgages as Share of All Housing Units (%)
Nevada	10.0	Pennsylvania	1.9
Arizona	7.7	Alabama	1.8
California	7.1	Louisiana	1.8
Florida	6.2	Arkansas	1.7
Rhode Island	6.2	South Dakota	1.4
Maryland	6.1	Vermont	1.4
Washington, D.C.	5.2	Montana	1.2
Illinois	4.8	North Dakota	1.2
New Jersey	4.3	West Virginia	0.9

Source: Federal Reserve Board.

An important intermediate step is to evict the current occupant. Because many homes for which legal owners fail to make payments are occupied by renters, not owners, this step has major welfare implications. It can often displace innocent victims of the owner's failure to pay, sometimes with very little or no advance notice.

The whole foreclosure process usually takes a long time and does not always end with the lender recapturing the properties involved. As a result, the number of foreclosed properties actually sold in any given month or year is much smaller than the number of initial foreclosure filings in that period. In the first three quarters of 2008, 2.523 million foreclosure actions were filed and 639,281 foreclosure sales occurred—or 25.3 percent of the actions filed, according to data from RealtyTrac.

How Many Foreclosures Have Already Taken Place?

There are two major data sources concerning the number, nature, and location of mortgage foreclosures in the United States. One is RealtyTrac, a California firm that provides detailed information about foreclosed properties to potential buyers. It reports foreclosures monthly and quarterly. It is not clear how completely RealtyTrac captures all foreclosures filed and their current stages of development. However, it does prepare frequent reports for states, counties, metropolitan areas, and cities. RealtyTrac's most comprehensive data seem to be on the monthly and quarterly number of filings made—that is, notices of delinquency followed by filing actions in courts.

For example, in the first three quarters of 2008, RealtyTrac data show 2.523 million new foreclosure filings were made in the United States. The average share nationwide of homes filed for foreclosure in the first three quarters of 2008 that were repossessed by banks was 25.3 percent.[2] Because of the time lag between filing and repossession, takeovers in a given time period may have originated with filings in an earlier period.

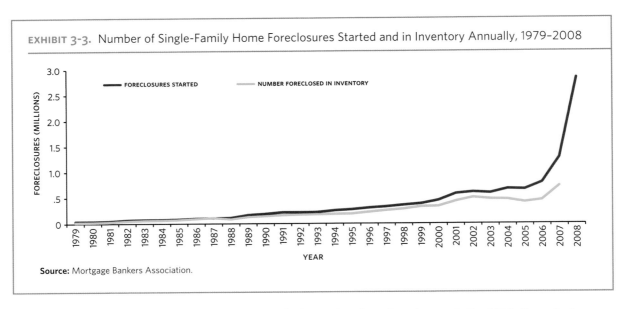

EXHIBIT 3-3. Number of Single-Family Home Foreclosures Started and in Inventory Annually, 1979–2008

Source: Mortgage Bankers Association.

The second reliable source of information about foreclosures is the MBA. It conducts a delinquency survey of the number of mortgages outstanding (not their dollar value), which reports the percentage of total outstanding mortgages in each quarter that have been filed for foreclosure or are somewhere in the foreclosure process. The MBA states that its survey covers only 85 percent of all mortgages outstanding, so the survey probably understates total foreclosures. But because it covers major areas, it probably underreports actual foreclosures by less than 15 percent.

Exhibit 3-3, based on MBA data, shows the numbers of single-family home mortgages that were filed for foreclosure in each year from 1979 to 2008. That annual number remained below 100,000 until 1987, gradually rose to 216,000 in 1991, steadily increased to 500,000 in 2001 and rose rapidly to 1.28 million in 2007. This compares with RealtyTrac's estimate for all of 2007 of 1.61 million new foreclosure filings. If the MBA estimate for 2007 is expanded by dividing it by 0.85 to allow for a 15 percent undercount, it would be 1.50 million—or just 7 percent below RealtyTrac's estimate for 2007. Thus both data sources estimate that new foreclosure filings in 2007 were in excess of 1.5 million. RealtyTrac estimated that 3.16 million foreclosure filings were made in all of 2008, of which 2.33 million were filed against separate properties. Foreclosures will likely keep rising in 2009 because more subprime mortgage rates will reset upward.

The Housing and Economic Recovery Act of 2008 (the Act), adopted by Congress and signed into law by President Bush in late July 2008, provides a way for lenders and borrowers to avoid foreclosure, as described in more detail below. However, Sheila C. Bair, head of the Federal Deposit Insurance Corporation (FDIC) at the time, told the press on October 23, 2008, that few mortgage lenders were willing to accept the "haircuts" on their loans that would be required by participation in the Act. Hence, the number of loans that have been restructured under the Act has been far below initial expectations. As a result, the federal government was considering guaranteeing the values of such mortgages so as to reduce the likely number of future foreclosures.[3] Also, the FDIC has developed a loan modification program that would enable many homeowners who are unable to make current payments to continue occupying their homes without undue losses to investors in the mortgages of those homeowners. This program is described in more detail below.

How Many Foreclosures Have Resulted in Home Sales?

As noted above, the MBA conducts quarterly delinquency surveys across the nation to determine how many foreclosures have been started and how many housing units are in the inventory of foreclosed homes.[4] I have converted the latter data into annual estimates by averaging the four estimates of foreclosed home inventories for each year. The results are shown in exhibit 3-3. The number of sales of foreclosed homes has also risen sharply since 2000. RealtyTrac states that 2.230 million properties had foreclosure filings made against them in all of 2008. Foreclosure sales had been running at about 19 percent of filings in the first three quarters. At that rate, there would be 423,700 foreclosure sales in 2008. Because there were about 114.7 million households in the United States in 2006, according to the Census Bureau, and the household population has been rising by about 1.1 million per year, there would have been 116.9 million households in 2008. This means that one foreclosed home would be sold in 2008 for every 276 households in the nation. Moreover, one additional foreclosure against a property would be filed for every 52.4 households. Until these statistics change, housing markets will continue to lose ground by gaining more units for sale from foreclosures than they lose by selling already foreclosed units.

How Are Foreclosures Distributed among States?

National ratios like those discussed above are not very useful, because foreclosures are distributed very unevenly across the country. They are not evenly distributed even within those states that have high levels of foreclosures. All such states contain great variations in the incidence of foreclosures from one city to another and from one neighborhood to another. RealtyTrac calculated the number of foreclosure filings in all states for which it had data and related foreclosures to the number of housing units in each state, as shown in exhibit 3-4. The first column in the table shows the ranking of states by which has the most foreclosures in relation to its housing stock, as shown in the last column. Nevada ranks first, since its foreclosures equal over 7 percent of its total housing units. Florida is second, Arizona third, and California fourth. They are followed by Colorado, Michigan, Ohio, and Georgia. Those eight states contained 63 percent of the properties with foreclosure filings against them in 2008, though they contained only 32 percent of all the households in the United States in 2006.

These eight states include five with very fast population growth (Nevada, California, Arizona, Georgia, and Florida), averaging gains of 15.23 percent from 2000 to 2006. Two others are currently suffering from major job losses and economic weakness (Michigan and Ohio). The remaining one is a moderately fast-growing state (Colorado). Four of the states had been heavily affected by immigration of relatively low-income Hispanics (California, Florida, Arizona, and Colorado), which had repercussions for their housing markets.

EXHIBIT 3-4. U.S. Foreclosure Market Data by State for 2008

Rate Rank	State	Total Foreclosure Filings	Change from 2007 (%)	Percentage of Housing Units in Foreclosure
–	**U.S.**	**3,157,806**	**81.2**	**1.8**
1	Nevada	123,989	125.7	7.3
2	Florida	501,396	133.1	4.5
3	Arizona	152,621	203.1	4.5
4	California	837,665	109.9	4.0
5	Colorado	66,795	27.9	2.4
6	Michigan	145,365	21.6	2.4
7	Ohio	146,099	26.2	2.3
8	Georgia	116,225	44.4	2.2
9	Illinois	115,063	54.7	1.9
10	New Jersey	69,612	101.2	1.8
11	Indiana	61,141	64.2	1.7
12	Tennessee	51,496	70.4	1.7
13	Utah	18,657	99.5	1.7
14	Massachusetts	53,797	150.0	1.6
15	Connecticut	25,510	84.9	1.5
16	Virginia	67,695	200.6	1.5
17	Rhode Island	7,334	258.2*	1.5
18	Maryland	41,582	71.3	1.4
19	Idaho	11,272	133.9	1.4
20	Missouri	42,054	33.0	1.2
21	Oregon	25,049	112.8	1.1
22	New Hampshire	8,018	436.0*	1.1
23	Arkansas	16,611	122.9	1.1
24	Texas	129,201	13.8	1.0
25	Washington	32,271	71.6	1.0
26	Minnesota	23,716	75.5	0.9
27	North Carolina	41,750	16.2	0.8
28	Wisconsin	25,164	62.3	0.8
29	Oklahoma	16,059	51.0	0.8
30	South Carolina	16,136	253.1*	0.8
31	Alaska	2,265	46.1	0.7
32	Pennsylvania	42,949	127.2	0.7
33	Delaware	2,998	151.9*	0.7
34	Hawaii	3,346	229.7	0.6
35	New York	55,641	29.3	0.6
36	Kansas	7,983	155.5	0.5
37	New Mexico	4,543	24.5	0.4
38	Maine	3,171	896.9*	0.4
39	Nebraska	3,326	-12.3	0.4
40	Iowa	6,405	31.3	0.4
41	Louisiana	7,837	79.7	0.4
42	Kentucky	8,820	41.9	0.4
43	Alabama	8,436	39.3	0.4
44	Montana	1,220	8.4	0.3
45	Wyoming	921	90.2	0.3
46	Mississippi	2,364	62.7	0.2
47	North Dakota	391	48.4	0.1
48	South Dakota	405	1575.0*	0.1
49	West Virginia	687	48.9	0.1
50	Vermont	124	372.4*	0.0
	District of Columbia	4,631	438.2*	1.5

Source: RealtyTrac.

*Actual increase may not be as high because of data collection changes or improvements.

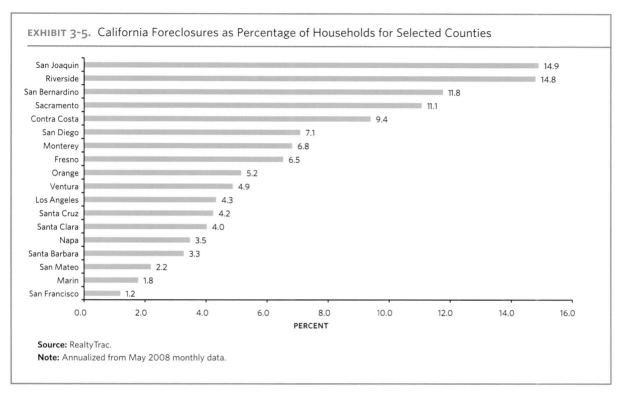

EXHIBIT 3-5. California Foreclosures as Percentage of Households for Selected Counties

Source: RealtyTrac.
Note: Annualized from May 2008 monthly data.

At the other end of the rankings are states with a relatively low incidence of foreclosure activities (that is, higher numbers of resident households per foreclosure filed). The six lowest-ranking states are heavily agricultural, have relatively small populations, and experienced relatively slow population growth from 2000 through 2006 (averaging 3.16 percent).

How Are Foreclosures Distributed within States?

Foreclosures are very unevenly distributed within states and within cities in each state. It is impossible to analyze those distributions for each of 50 states. So I have chosen California—the largest state in population with by far the largest number of foreclosures—to illustrate intrastate diversity. RealtyTrac reported the number of foreclosure starts in each California county for May 2008. Exhibit 3-5 estimates for each of 18 counties (of 58 total) the number of 2008 resident households for each foreclosure likely to be initiated in all of 2008, annualized by multiplying the number in May times 12. As shown, San Francisco County (identical to the City of San Francisco) had only about 1 percent of households in foreclosure, whereas San Joaquin County, a primarily agricultural county in the Central Valley just south of Sacramento, had nearly 15 percent of households in foreclosure. San Joaquin County had one foreclosure filed for every 6.71 resident households; whereas San Francisco had one foreclosure filing for every 84 resident households. Thus, foreclosures are 12.5 times as high per resident household in San Joaquin County as in San Francisco. Other counties with relatively high foreclosure rates are Riverside, San Bernardino, and Contra Costa. All three are inland counties that have grown rapidly from expansion out of Los Angeles, Orange, and San Francisco counties, respectively. Other counties with a low incidence of foreclosures are Marin and San Mateo (both high-income suburban neighbors of San Francisco), and Santa Barbara (a high-income coastal community north of Los Angeles).

How Are Foreclosures Distributed within Cities?

Similar variations in foreclosure activity appear within cities or other communities within counties. For example, San Joaquin County had the highest incidence of foreclosure activity of all the counties listed in exhibit 3-5. The largest city in that county is Stockton. The state government estimates that its population in 2008 was 289,987, up from 243,771 in the April 2000 census. That is an increase of 42,216 persons in slightly over eight years. Converting that population gain to added households and adding housing for them to the 78,522 occupied housing units in Stockton in 2000 yields a total of 91,923 occupied housing units in Stockton at the end of 2008—say 92,000.

RealtyTrac keeps an ongoing account of how many housing units are in various stages of the foreclosure process and sets forth data about individual communities on its Website. As of July 14, 2008, Stockton had 9,160 homes either in preforeclosure proceedings (3,325), at auction (1,861), already owned by banks (3,882), or owned by a government (3). That is a total of one unit in the foreclosure process per 10.04 households in the entire city. That incidence score is slightly greater than Nevada's score of one unit per 11 households—the highest score among all 50 states considered as wholes. It is difficult to compute separate scores for ZIP codes within Stockton because accurate current data on population or households for individual ZIP codes are not available. Based on current foreclosure activities and 2000 ZIP code populations, the foreclosure incidence scores within Stockton vary from a low of 11.15 households per one foreclosure activity (in ZIP code 95207; 2000 population 49,958) to a high of 2.41 households per one foreclosure activity (in ZIP code 95212, 2000 population 9,634).

In fact, there is an inherent tendency for foreclosure activities to become concentrated within neighborhoods. That can occur because the presence of a certain amount of foreclosures within a neighborhood can cause "contagion" to other units. If a foreclosed home is abandoned by its occupants for any length of time, it tends to deteriorate, at least in appearance. No one takes care of the lawn and the trash that accumulates, and no one repairs damages to the home. Such homes often become targets for vandals. This makes the entire neighborhood look less valuable and may cause declines in the market values of nearby homes. If their values fall enough, the remaining owners may find that those values are less than the debt they still owe on their mortgages. This could motivate some to stop making mortgage payments, spreading the prospect of eventual foreclosure to more homes in the neighborhood.

As the appearance of the area deteriorates, it becomes more and more difficult for remaining residents to sell their homes at "decent" prices if they have to move, and fewer and fewer people looking for good homes are attracted to the area. Moreover, if the assessor reduces the assessed values for the area, property taxes fall and there is less public money for maintaining the local infrastructure and schools. Even if assessed values do not fall, tax collections will fall because so many homes are not occupied by working residents. In short, any heavy concentration of foreclosures in a single neighborhood can start a self-fulfilling downward spiral in local property values, eventually generating more foreclosures.

The foreclosure situation in parts of the San Francisco Bay Area in 2007 is exemplified by this excerpt from SFGate, a Website run by the *San Francisco Chronicle*, from October 14, 2007[5]:

> *With 271 homes—or more than 2 percent of all residences—already foreclosed upon in the first eight months of this year, the 94531 ZIP code . . . has the Bay Area's highest foreclosure rate, according to a Chronicle analysis of housing data provided by DataQuick Information Systems, a La Jolla (San Diego County) research firm. In this southeastern corner of Antioch, another 671 households—or 6 percent of the total—have received bank notices this year that they are behind in their payments, the first step of the foreclosure process.*

> *The foreclosure rate here is seven times that of the region as a whole and nearly 1,000 percent higher than it was a year ago. This small area of Antioch, with 23 foreclosures for every 1,000 homes, has twice the bank repossession rate of greater Stockton, an area often cited as the No. 1 foreclosure spot in California. . . . At the eastern end of Catanzaro Way, the numbers are even grimmer. Nine out of 40 properties have been repossessed by the lender; another four are in default. That means almost one-third of the homes are in or facing foreclosure. You wouldn't know it if not for the dead lawns and for-sale signs that line the street. The neighborhood of spacious Mediterranean-style homes appears placid and pleasant, no different than any other California subdivision*

> *Catanzaro Way and the 94531 ZIP code are a virtual petri dish for foreclosures because they share so many of the factors that fuel the trend: oversupply of homes, rampant price run-ups followed by swoons, lower-income residents, subprime adjustable-rate mortgages. . . .*

Such conditions are typical in high-foreclosure neighborhoods within all of the highest-foreclosure states, as well as in many other states with relatively low overall foreclosure rates.

How Foreclosures May Affect State and Local Governments

Cities with high levels of foreclosures are encountering fiscal difficulties. Stockton is suffering from losses of property tax collections caused by lower assessed values, which are due to falling home prices, as well as from declining sales tax revenues, spreading foreclosures, and increasing property tax collection defaults. Yet the city government has fixed-payment contracts with many of the labor unions that provide key services like police protection, fire protection, and garbage collection. Moreover, neighborhoods that have multiple foreclosed homes tend to require greater protective services, rather than diminished ones. If revenue collections fall below the city's fixed expenses, acute shortages of money could lead to bankruptcy. Vallejo, California—a city of 117,000 residents—declared bankruptcy in May 2008 because it did not have enough tax revenues or reserves to keep paying its city workers their union-negotiated wages. Proponents of city bankruptcies claim that Chapter 9 filings are the only way for cities burdened with high-wage contracts to stay in business in this period of falling housing values and shrinking tax collections. Those proponents claim that bankruptcies invalidate past contracts that employee unions made with city governments, allowing cities to renegotiate worker wages at lower levels.

Many other California cities face similar budget problems because of falling property and sales tax revenues but fixed labor union contracts. The state government's fiscal position is even worse, because it is experiencing a massive budget deficit for 2008. Governor Arnold Schwarzenegger estimated a budget shortfall of $14.5 billion for the fiscal year ending in June 2009 but does not want to increase taxes to cope with this deficit. Legislative analyst Elizabeth Hill said the budget deficit was more like $16 billion and should be attacked with both spending cuts and new tax revenues. In any event, it appears that the government of California is in no position to aid city governments that encounter serious deficits themselves, as it seems will happen in many areas. As the nation slides into a serious recession, this problem will appear in cities and states all across the United States.

Other Adverse Impacts of Concentrated Foreclosures

The Urban Institute held a meeting in July 2008 to discuss the adverse impacts of subprime and other mortgage foreclosures upon local communities. Attendees from around the nation revealed a host of ways in which such foreclosures harmed both the households and the areas concerned. Among these adverse impacts are the following:

- *Disruption of family life from displacement.* Families who are displaced by foreclosures must move to some other location, often with little or no warning. Schoolchildren must leave classes and friends and adjust to new schools in different locations, something that impedes normal learning. If such disruption happens often to a family, it can hinder children's long-run school performance and their economic chances in life. Also, elderly family members often must leave friends and move to areas where they have no familiar contacts.

- *Degradation of school classes by constant turnover of children.* In some cities, inner-city schools already have very high turnover rates among children, which make effective teaching extremely difficult. When 50 percent or more of the children in a class move during each school year, teachers and remaining students have difficulty maintaining continuity of instruction and relationships.

- *Unexpected eviction of renters.* A significant proportion of all foreclosed homes are occupied by people renting from the legal owners, who bought those homes on speculation. One housing expert stated that in New York City, about half of all foreclosure evictions involve such renters. In 2006, more than 30 percent of high-price purchase loans (mainly subprime or Alt-A loans) were made to speculators, most of whom then rented the properties to others. In the same year, those fractions were 27 percent in San Antonio, 19 percent in Memphis, and 9 percent in Riverside–San Bernardino, according to the Urban Institute.

- *Lack of legally enforced and timely eviction notices to renter families.* Renters who will be displaced by foreclosure need time to plan where they will move, how they will shift their children's schools, how they must alter their daily travel, etc. Yet in many cases there are no legally enforced requirements for owners who have failed to make payments on their loans to notify their tenants well in advance that they will have to move. This can create great hardships and family disruptions for such renters, even forcing some to become homeless for significant periods.

■ *Aggravation of a general shortage of low-income rentals.* The eviction of renters from foreclosed homes frequently exacerbates the general shortage of rental housing for relatively low-income households. Several million U.S. renter households already pay well over 30 percent of their annual incomes for shelter, and the nation's supply of low-rent housing is gradually diminishing, according to the Joint Center for Housing at Harvard University.

■ *Inability by renters to reclaim their initial security deposits.* Renters are often given little or no advance notice by the landlord owners of their likely eviction. In many cases, such landlords simply disappear without repaying the tenants' initial security deposits and leave no forwarding addresses.

■ *Lack of counseling resources for displaced households.* Families faced with displacement need advice about what remedies they might have, where they might be able to find decent living quarters, and how to cope with economic difficulties that have forced them to miss key payments on their loans. However, local resources for providing such advice are often in very short supply. Moreover, many households do not want to admit they are in foreclosure and will not seek counseling even though they need it badly.

■ *Unwillingness of banks that own foreclosed homes to maintain them adequately.* Many foreclosed homes are now owned by banks that are trying to sell them but having difficulty finding buyers who will pay what the banks want to receive. Meanwhile, banks are typically investing little or no time and money to maintain the vacant homes they own or protect those homes from vandals. That causes such homes to gradually deteriorate, putting a downward pressure on the values of surrounding homes still occupied by owners or renters.

■ *Inability of owners to learn who to negotiate with in order to work out financial difficulties.* The massive securitization of mortgage loans scattered the ownership of individual homes among many buyers of mortgage-backed securities. Although special servicers are supposedly appointed to deal with owners who have delinquent payments, it is often hard for delinquent owners to discover with whom they can negotiate some type of workout arrangement. Also, many special servicers find themselves overwhelmed with more cases than they can handle effectively. This makes avoiding foreclosure through some type of workout plan more difficult than in past economic downturns.

■ *Lack of concern by banks about the negative impacts of foreclosures spilling over on local neighborhoods.* Many banks that formerly served their communities and held the loans they made to local residents have recently securitized all such loans. Hence they have little concern about what happens to local neighborhoods, because they no longer are responsible for what happens to the payments on the loans they put into securitized form.

■ *Spreading of foreclosures out of low-income neighborhoods to many middle-class areas.* The high concentration of foreclosures has spread from low-income areas to many outlying suburbs where new growth was concentrated and even to middle-income neighborhoods that are suffering from an increasingly weakening economy. Antioch, California, an outlying suburb in the East Bay, is an example of such a community. People in these areas who are facing foreclosure need counseling too but are often unwilling to admit or seek it.

- *Loss of elderly households' main repository of wealth.* Elderly households hit by foreclosures may lose all the wealth they had built up in their homes to support themselves during retirement. Perhaps we need a new legal concept: a foreclosure with the debtor remaining in possession of the home. But that would require some means of negotiating a workout with the lenders involved and might wipe out the values of second mortgages or other liens. Yet many owners in financial difficulty are elderly people who need counseling and perhaps financial assistance.
- *Inability to bring homes that are being foreclosed up to present legal standards because of lead paint and other deficiencies found in older structures.* When such buildings are foreclosed, future buyers will want them to meet current legal standards, but making that happen may be very expensive. Who is to pay for this improvement, since the defaulting owners clearly cannot do so? This poses a serious problem for communities that contain many homes that were built decades ago.
- *Failure of assessors to adjust assessments downward to reflect present lower market values.* Many older homes in particular are being assessed at values that are actually well above their true present market values. One reason: some assessors are removing foreclosed real estate sales from their databases and therefore estimating current market values based on comparables at levels that are too high. This imposes continuing high taxes on remaining homeowners and may contribute to some of them defaulting on their current mortgage payments.
- *Local governments' lack of awareness of the major problems they will see springing from foreclosures.* Local officials in many suburbs, in particular, have not experienced high levels of foreclosure or suffered from declining property tax revenues—yet. But rising foreclosures are likely to generate adverse neighborhood effects in more communities than have yet recognized them. Local governments should begin tracking foreclosures by location in all their neighborhoods to get ahead of the problems they may well encounter in the future.
- *Inability or unwillingness of metropolitan-level government agencies to track foreclosures throughout their own metropolitan areas.* Hence almost no metropolitan areas are identifying emerging areas of potentially great concern, not only to local governments, but to the entire region. This adverse impact is part of the larger issue of the lack of effective governance structures at the metropolitan-area level throughout most of the nation.
- *Diminishing fiscal resources of state and local governments as the U.S. economy moves into a weaker phase.* Such governments are the logical points where remedies to foreclosure could and should be developed. But they are suffering from declining revenues with which to address many other problems that seem even more compelling than housing foreclosures. Examples are rising unemployment, inadequate transportation facilities, and increasing health care costs. The result is a tendency for state and local governments to shift all remedial actions to the federal level, even though its fiscal resources are equally limited and under other great demands.

Possible public policies aimed at coping with these adverse impacts of foreclosures are discussed in chapters 6 and 7.

Most of the above adverse impacts of foreclosures—especially their effects on whole neighborhoods—are much more serious for 1-4 family homes than high-rise condominium units. One high-rise condominium building containing 200 mostly foreclosed units is less likely to devastate a neighborhood as much as 200 foreclosed single-family homes concentrated in a single neighborhood. However, most foreclosures concern single-family homes rather than high-rise condominiums; so the above observations apply to the majority of foreclosed dwellings.

Some Ameliorating Factors

Some less negative byproducts of home foreclosures arise because so many foreclosed units were not owner-occupied but belonged to speculators. Those investors initially rented them or left them standing vacant. Many owner-occupants who default will be able to strike deals in some type of workout arrangements with the local sheriffs who do the foreclosing. Many foreclosed units that were rented by speculator-owners may continue to be rented to the same renter-occupants by new owners who buy them for investment purposes. These outcomes are reasons why the number of foreclosure sales is much smaller than the total number of foreclosure filings in almost every jurisdiction.

Traumatic Period

The United States is going through a period of relatively massive numbers of home foreclosures, exceeded in the past only during the Great Depression of the 1930s. This will slow the recovery of the entire housing sector by flooding many local markets with foreclosed homes for sale at below-market prices. It will also strain the capacity of rental housing markets to cope with the sudden increase in households ejected from their owned or rented homes. To some extent, these adverse trends may be partly offset by recently enacted federal legislation and programs to help homeowners in jeopardy of foreclosure. But there is little doubt that housing markets in many communities will go through a traumatic period of adjustment to conditions not seen for more than 60 years, if ever.

NOTES

1. Chris Mayer and Karen Pence, "Subprime Mortgages: What, Where, and to Whom?" Paper 2008-29 in the Finance and Economics Discussion Series, Division of Research and Statistics and Monetary Affairs, Federal Reserve Board, Washington, D.C.
2. www.realtytrac.com/states. Viewers can look up statistics for states and get national summary data as well. RealtyTrac is a California firm that monitors foreclosures and keeps an inventory of data on properties that are undergoing foreclosure in all 50 states and the District of Columbia.
3. Peter Whorisky and Zachary A. Goldfarb, "Treasury Considers Backing Mortgages: FDIC Proposal Aims to Help Homeowners," *Washington Post*, October 24, 2008, page 1.
4. Mortgage Bankers Association, "Foreclosure Starts and Foreclosure Inventories for the U.S. (Not Seasonally Adjusted)," 2008.
5. Erin McCormick, Carolyn Said, and Kelly Zito, "Mortgage Meltdown: Neighborhoods Crumble in Wave of Foreclosures," October 14, 2007; http://www.sfgate.com/cgi-bin/article.cgi?file=/c/a/2007/10/14/MNEG-SE50Q.DT.

The Financial Crisis and Commercial Property Markets

AS OF EARLY 2009, COMMERCIAL PROPERTY MARKETS have seen far fewer mortgage problems than the residential sector, and thus far commercial markets have not become directly involved in massive defaults and foreclosures and related problems. Nevertheless, commercial property markets were directly affected by the immense expansion in investor borrowing after the 2000 stock market crash and by the credit freeze in 2007 and 2008. Those markets benefited greatly from the low interest rates, generous appraisals, securitized fundraising, careless underwriting, cheap debt, and compressed capitalization rates caused by the massive flow of money into real estate, especially after 2000. And they also suffered from a credit crunch similar to that afflicting residential markets. The lack of lending and the need to refinance many existing loans coming due, especially those that had beem securitized, is a major problem for the commercial real estate industry that will likely lead to substantial increases in delinquencies and foreclusures through 2010.

Supply and Demand in Commercial Property Space Markets, 1989–2000

Commercial real property markets in the United States went through a downward economic cycle in the first part of the 1990s. They recovered after about 1998, encountering an expansion of new construction and a tightening of availability from 2003 through 2006. These movements are depicted in exhibit 4-1, based on data from CB Richard Ellis. This exhibit shows that the national office vacancy rate was a high 17.8 percent in 1988, then rose to a peak of 18.7 percent in 1991. This increase resulted from the collapse of real property space markets and market values in 1990. That crisis occurred because of huge overbuilding in the late 1980s, followed by the recession of 1991. New office space construction completed each year fell 93.8 percent, from 119.9 million square feet in 1989 to 7.4 million square feet in 1994, then began to recover. With new construction disappearing for a while, vacancy rates dropped from 18.7 percent in 1991 to 8.3 percent in 2000. Then vacancy rates rose sharply as a result of the stock market crash of 2000, followed by the 9/11 attacks in late 2001 and

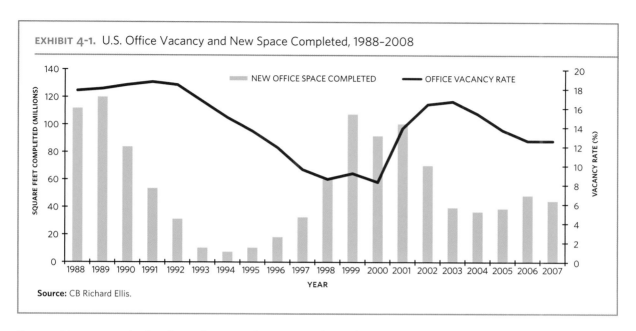

EXHIBIT 4-1. U.S. Office Vacancy and New Space Completed, 1988–2008

Source: CB Richard Ellis.

the resulting economic slowdown. But once the economy heated up after about 1994, new office construction began to come onto the market in greater volume in 1998 and 1999. That was part of a strong general economic expansion, stimulated by the Internet stock market bubble through 1999. From 2000 onward, commercial property market conditions went into an unusual phase because of both the stock market crash and the massive flow of financial capital into real estate.

Effects of the Flood of Capital into Commercial Property Markets after 2000

After the stock market crash of 2000, financial capital from around the globe flooded into U.S.—and worldwide—commercial property markets, as explained in chapter 1. This had the following crucial consequences for what happened in commercial markets:

■ Increased competition among capital suppliers (any investors with capital to use in lending on or buying properties);
■ A shift from cash flow valuation to price momentum valuation;
■ Heavy borrowing short to buy long, owing to the search for yields among investors;
■ A disconnect between space markets and investment markets;
■ Rising prices of commercial properties through capitalization rate compression; and
■ Rising debt in commercial property markets.

Increased Competition among Capital Suppliers

The first consequence of the capital flood was intensely increased competition among capital suppliers to buy quality real estate properties or to make loans to people who wanted to buy them. As explained in my earlier book *Niagara of Capital*, this competition among capital suppliers radically reduced the high quality of underwriting done by both property buyers and major lenders after commercial real estate values crashed in 1990–91. After 2000, those capital suppliers took less time to perform due diligence on deals presented to them, slashed the number and stringency of the covenants they placed on making their capital available, reduced the interest rates on loans or the yields on purchases of property that they were demanding, and generally made it much easier to borrow money from them or sell properties to them. This decline in underwriting standards was not the result of lender or investor stupidity or ignorance. Rather, it arose because there were so many capital suppliers trying to buy properties or make loans on them that each was under great pressure to act quickly and reduce terms, in order to be able to make any deals at all. This competition emerged after 2000 but gradually increased in intensity until 2005, 2006, and early 2007. It had a profound impact on commercial property markets all over the world, especially in the United States.

Shift in Valuation from Cash Flow to Price Momentum

There was a shift of property valuation from cash flow realities to "momentum investing" based almost solely on rising market values. Competition among investors that drove property prices upward also caused a change in their method of evaluating whether to buy specific properties. Investors shifted from computing future profits on the basis of realistic cash flow estimates to computing them on the basis of the ability to resell the properties at higher prices, almost regardless of cash flow realities. This type of momentum investing is a recipe for future disaster that is typical of bubble-type thinking by investors. It happened in Japan during the bubble period leading up to a collapse in values in 1989–90 and the subsequent long period of slowing growth. It also happened during the Internet bubble in U.S. stock markets in the late 1990s, until the collapse of stock market values in 2000. This is really part of what economist Hyman Minsky characterized as increasingly optimistic thinking by lenders, borrowers, and property owners during long periods of prosperity, as measured by rising property prices.

Borrowing Short to Buy Long

The second consequence of the capital flood was that investors seeking real properties discovered that short-term interest rates were very low after 2000–02. The three-month commercial paper rate fell as low as 1.13 percent in 2003. So investors shifted their buying or lending toward longer-term assets that had higher yields, such as commercial real estate. Because short-term interest rates were very low, many investors borrowed short to buy longer-term assets with higher yields, especially after 2002, when short rates actually became negative in real terms. As time passed, competition among buyers pushed yields on long-term real estate properties downward through capitalization rate compression. This made it more difficult for investors to benefit from the upward slope of the yield curve.

Nevertheless, many investors borrowed even more to increase the net yield on the equity they were putting into their deals. Such leveraging increased the risk to investors, but that did not stop them from playing the yield curve. When the yield curve became almost flat in 2007, the ability to pay for long-term assets by borrowing short at lower rates disappeared. That left highly leveraged investors with large short-term liabilities that often exceeded their equity positions. Wharton economist Peter Linneman believes this was one of the two key factors underlying the credit crunch. The second key factor was a widespread lack of transparency among lenders, property owners, and the financial instruments used by both that created nearly universal uncertainty about who was solvent and who was not, and therefore about what real properties and securities were really worth.

Disconnect between Space and Investment Markets

The third consequence of the capital flood was a major disconnect between the space market and property sale conditions in commercial property markets. As stock prices plunged in 2000 through 2002 and after the 9/11 attacks in 2001, vacancy rates in offices rose sharply, as shown in exhibit 4-1. National office vacancy rates shot up from 8.3 percent in 2000 to 16.7 percent in 2003. One reason is that hundreds of new Internet-related firms simply disappeared overnight. They left large amounts of leased office space vacant. Also, the sharp fall in travel after 9/11 hurt airlines, resorts, and hotels and slowed the overall economy, causing more space vacancies. Yet the prices of office buildings and other commercial properties started rising significantly at the same time that conditions in their space markets were deteriorating.

This was the first time in the memory of most real estate operators that office buildings and other commercial properties became more valuable while they were producing lower net incomes. Normally, deteriorating space market conditions had always meant falling property prices, as occurred from 1990 to about 1993. But this time the opposite happened. Why? Because the massive flow of financial capital into all real estate markets—including commercial property markets—drove property prices upward. Buyers could borrow money so cheaply they were willing to purchase properties that were not performing well because they could do so with very little equity. Surprisingly, that happened almost without regard to the balance between supply and demand for space in those markets.

This imbalance or disconnect between conditions in space markets and those in property markets did not last long. Commercial space markets began to recover when stocks began to recover in 2003. The economy as a whole was rebounding from the adversities of 2000 through 2002, so demands for space in commercial property markets began to rise. The national office vacancy rate fell from 16.7 percent in 2003 to 12.7 percent in 2006 and declined slightly more in 2007. This situation reversed itself in late 2007 and especially in 2008–09 when an intensifying recession in the U.S. economy caused vacancy rates to climb again.

Rising Prices of Commercial Properties

The fourth consequence of the flood of capital into commercial real estate was that this flood drove up prices for most types of property. This can be seen in exhibit 4-2. The lines show average prices for the four types of property, indexed so that prices in December 2001 equal 100. The specific price index increases and decreases by four property types are listed in exhibit 4-3. Prices of all four types of properties rose steadily from 1998 onward and hit peak index values in either 2007 or 2008. Hence they all rose for nine to ten years before seeing declines.

Most of this increase in commercial property prices was caused by capitalization rate compression, rather than by increases in net earnings. That is, about the same amount of net

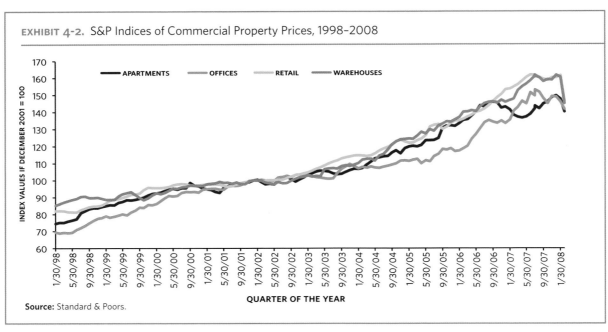

EXHIBIT 4-2. S&P Indices of Commercial Property Prices, 1998–2008

APARTMENTS　　OFFICES　　RETAIL　　WAREHOUSES

INDEX VALUES IF DECEMBER 2001 = 100

QUARTER OF THE YEAR

Source: Standard & Poors.

EXHIBIT 4-3. Rise and Fall in Value by Property Type, 1998 and 2008

Property Type	Index on 1/98	Peak Value	Index on 3/08	Rise (%)	Fall (%)
Apartments	74.56	149.53	140.09	100.55	6.31
Offices	69.42	152.94	141.6	120.28	7.42
Retail	81.97	161.80	145.86	97.40	9.87
Warehouses	85.24	161.65	144.98	89.64	10.31

Source: Standard & Poors.

income from a property was evaluated as worth much more at the peak in 2007 or 2008 as in 1998. The reason is that intense competition among property buyers pushed up the amounts they were willing to pay for every percentage point of net income that a property provided in a year. In other words, property buyers were willing to accept lower yields on their investments in order to get the properties they wanted, which means they were willing to pay higher prices. Property price changes caused by falling capitalization rates are illustrated through analysis of a sample property producing a net annual income of $100,000, without any debt leveraging. To get the market price at a given capitalization rate, I have divided the net income of $100,000 by the high and the low capitalization rates in decimal terms, using NCREIF capitalization rate data from 1995 and 2007. The results are shown in exhibit 4-4.

For those properties that also had rising net incomes, market price increases were larger than shown in this exhibit. That group probably included most of the properties bought or sold in this period. Why? Because after about 2003, the economy began to recover strongly from

EXHIBIT 4-4. Net Borrowing by Financial and Nonfinancial Sectors, 1996–2008

Property Type	Annual Income ($)	Capitalization Rate High 1995	Property Value ($)	Capitalization Rate Low 2007	Property Value ($)	Increase in Value Resulting from Cap Rate Decline (%)
Apartment	100,000	0.0808	1,237,623	0.0510	1,960,784	58.4
Industrial	100,000	0.09138	1,094,331	0.05984	1,671,122	52.7
Office	100,000	0.09329	1,071,926	0.05622	1,728,726	65.9
Retail	100,000	0.09403	1,063,490	0.05875	1,702,128	60.1

Source: Capitalization rate data from NCREIF.

EXHIBIT 4-5. Net Borrowing by Financial and Nonfinancial Sectors, 1996–2008

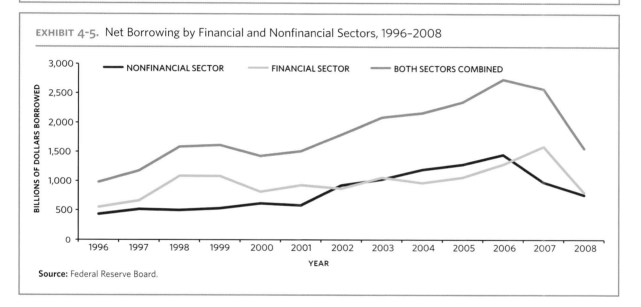

Source: Federal Reserve Board.

the negative effects of the stock market crash and 9/11. Office vacancy rates had soared after bottoming out in 2001 at 6 percent in downtown areas and 8 percent in the suburbs. They leveled off at 15 and 18 percent in 2004, then began falling again. Even some rents then began rising, doubly improving property net incomes from their low points.

Capitalization rates for other types of properties not shown in the exhibit moved in similar patterns. Hotels did not recover quite as fully because they suffered more than most other types from the disruption of airline and tourist travel after 9/11. But by 2004 to 2006, hotels were booming and their prices were rising notably.

Rising Debt in Commercial Property Markets

The fifth consequence of the flood of capital into commercial property markets was a tremendous increase in the use of debt. Data from the Federal Reserve Board's flow of funds accounts are shown in exhibit 4-5, though the figure for 2008 is for only the first quarter.

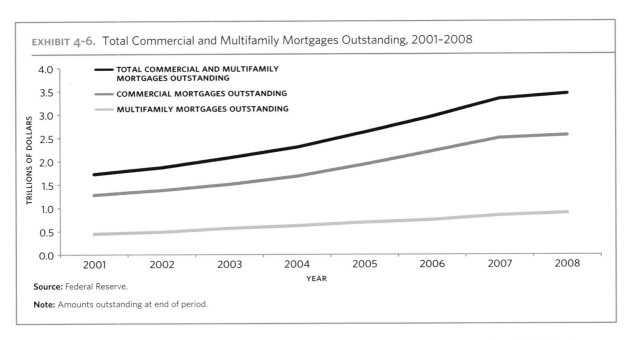

EXHIBIT 4-6. Total Commercial and Multifamily Mortgages Outstanding, 2001–2008

TOTAL COMMERCIAL AND MULTIFAMILY
MORTGAGES OUTSTANDING

COMMERCIAL MORTGAGES OUTSTANDING

MULTIFAMILY MORTGAGES OUTSTANDING

TRILLIONS OF DOLLARS

4.0
3.5
3.0
2.5
2.0
1.5
1.0
0.5
0.0

2001   2002   2003   2004   2005   2006   2007   2008

YEAR

Source: Federal Reserve.

Note: Amounts outstanding at end of period.

Clearly, the nonfinancial sector suddenly increased its net borrowing after 2001. That borrowing more than doubled, from just under $600 billion per year in 2001 to a peak of $1.451 trillion in 2006. This exhibit excludes all borrowing by households and governments, so it focuses only on private nonhousehold borrowing by nonfinancial and financial firms. If household borrowing is included as part of the nonfinancial sector, an even greater increase in nonfinancial sector debt can be observed, from about $1.0 trillion in 1999 to $2.4 trillion in 2007. Debt on commercial and multifamily properties also increased tremendously since 2001. The total amount of outstanding commercial mortgages alone rose from $1.282 trillion in 2001 to $2.553 trillion by the third quarter of 2008, an increase of 99.1 percent, according to Federal Reserve Board data (see exhibit 4-6). This clearly shows a tremendous shift away from equity finance to debt finance, as a result of low interest rates and a flood of readily available debt capital into commercial real estate markets after 2000.

Increasing Use of Financial Derivatives in Commercial Property Markets

As real estate–related borrowing soared in commercial property markets, so did the use of financial derivatives. More borrowers used interest rate swaps to shift from variable interest rates to fixed long-term rates in order to stabilize their future interest expenses. The rapid expansion of derivative usage is shown in exhibit 4-7. Data for this exhibit came from the International Swaps and Derivatives Association (ISDA). The portions of the lines that depict interest rate swaps, cross-currency swaps, and interest rate options after 1997 were created by assuming that each of those products formed about the same percentage of the total of all three from 1998 to 2007 that they had formed from 1987 to 1997. This extrapolation was necessary because the ISDA's data did not break out those three types of derivatives from the

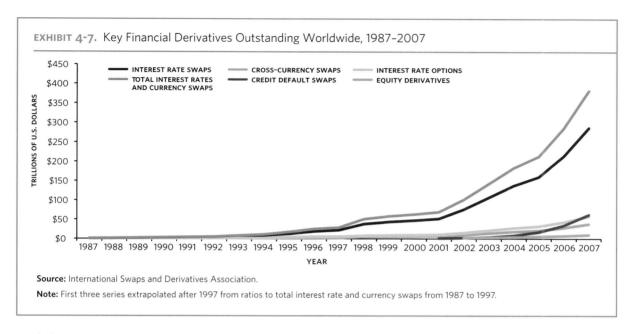

EXHIBIT 4-7. Key Financial Derivatives Outstanding Worldwide, 1987–2007

Source: International Swaps and Derivatives Association.

Note: First three series extrapolated after 1997 from ratios to total interest rate and currency swaps from 1987 to 1997.

total after 1997. Moreover, this exhibit applies to use of these derivatives worldwide, not just in the United States. Also, it does not cover derivatives created over the counter rather than on established exchanges. Nevertheless, despite those data limitations, there were clearly dramatic increases in interest rate and currency swaps after 2001 and even more spectacular increases from 2005 through 2007.

These huge increases in derivative use were caused by similarly huge increases in total borrowing during the same periods. However, because exhibit 4-7 deals in many trillions of dollars of derivatives, it involves much larger sums of money than the underlying borrowing that stimulated the use of such derivatives. Thus, the exhibit shows that almost $300 trillion of interest rate swaps, in notional terms, were outstanding in 2007—an increase of 356 percent over the 2001 total, all in just six years.

Another widely used derivative is the credit default swap (CDS), a form of insurance. One party bets that a security that is supposed to pay off at the end of a specified term pays a second party a monthly fee in return for the second party's agreement to make that payment to the first party if the security defaults. Neither party need actually own the security or have any direct interest in it. Banks and other lenders—and many pure speculators—purchased trillions of such CDSs as protection against defaults.

The amount of these derivatives used by Americans is surely much smaller than that shown in the exhibit. But that American total probably followed a similar course of rapid expansion after 2001, stimulated by the huge flow of financial capital into U.S. real estate markets. The existence of such large amounts of relatively new and untested financial instruments related to commercial property markets is one of the reasons that the Federal Reserve Board became concerned about the possible financial failure of the investment bank Bear Stearns in 2008. Bear Stearns was a counterparty on many financial derivatives; that is, an agent who took the other side of deals in which normal investors used a derivative. Bear Stearns was also an example of a firm heavily into short-term-financed purchases of risky, longer-term, and illiquid assets. So the Fed was concerned that a Bear Stearns failure might cause the collapse of many derivative deals it had made with other parties. To avoid that disruptive outcome, the Fed forced Bear Stearns to sell out to JPMorgan Chase at a stock price that wiped out much of the value of Bear Stearns stock. In fact, the Fed put up billions of dollars of capital to help JPMorgan Chase cope with Bear Stearns assets that were underwater.

The use of financial derivatives in the United States and all over the globe has grown extremely rapidly to enormous totals of financial paper outstanding, as exhibit 4-7 illustrates. Yet this whole mass of new and largely unregulated financial investments has never been put to the test of a major economic downturn or any type of large-scale financial crisis. The purveyors of those instruments exhibited the hubris of financial "wizards," believing that what works in some esoteric theory will invariably work in practice—even though it must be implemented by flawed human beings. Apparently those wizards had learned nothing from the experiences of prior financial crises. Until mid-2008, even the credit crunch had not subjected the immense amount of financial derivatives outstanding to any real test of their ability to withstand a financial crisis. That poses a significant potential worry for U.S. and other financial regulators around the world, because so much capital has been invested in these new and obscure forms of "virtual assets."

Contagious Spread of Credit Uncertainty from Housing Markets

Even though commercial property markets had no major source of credit defaults comparable to subprime lending in housing markets, by 2008 the availability of credit in commercial property markets had also virtually shut down. Apparently flu, measles, smallpox, and other contagious diseases have their parallels in the world of finance, for the shutdown of credit availability certainly spread from housing markets to commercial markets. How did that happen?

The biggest causes were the poor underwriting of all types of real estate transactions, the widespread lack of transparency in financial dealings and instruments, and the mismatch of durations between borrowing short and lending or investing long. The flood of financial capital into residential markets occurred with equal force in commercial property markets. At least one result was the same: capital suppliers reduced the quality of their own investment underwriting under the pressure of competition from other well-heeled investors who were eager to make deals. Thus greed reared its head in commercial markets as well as residential ones, though there were fewer equivalents in the commercial markets of relatively naive low-income homebuyers. The pressure to make deals without adequate due diligence was reinforced by investors' acceptance of quality ratings by such established credit rating firms as Moody's, Standard & Poor's, and Fitch. Capital suppliers in commercial property markets often justified their own lack of sound underwriting by relying on high quality ratings from those agencies. This carelessness was part of the rising optimism that occurs in long periods of financial prosperity and causes investors to be more trusting of the views of others than prudence would normally dictate. This led to immense upward pressure on commercial property prices—and thus downward pressure on capitalization rates—from 2000 through 2006.

It was not any failure of commercial property owners to make their debt payments that changed this situation. Rather, it was the obvious problems being experienced by lenders in housing markets, especially concerning U.S. subprime lending. Those problems had two impacts crucial to commercial property markets. First, subprime lending difficulties caused major investment and commercial banks to experience large losses. By mid-2007, those losses affected the banks' willingness and ability to provide capital to commercial property markets. That in itself caused a notable diminution in the availability of credit in those markets. Equally important, people and firms that had been supplying capital to commercial property markets suddenly recognized that they had not done adequate due diligence concerning their loans or purchases. Clearly, both commercial and investment banks had been hurt by their poor underwriting in housing markets. So why could not firms that had done equally poor underwriting in commercial markets also get hurt, at least in the not too distant future? Capital suppliers who had stayed out of residential lending or buying woke up to the fact that they, too, were vulnerable to future problems with commercial properties—especially if the U.S. economy entered a recession.

As a result, people and firms that had been supplying capital to commercial property markets began to reexamine the terms on which they should continue to do so. Moreover, many commercial and investment banks that had been lending money in commercial property markets discovered that their asset portfolios were heavily laden with real estate deals. By 2007, commercial banks had more than 37 percent of their assets in real estate, compared with 25 percent before 2000.

Another factor that woke up capital suppliers to a greater perception of the risks they had been taking was the fact that housing prices began to slow and even decline in many markets. Yet housing prices on a national basis had been rising continuously from 1968 to 2006. If that could happen in housing markets because prices there had been bid up so high, why could it not also happen in commercial property markets? Thus, the perception of flattening or even falling housing prices stimulated suppliers of capital to commercial markets to reevaluate their willingness to continue accepting the high prices to which properties in those markets had risen.

Another factor affecting commercial property markets was the accounting requirement that property owners and investors must mark their assets to their fair or true market values when computing their balance sheets and making annual or quarterly reports. This requirement is even more central to the international accounting standards that the Securities and Exchange Commission (SEC) promotes than it is to traditional U.S. real estate accounting practices. Yet because of the credit freeze, whole markets for various types of real properties and securities vanished almost overnight after about mid-2007. So how could investors who owned securities based on those markets determine the fair market values of those securities? When there are neither buyers nor sellers of past CMBS issues and virtually no new CMBS issues, how can the market value of an investor's CMBSs be even roughly estimated?

If the law or the SEC or the Internal Revenue Service nevertheless requires verifiable estimates of market value, those estimates are likely to be either zero or some number lower than they will be when markets return to life. That will tend to exaggerate the actual losses of the owners of those securities or properties, perhaps even forcing them into insolvency for dubious reasons. The industry's spokespersons are clamoring to have the mark-to-market requirement suspended at least until normal market relations are reestablished. But until that happens, the strict application of this rule is, in my opinion, grossly exaggerating the extent of economic losses of many investors and financial institutions.

A final straw for commercial property markets was the revelation that the established credit rating agencies had miserably failed to perform their basic function reliably. Those agencies consistently made large errors in accurately assessing the soundness and value of dozens of issues of securities brought to them for ratings, and even some significant computational errors. This news cast doubt not only on capital suppliers' future deals in commercial markets but also, even more strongly, on deals they had already made.

As a result, nearly all capital suppliers decided that it was time to reassess their behavior in real estate markets, commercial as well as residential. Even if they had suffered no losses in commercial markets—yet—there certainly was a chance that they might do so, because they had gravely underestimated the risks that they had already accepted. So they paused in making new deals until they could resolve all these uncertainties.

The Revised Viewpoints of Capital Suppliers on Commercial Property Markets

It did not take long for most major suppliers of capital to commercial property markets to reach five fundamental conclusions. First, if they were to loan money to real estate investors, they needed to demand higher rates of return on the capital they supplied in order to offset the greater, often unrecognized risks they had been taking. That meant they would need to charge higher interest rates and spreads on capital they lent to others. They would have to overcome or ignore the pressure of competition from other capital suppliers and insist on higher yields, or they would not supply capital to investors or property owners.

Similarly, equity investors also recognized the deteriorating prospects for growth in both income and property values, leading buyers to demand higher yields/cap rates to compensate them for their risk and provide adequate returns. These higher yields meant that the market value of commercial properties would be reduced so as to provide higher capitalization rates for a given net income; that is, higher yields to buyers or investors. The compression of capitalization rates was replaced by an elevation of capitalization rates in all commercial property transactions. That would require owners of commercial properties to accept at least some rollback of the high prices they had been receiving from 2000 to early 2007.

Second, capital suppliers would have to carry out much more thorough due diligence in analyzing the deals into which they put their money. Yes, that would take them longer than before and cost them more. But they could no longer depend almost entirely on credit rating agencies to determine whether proposed investments were sound.

Third, capital suppliers needed to include both more and more rigorous covenants in any loans or any purchases they made, including amortization of the loan principal. The days of "covenant light" and interest-only loans were over. Capital suppliers needed to ensure that borrowers would not overcommit themselves to spending more on properties than they were worth or enter so many deals that they might not be able to repay all of them, or place other repayment commitments ahead of those to themselves.

Fourth, capital suppliers whose portfolios were already heavily loaded with real estate loans or direct investments needed to slow down or even stop making any more such investments. This was especially important for commercial banks, which needed to keep diversified portfolios of their uses of capital for both legal and prudential reasons. Such slowdowns implied that these capital suppliers would reinforce their insistence on much more stringent terms for entering any deals than they had been getting in the past five years or so.

Fifth, capital suppliers needed to attain more certainty about how much real properties were actually worth. That was hard to do in an environment marked by so much stock volatility, asset losses, stock declines, a looming recession, threatening inflation, and public policy indecision about what actions the government ought to take. Investors would have to demand more transparency concerning the properties and securities they were being asked to finance. They needed more and clearer information about the nature of those properties and securities, and the risks involved in investing in them. Capital suppliers were also threatened by the thought of making a deal in the near future on what seemed like good terms, but then soon after finding that they could have gotten much better terms when all that uncertainty cleared away.

By mid-2008, the net result of all these factors was a freezing of financial capital in the hands of capital suppliers. Suppliers became unwilling to make deals until all those sources of uncertainty largely disappeared. In reality, there was still a lot of financial capital around looking for somewhere to invest. Moreover, the stock market did not seem appealing, as stock values dropped steadily in mid-2008. Bond markets might produce higher immediate yields if interest rates rose, but that would also reduce the market value of bonds already held or those purchased soon before interest rates rose. So commercial real estate still had some attraction as a place to invest capital if all those sources of uncertainty could be overcome.

Ironically, this freeze in capital sources removed one of the central causes of all the economic problems in real estate markets, especially for commercial properties: the oversupply of capital seeking immediate investment. That oversupply had generated intense competition among capital suppliers, causing the competitive deterioration in underwriting standards discussed earlier. That in turn led to inadequate compensation to capital suppliers for the risks they were undertaking—which was also the direct cause of all the difficulties investors had encountered in housing markets. Once the capital freeze occurred, the supply of capital actively seeking investment in real estate largely dried up. One positive result was that the freeze removed the incentives for intense competition among investors who supplied capital. But this "correction" went too far, causing an intense shortage of capital for real estate transactions. Thus an initial oversupply of capital led to an eventual undersupply. That shifted the prevailing problem from excessive investing to almost no investing. Yet at least some sizable reduction in the available supply of capital ready to invest in real estate was a necessary ingredient in the cure for the problems generated by the initial oversupply.

Property Owners' and Borrowers' Responses to Capital Suppliers' New Requirements

The fact that all the suppliers of capital suddenly developed a new and nearly universal set of requirements for providing that capital—requirements more favorable to them—had no immediate effect on the attitudes of property owners. Those owners had been enjoying the benefits of the poor underwriting and low yields that capital suppliers had been accepting from 2000 to early 2007. Clearly, those trends had raised the market value of the properties owned by those selling or holding them. When the capital suppliers suddenly shifted their requirements to a set far less favorable to property owners, the owners naturally resisted this change. They preferred holding onto the high market values of their properties that had been generated by falling capitalization rates and easy availability of credit. There was no pressing reason why property owners should accept new terms that required them to lower their prices, so most did not voluntarily lower those prices. They simply stood fast with the prices that had been generated by the falling capitalization rates. In the same way, many bankers held onto securitized paper that had become worth far less than 100 cents on the dollar because they did not want to accept the reality of lower prices.

One factor that made it difficult for some property owners to stand fast with the high prices that emerged from the capitalization rate compression was the rolling over of debt that they had placed on their properties with high degrees of leverage. An example would be an owner who financed acquisition or construction of a property worth $100 million by obtaining loans for 90 percent of that value before 2006—short-term loans for which full refinancing would be necessary in 2009. But by 2009, in the eyes of lenders, the market price for that property would have fallen by, say, 10 percent to $90 million. If the owner tried to refinance the property so as to roll over the loan, he would find that the few lenders willing to advance capital would require a loan-to-value ratio of no more than 65 percent. That would give the owner a $58.5 million loan to finance a debt of $90 million—leaving the owner an "equity gap" of $31.5 million, or more than three times the equity the owner had in the property. In many cases, such owners would find it necessary to turn over the keys on the property to the original lender, because it was so difficult to come up with the required $31.5 million, since other lenders would not provide it. One well-known commercial developer in California has observed that he may lose almost half of his commercial properties in that way during 2009 if the credit situation does not improve. This problem was less prominent in apartment markets, where leverage was not so high and prices had not fallen so far as in office markets.

REIT Share Prices and Private Commercial Property Prices

The collision between new transactional terms more favorable to capital suppliers and the desire of property owners to retain existing prices is dramatically illustrated by what has happened recently to real estate investment trust (REIT) stock prices. The FTSE NAREIT Index is a composite measure of all equity REIT stocks that meet criteria established by FTSE (the Financial Times and London Stock Exchange) and the National Association of Real Estate Investment Trusts (NAREIT). From 1999 to early 2007, REIT share prices as measured by the

EXHIBIT 4-8. Stock Price Index Changes from December 1998 to February 2008

Index	December 31, 1998	February 7, 2007	Change (%)	October 9, 2002	February 7, 2007	Change (%)
FTSE NAREIT	2,491.53	10,980.62	340.71	3,187.46	10,980.62	244.49
Dow Jones	9,181.43	12,666.87	37.86	7,286.27	12,666.87	73.84
S&P 500	1,229.29	1,450.02	17.95	776.77	1,450.02	86.67
NASDAQ	2,192.69	2,490.50	13.58	1,114,11	2,490.50	123.54

FTSE NAREIT index rose steadily, even when all three major stock indices plunged in the stock market crash of 2000. In the eight years from December 31, 1998, to February 7, 2007, FTSE REIT share prices rose 340.7 percent. In contrast, the other three stock indices first collapsed, then recovered for net gains of less than 38 percent, as shown in exhibit 4-8. This reflected the massive flow of financial capital into real estate and away from other stocks after 2000.

I believe this divergence of real estate stock prices from most other stock prices was evidence of a major paradigm shift among institutional and other investors concerning their view of real estate. Before the stock market crash, many investors had largely avoided real estate for two reasons. One was their memory of the collapse of real estate property values in 1990 after huge overbuilding in the 1980s. The property value collapse was so bad that federal regulators prohibited banks, savings and loans, and insurance companies from making further real estate loans after 1990 for several years. That prohibition is what drove many real estate owners and developers into switching their properties from private ownership into publicly held REITs. They did so because raising money on the stock market was the only way they could get significant amounts of capital. Real estate did not recover from those adverse investor attitudes until about 1994, when space markets began showing strong improvements as the general economy expanded. The second reason investors avoided real estate was that Internet and other high-tech stocks were doing so well in the stock run-up to 2000 that investors poured their cash into those sectors, not real estate.

But the stock market crash of 2000 changed all that. In fact, I believe it helped cause a paradigm shift in the attitudes of institutional and other investors toward putting funds into real estate. They decided that real estate was one of the only sound places to put large amounts of their capital. Their funding drove REIT share prices, as measured by the FTSE NAREIT index, steadily upward for the next seven-plus years.

The performance of the FTSE NAREIT and the three major stock indices up to February 7, 2007, are shown in exhibit 4-8. The second, third, and fourth columns show the indices' movements from December 31, 1998, before the stock market crash, until February 7, 2007. The prices of FTSE NAREIT shares rose almost continuously in that period. All three of the other indices plunged in value at different moments in 2000 and kept falling until October 9, 2002, after which they all began rising again. The fifth, sixth, and seventh columns show the performance of these indices from the low point after the crash of 2000 until February 7, 2007. Even during this recovery period, the FTSE NAREIT index greatly outperformed the three major indices, as financial capital continued to flow into real estate. In fact, for the first

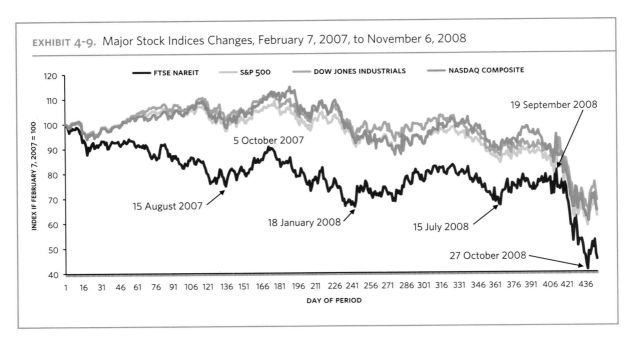

EXHIBIT 4-9. Major Stock Indices Changes, February 7, 2007, to November 6, 2008

few years, real estate prices were catching up to other asset prices—then they somewhat overran their true relative value in relation to those other asset values.

After February 7, 2007, when the FTSE NAREIT hit its all-time high of 10,980.62, FTSE NAREIT shares fell sharply both absolutely and in relation to shares in the other three indices. This can be seen in exhibit 4-9. The FTSE NAREIT's decline continued for almost a year until about January 18, 2008, when it suddenly reversed course. It rose until about the middle of May 2008, when it began falling again with the other three indices. The statistical correlation between FTSE NAREIT index values and S&P 500 index values between May 18 and July 18, 2008 was 0.97718. Clearly, FTSE NAREIT shares had stopped either rising or falling in relation to the other three indices and were instead moving very closely along with those other indices. However, after September 19, the FTSE NAREIT index plunged dramatically, much faster than the other stock indices, as discussed further below.

Thus, from 1999 through February 7, 2007, FTSE NAREIT share prices had gained in value at least 387 percent more than the highest of the other three indices (the Dow Jones Industrial Average). But after that, for 15 months, FTSE NAREIT share prices fell in percentage terms more than twice as much as Dow Jones Industrial shares and almost three times as much as S&P 500 shares.

Then from May 19 until September 30, 2008, the FTSE NAREIT index fell 8.13 percent while the Dow Jones fell 16.7 percent and the S&P 500 fell 18.36 percent. In that period, REIT shares notably outperformed stocks in general, though all three indices declined. From September 19 to October 27, as shown in exhibit 4-9, stock prices in general collapsed sharply. These indices were down 66.4 percent for the NASDAQ, 49.1 percent for the FTSE NAREIT, 32.3 percent for the S&P 500, and 26.4 percent for the Dow Jones—all in 38 days.

From this detailed analysis, the following significant conclusions can be drawn:

■ Relative to other asset classes, the market values of commercial real estate (as represented by FTSE NAREIT shares) increased tremendously more than those of other types of stocks, bonds, and other assets between the end of 1999 and February 7, 2007. Even as of late July 2008, the market values of FTSE NAREIT shares had still risen much more than the market values of the other stock indices since December 1998. These movements showed—at least to me—that a paradigm shift had occurred concerning the attitude of institutional and other investors toward putting money into commercial real estate. Most such investors determined that commercial real estate was a separate asset class into which they ought to invest a significant share of their total assets.

■ From February 7, 2007, to September 19, 2008, the market value of commercial real estate as reflected in the FTSE NAREIT declined by about 19.1 percent. The absolute market values of stocks represented by the other three major indices also declined in that period but by smaller percentages, ranging from 4.7 to 13.4 percent. After September 19, the values of all four indices plunged dramatically, but the FTSE NAREIT and NASDAQ indices fell more than either the Dow Jones or the S&P 500 (but less than the NASDAQ, as noted above). From early 2007 to the end of October, commercial real estate as an asset class had lost a significant amount of relative attraction in the minds of investors compared with other asset classes represented by stocks.

■ The market values of commercial properties held outside REITs have also declined since September 2, 2008, as evidenced by a 9.54 percent decline in value in the NCREIF Property Index for the fourth quarter of 2008. However, as shown in exhibit 4-9, for stocks in the S&P 500 and the Dow Jones Industrials, declines have not been as great as the decline in FTSE NAREIT share prices. The decline in property values for direct property investments has been slower to develop in part because these values are based on appraisals, and with the drastic lack of transactions in commercial real property caused by the credit crunch, it is difficult to estimate reliably what has happened to the prices of properties.

■ Even as of November 6, 2008, the current values of the FTSE NAREIT index were still more than 70 percent higher in relation to those of the other three indices than they were at the end of 1998. This implies that the favorable attitude of investors in general toward real estate has not completely disappeared. Thus, some important vestiges of the pro–real estate paradigm shift in attitudes among investors that occurred in 2000 remain as of late 2008, though in much smaller amounts than a year earlier. Therefore it is not likely that all the financial capital that flowed into real estate between 2000 and early 2007 will be completely withdrawn from real estate in the foreseeable future.

Of course, the reliability of the last conclusion depends upon whether FTSE NAREIT shares in the future move in close lockstep with the other, more general stock indices or continue to fall in value to a much greater degree. For 2008, total returns for the FTSE NAREIT Equity REIT Index were –37.73 percent, and the price index was off 41.12 percent, similar to the drop in other stock indices.

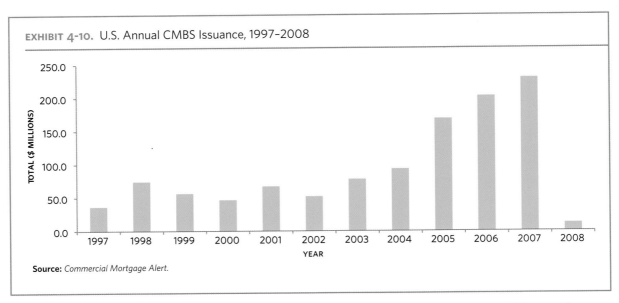

EXHIBIT 4-10. U.S. Annual CMBS Issuance, 1997–2008

Source: *Commercial Mortgage Alert.*

The Decline in CMBS Activities and the Shortage of Lendable Funds in Commercial Property Markets

During the boom in commercial property prices from 2000 through early 2007, buyers and sellers of such properties became increasingly reliant on CMBSs, as shown in exhibit 4-10. Annual issuances of such securities soared from about $46.9 billion in 2000 to $230.2 billion in 2007—a rise of 490 percent in seven years. This source of borrowing against commercial properties was a major factor in the giant run-up of total debts against such properties in the same period.

Yet in 2008, only $12.1 billion in CMBSs were issued, all in the first six months; there was zero issuance in the latter half of the year. That is a decline of 95 percent. The big problem was that potential buyers of CMBSs were unwilling to commit to purchasing securitized versions of multiple loans, unless they received much stronger assurances from the issuers that the properties involved were worth what the packagers said they were—because adequate due diligence and proper underwriting had been performed. Those potential investors had lost faith in the quality ratings placed on CMBS issues by established credit rating agencies. In addition, they thought CMBS issues provided insufficient data about the properties concerned to permit adequate due diligence. Tranching of these securities added further complications. Finally, capital suppliers were gripped by uncertainty concerning future property values for the reasons discussed above.

Probably even more devastating to property owners seeking to sell or borrow against their properties was the unwillingness of potential lenders to accept traditional mortgages. As the chief financial officer of a major REIT said, "Without mortgages, real estate markets cannot function." Traditional mortgages provided security to the lenders, with their ability to seize the properties involved if the borrowers failed to repay. That ability had been compromised by securitization, which split the responsibility for ownership among dozens or even hundreds of different parties. In case of default, each such fractional owner could claim only a small piece of the properties involved. To cope with the resulting difficulties of seizing properties under such conditions, defaulted securitized loans were turned over to special servicers. They were supposed to work out deals with the borrowing parties and distribute the results among the multiple investors. But that was a complex arrangement that was not at all certain to work. It works well in theory, but in practice it depends on the volume of loans that those special servicers must deal with. In many housing markets, the servicers have been overwhelmed by large numbers of defaults and have been unable or unwilling to work out individual recovery plans with specific borrowers. In commercial property markets, the volume of defaults has been much smaller, and servicers have been more able to work out effective recovery plans with individual borrowers. However, many more defaults will ocurr and these will test this market severely.

Therefore, if borrowers made traditional mortgage deals with individual lenders for each separate property, the perils of securitization could be avoided. Assuming each lender held on to the mortgages it made until it was repaid, each lender could seize the property concerned in case of default or develop workouts with the borrowers directly. But many lenders refused to hold onto even such traditional deals. True, some life insurance companies and commercial banks were willing to lend against individual properties of high quality under traditional conditions. But even traditional mortgage loans against high-quality properties were rejected by many potential lenders. Either they had too many real estate loans on their books, or they were simply unwilling to accept the property valuations implicit in traditional mortgages because of prevailing uncertainty about what properties were really worth. So sources for traditional mortgages shrank to far fewer than needed to meet the demands for them. This raised problems for owners of real estate, which had loans on many of their properties that were rolling over during the credit crunch. How could they refinance those properties? As of this writing, there is no easy answer to that question.

This situation will pose great difficulties for owners of many commercial properties that were heavily financed with debt in the past few years. An official with the Real Estate Roundtable estimated in December 2008 that all U.S. commercial real property was then valued at roughly $6 trillion, of which $3.2 trillion was debt. He also estimated that in each year in the near future about $400 billion of that debt would mature. That $400 billion due each year equals 12.5 percent of the total debt of $3.2 trillion, so the original market value of the properties coming due each year was 12.5 percent of the total $6 trillion, or $750 billion. But by the time the debt comes due, those properties may have declined in market value by, say, 30 percent. So the property with loans coming due each year would have a current market value of $525 billion.

The $400 billion in loans coming due each year were made on properties originally worth $750 billion, for an average loan-to-value ratio of 53.3 percent. The borrowers would like to renew those loans for the same $400 billion on property that will then be worth $525 billion, which would be an average loan-to-value ratio of 76.2 percent. But lenders would then demand loan-to-value ratios of no more than 60 percent; so they would advance only $315 billion. That would leave a gap of $85 billion for the borrowers to fill in order to roll over their original debts. If it is as difficult to borrow money then as it is now, where will they get that money?

This complicated calculation shows the difficulty that is likely to confront owners of many commercial properties that were heavily financed with debt in the past few years, as that debt becomes due. They will be caught in a trap resulting from

- A notable decline in the market values of their properties,
- Another decline in the loan-to-value ratios available from lenders—if there are any lenders left who are willing to make loans—and
- Higher interest rates and stronger loan covenants demanded by the remaining lenders.

Hence, further declines in values and many foreclosures seem likely to arise in commercial property markets at least in 2009, and perhaps even beyond that year.

One possible way out of this dilemma for property owners would be to sell their properties to someone else. But in the past, most property sales involved significant borrowing by the purchaser. Where would purchasers get the money? One answer is from the sellers, through seller financing of deals. Thus, it is likely that seller financing will become more prominent in the near future, when property owners facing such debt rollover problems have to do something better than defaulting.

However, a second key implication of the analysis above is that the loss of private sources of funding for the rollover loans for real estate purchased at the height of the debt expansion phase of this cycle will have to be made up for in some manner with funds from the public sector. With asset prices falling, interest rates demanded by lenders rising, and loan-to-value ratios falling, the borrowers who financed new purchases at the height of low-cost debt availability (up through 2007 and early 2008) will be unable to support the rolling over of that debt under newly prevailing market conditions. Nor will they be able to obtain private financing from other sources, which have disappeared. Creating new forms of public debt to fill these rollover gaps will be a major part of the restructuring of real estate finance produced by the credit crunch of 2007–08. If no such restructuring occurs, many such rollover gaps will not be able to be filled by the private sector. Hence, those firms that borrowed under minimum debt-cost conditions will find themselves facing bankruptcy or at least defaulting on major parts of their debt.

The Dearth of Public Policy Responses to Credit Problems in the Commercial Property Market

A final difficulty facing commercial property markets during the credit crunch was the low priority that the federal government gave to ameliorating credit problems in those markets, compared with its willingness to pour billions into propping up housing markets. Politically, there was no contest between housing and commercial property markets. Almost every household occupies a dwelling unit, and there are more than 125 million dwelling units in the nation. Most of those occupants are potential voters, and over 65 percent of them were homeowners. When a significant fraction of such households seemed in danger of real financial problems from housing market ailments, politicians leapt to the rescue—all the more eagerly in an election year like 2008. Both Congress and the Bush Administration put forward several bills that would provide emergency aid to millions of households facing foreclosure on their homes, mainly because of subprime mortgage problems.

The Federal Reserve Board had also leapt into action on commercial property problems when Bear Stearns seemed likely to collapse. But the main cause of Bear Stearns' difficulties was the huge losses it sustained in the subprime mortgage sector, although it also had losses involving commercial properties—as did Lehman Brothers, which succumbed to bankruptcy. Yet because Bear Stearns also had many counterparty connections in commercial property markets and with commercial derivatives, the Fed's actions helped such markets, at least indirectly. In particular, the Fed's willingness to lend short-term capital to both investment and commercial banks that were in trouble aided many firms that operated in commercial markets. But most of their difficulties, too, had arisen because of housing defaults, not commercial property defaults.

Consequently, no federal assistance was offered to potential private borrowers in commercial property markets to find available sources of capital when other forms of lending dried up in 2007 and 2008. This left many such borrowers in difficult situations when their loans on commercial properties came due through what until then had been normal loan rollovers. Everyone was told to "hunker down" and cut operating costs in order to free up capital without explicit federal aid or to find new capital investors. As of early 2009, relatively few commercial property markets operators had announced that they would have to cease operations. But many such operators were desperately struggling to find capital from one loan due date to the next in order to avoid defaults that would impair their long-term credit reputations.

After the massive declines in stock prices in September and October 2008, the federal government began to consider injecting capital into commercial firms and properties, as discussed further in chapter 7.

Unexpected Declines in Private Lenders' Willingness to Make Loans on Commercial Properties

During 2008, the federal government took many dramatic steps aimed at increasing the willingness of banks and other private investors to make loans, both in housing markets and in commercial property markets. Those dramatic steps were described in detail in chapter 1. They included a quasi-nationalization of the U.S. system of large private commercial banks through injection of federal money into

- Purchases of certain classes of assets, including some toxic loans held by banks;
- Federal guarantees backing private purchases of other assets, such as money market funds and bank deposits;
- Purchases of preferred stock in major banks as a means of increasing the capital of those banks; and
- Encouragement of Fannie Mae and Freddie Mac—now owned by the federal government— to continue securitizing home mortgages.

However, an unexpected result of these federal actions and other recent events was the continued unwillingness of many private banks and other potential lenders—even those aided with federal funds—to make loans to private borrowers, except at interest rates and with other conditions that most borrowers either could not or would not pay. Like almost all other private lenders, banks had determined to get higher yields than they had been demanding from 2000 to 2006 so as to compensate them for the significant risks they had been taking— and had not been adequately paid for. So they essentially stopped making loans on commercial properties except at interest rates and loan-to-value ratios that discouraged potential borrowers from making deals or borrowing money.

This reluctance to lend was further encouraged by the negative future outlook in most sectors of the economy as the nation plunged into a strong recession. At a recent Urban Land Institute meeting, a banker from one of the nation's largest banks asked the assembled experts if they thought the economy in their specialized sectors was getting worse, and everyone there agreed it was. He then asked them if they wanted to borrow money from him, and they all did. But, he asked, why should a prudent lender invest money in companies whose businesses were getting worse? In fact, that same banker said he could get a 21 percent return from buying up the discounted bonds issued by some of the same clients that were trying to borrow money from him at 7 to 8 percent interest. So why should he make such loans? Yet the banker also said that to keep regular clients in business his bank was willing to roll over existing loans—but at higher rates than before.

Why are commercial bankers so unwilling to make loans to private borrowers? One reason is that the values of most types of assets in the U.S. economy—including stocks, housing, business firms, and other financial assets—have been falling dramatically, especially since September 2008. And levels of business activity in housing, retailing, and automobile sales have also plunged. So what can a banker accept as collateral for a loan that he can have any confidence will retain its value in the future? Also, many bankers are trying to recover from being overleveraged with loans in comparison with their reserve capital. Hence they need to reduce the total amount of loans on their books that can be supported by their limited capital. That discourages them from making more loans. Furthermore, they do not know what the reserve capital requirements are likely to be in one or two years, because the financial authorities may want to increase reserve requirements in the future to prevent a recurrence of excessive leveraging. This uncertainty also discourages them from making more loans.

The final factor that is preventing bankers from making more loans is the dilemma faced by owners of commercial properties who borrowed against those properties with short-term loans made from 2000 through mid-2007, as discussed earlier. Those loans were made with low interest rates and high loan-to-value ratios typical of the lending activity in that period, as discussed earlier. When such loans come due today or in the near future, the borrowers discover that lenders now

- Have reduced their view of the market values of the properties involved,
- Want higher interest rates and more stringent loan covenants than formerly, and
- Will only advance funds with lower loan-to-value ratios.

The resulting gap between the amount of the loans made originally and the amount banks will now advance makes it either very difficult or impossible for many borrowers to meet these terms without borrowing added funds from someone else. Yet that is virtually impossible to do in today's financial climate. Under these conditions, it is quite likely that commercial lending defaults will rise significantly in 2009 and beyond.

So despite federal efforts to encourage more private lending, there has been a reduction in the willingness of many private banks and other lenders to make loans on commercial properties, unless they are merely extending existing loans to well-established clients. In fact, as of December 2008, there seem to be almost no available sources of borrowing for owners of commercial properties—especially for first mortgage loans. Moreover, few banks are willing to make construction loans for new developments, especially because the prospects for new projects becoming profitable in the near future appear very dim.

Yet the federal government cannot feasibly absorb all the losses in value that have occurred to either residential or commercial real properties since 2006 or will occur in the next few years. It does not have enough capital on hand to do so, and simply printing more money to absorb such losses—which the government could do—would both devalue the American dollar and possibly lead to strong inflationary pressures. So what is to be done? This question is discussed in detail chapter 7.

In This Financial Standoff, Who Is Going to Blink First?

In normal financial real estate markets, both lenders and borrowers have strong motives to continue making deals, rather than to sit on the sidelines. Lenders and other capital suppliers have lots of funds they want to put to work so as to earn decent yields on those funds. If they do not invest those funds in profit-making ways, they will disappoint the persons and firms who placed their funds with those potential lenders to invest. Yet that is just what most potential lenders who still control or have access to large amounts of money have been doing in the fall of 2008. Rather than putting their funds into traditional real property purchases or loans, they have been sitting on them. That means they have been parking their funds in U.S. Treasury securities or money market funds, because those uses pay at least some return while seeming relatively safe from any default.

Such behavior has long been traditional during the most turbulent phases of American business cycles. The impacts of this behavior on total U.S. Treasury securities outstanding can be seen in exhibit 4-11. The most variable type of Treasury security shown is Treasury notes. The volume of such notes outstanding, as a group, declined from $2.122 trillion in 1997 to $1.433 trillion in 2001, a fall of 32.5 percent. But then that volume rose significantly from 2001 to more than $2.458 trillion in 2007, a significant gain.

This increase in Treasury notes outstanding was partly related to the interest rates being paid on such notes, set forth in exhibit 4-12. After 2000, the Treasury slashed nominal interest rates on its one-year, five-year, and ten-year notes, clearly to help offset the negative impact of the stock market crash on economic activity. The rate on the one-year note dropped from 6.11 percent in 2000 to 1.24 percent in 2003, a fall of 4.87 points in three years. However, that rate then zoomed back up to 4.94 percent in 2006, a gain of 3.70 points in three years. But from February 29 to May 9, 2008, the one-year note interest rate was continuously below 2.0 percent, averaging 1.69 percent and getting as low as 1.33 percent. This resulted in part from a flood of private financial capital into Treasury notes (not shown in the exhibit), especially the one-year note.

That flood was caused by lenders parking their funds in Treasuries in early 2008 rather than investing them in other securities or properties. Those investors were avoiding risks

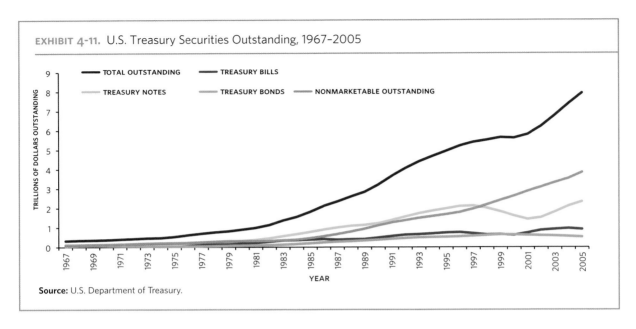

EXHIBIT 4-11. U.S. Treasury Securities Outstanding, 1967–2005

Source: U.S. Department of Treasury.

rather than seeking desirable returns. The five-year note shown in the exhibit also had a declining interest rate and a recovery in the same periods, which are not shown on the graph. The interest rate on the ten-year Treasury note, after remaining above 4.0 percent for several decades, began to fall below 4.0 percent briefly in November 2007. It dropped below 4.0 percent again on January 2, 2008, and stayed below 4.0 percent continuously until May 27, hitting a low point of 3.34 percent. This drop in interest rates was also the result of a flight of capital from normal investment channels into safe Treasuries. More recently, investors have moved funds out of bank notes and into Treasury securities, even at very low returns, in order to escape private securities with low transparency.

With capital suppliers parking their money in safe, low-rate instruments and property owners fighting against accepting lower prices for their assets, who is going to blink first in this standoff on both sides of real estate transaction markets? The answer involves two points. First, I believe there will be no instantaneous end to this impasse. Rather, at first a few deals will be made by people on both sides who desperately need to complete transactions. Gradually, as the people who pioneer such deals seem to survive without dire results, more and more lenders and property owners will come out of the woodwork and enter into transactions. Second, who blinks first and when that happens will vary from one local market to the next, depending on specific supply-demand balances in each. In regions with big oversupplies of space, property owners are likely to blink earlier than they will in regions where space supplies are tight. Ironically, one cause of some big regional space oversupplies is the collapse of many mortgage banking firms, as in the Orange County, California market.

In general, the standoff will dominate in real estate markets for at least one year after this was written (in November 2008), and perhaps even longer. Since the nation's economy definitely entered a recession in late 2008 that will surely worsen in 2009, it will take longer for

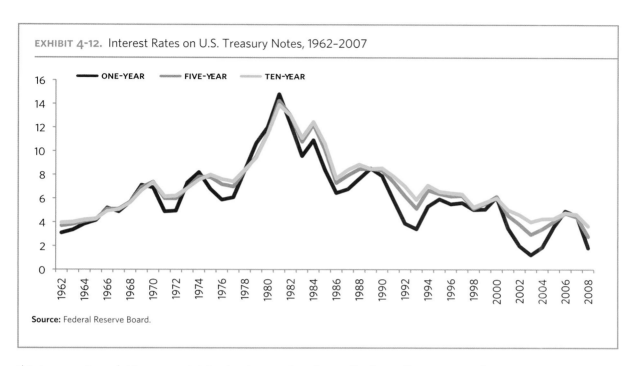

EXHIBIT 4-12. Interest Rates on U.S. Treasury Notes, 1962–2007

Legend: ONE-YEAR FIVE-YEAR TEN-YEAR

Source: Federal Reserve Board.

this impasse to end. More uncertainty about property values will arise as the economy slows and jobs are cut.

As 2009 began, real estate industry leaders were trying to persuade officials in the U.S. Treasury and the Obama administration to provide large amounts of government financial aid to help property owners fill the loan rollover gaps described here. If they did not do so, it appeared quite likely that the owners of thousands of large commercial properties would default on their loans. Hence those properties might be taken over by those who had lent money to those owners, even if such lenders had no property management experience. Such a development could result in relatively chaotic conditions in commercial property markets throughout the nation. Whatever happens, interesting times lie ahead for commercial real estate.

The Basic Instability of U.S. Financial Markets

A CRUCIAL CAUSE OF THE CREDIT CRUNCH has been the fundamental instability of the U.S. financial sector, including real estate markets. That trait consists of an inherent tendency to generate excessive debt leverage in prosperous times. Such leverage then results in downward credit spirals when unexpected events suddenly arise and force many borrowers to repay before they are ready. This chapter explores the major factors underlying this instability.

The Expansion of the Financial Sector since 1950

Since World War II, the financial sector of the American economy has steadily increased in both relative and absolute importance. The Bureau of Economic Analysis of the U.S. Department of Commerce defines the financial sector as including the following major parts:

- Financial activities
  - Finance and insurance,
  - Federal Reserve banks, credit intermediation, related activities,
  - Securities, commodity contracts, and investments,
  - Insurance carriers and related activities, and
  - Funds, trusts, and other financial vehicles.
- Real estate and leasing
  - Real estate and
  - Rental and leasing activities and lessors of intangible assets.

The real estate and leasing portion of this sector has always been much larger than the finance and insurance portion. The growth of both major segments is shown in exhibit 5-1. In 1950, the real estate and leasing sectors constituted 8.68 percent of gross domestic product (GDP, as measured in current dollars), while finance and insurance activities constituted 2.69 percent. So both segments of the finance sector together made up 11.37 percent of current GDP. Over time, the finance and insurance portion steadily increased as a percentage of GDP,

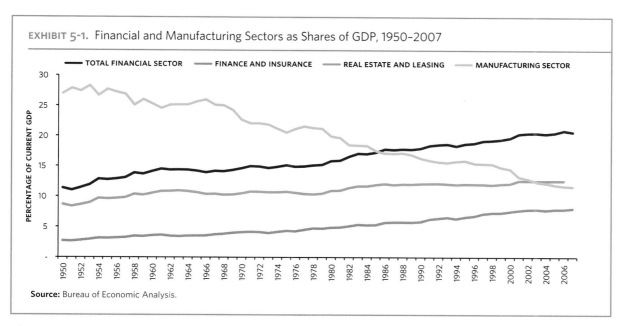

EXHIBIT 5-1. Financial and Manufacturing Sectors as Shares of GDP, 1950–2007

Source: Bureau of Economic Analysis.

whereas the real estate segment rose steadily until about 1986 and has remained at about 12.5 percent of current GDP since then. Since 2000, these segments combined have exceeded 20 percent of current GDP, which makes them the largest single industry sector in GDP. Their relative importance is illustrated by the long-term decline in the share of manufacturing in GDP from 27.0 percent in 1950 to 11.67 percent in 2007, as also shown in the exhibit.

Since 1986, the overall financial sector has exceeded manufacturing and all other sectors of the American economy as a percentage of both current and real GDP. Exhibit 5-2 shows that the finance sector greatly surpassed all other sectors in 2007. The real estate subsector alone was a larger percentage of GDP in 2007 than any other complete sector. The importance of the financial sector is not based solely on its overall size but also on the key role it plays in enabling other sectors to function well. All the other sectors depend on financing in some crucial way, so the influence of that sector permeates the entire economy.

Chronic Instability in the Financial Sector

One reason the financial sector is important to all other sectors of our economy is because of its own chronic instability. By instability, I do not mean that the financial sector is unable to sustain its own existence over time. Rather, that sector generates highly volatile conditions that periodically create high profits for most of its members and then plunge many of them into great financial difficulties. Peter Linneman of the University of Pennsylvania explains this volatility as follows: "We swing from greed to fear; and nontransparency means we overvalue what we cannot see when greed wins, and we undervalue what we cannot see when fear wins."[1]

Moreover, the financial sector's periodic setbacks and crises have large repercussions on other sectors. As evidence of this instability, stock market trader Satyajit Das lists specific

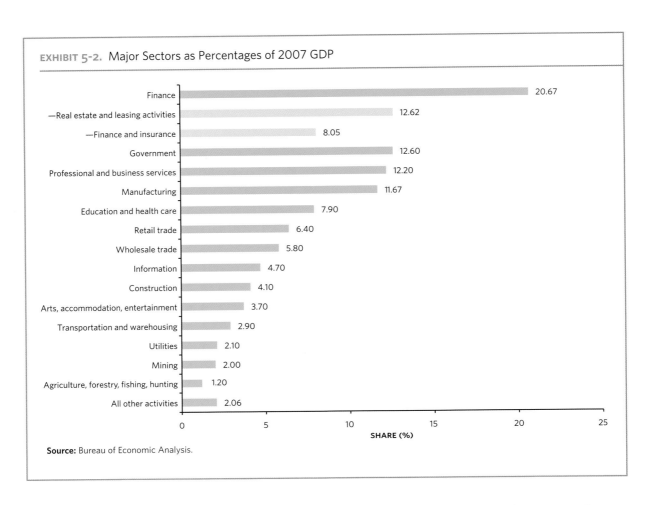

EXHIBIT 5-2. Major Sectors as Percentages of 2007 GDP

Sector	Share (%)
Finance	20.67
—Real estate and leasing activities	12.62
—Finance and insurance	8.05
Government	12.60
Professional and business services	12.20
Manufacturing	11.67
Education and health care	7.90
Retail trade	6.40
Wholesale trade	5.80
Information	4.70
Construction	4.10
Arts, accommodation, entertainment	3.70
Transportation and warehousing	2.90
Utilities	2.10
Mining	2.00
Agriculture, forestry, fishing, hunting	1.20
All other activities	2.06

Source: Bureau of Economic Analysis.

crises in his insightful book, *Traders, Guns & Money*. These events include economic distress from oil price increases and high inflation in the 1970s; the savings and loan crisis in the late 1980s and early 1990s; the Asian financial crisis, Russian default, and Long-Term Credit Management failure in the late 1990s; and the bursting of the Internet bubble and September 11 terrorist attacks in the early 2000s.[2]

Many of these adverse events were thought to have very low probabilities by those who designed the mathematical trading models used by investment firms. Yet such events occurred frequently enough to question the belief that such disruptions are truly unlikely.

A big difference between more recent crises and earlier ones results from the huge degree of consolidation of financial sector firms that has occurred over time. Today many such firms are so large that just a few going under makes international news, whereas prior to the consolidation, many small firms went under without creating more than local news. Thus, in the 1980s and early 1990s, the entire savings and loan sector virtually disappeared, but because it consisted of many relatively small firms, it did not attract as much attention as many more recent but smaller crises.

Why Has the Financial Sector Been So Unstable?

Classical economic theory denies that a relatively free market economy should be as unstable as the data above show the U.S. economy to have been recently. True, the U.S. economy has suffered from fewer major destabilizing shocks since World War II than it did before then. The National Bureau of Economic Research (NBER) keeps track of cyclical movements in the American economy and is the official designator of which ones count as recessions (usually defined by the NBER as two consecutive quarters in which real GDP declines). From 1854 through 2001, the NBER counted 32 cycles, with an average duration (from one peak to the next peak) of 56 months (about 4.5 years). Eleven cycles occurred from 1854 to 1900, or one every 4.1 years. From 1900 to 1945, ten more occurred, or one every 4.5 years. From the end of World War II in 1945 to 2001, NBER has identified 11 such cycles, with an average duration from peak to peak of 67 months, or 5.6 years. Moreover, the most recent troughs in 1991 and 2001 were relatively mild compared with many previous troughs—such as those in the Great Depression of the 1930s.

Nevertheless, many periods of financial instability have recently occurred. Most do not qualify as full recessions, but they certainly produced adverse results in the financial sector— in many cases including real estate markets. Is there some systematic way in which such periods of instability arise? I believe that several major, built-in causes of such instability can be identified, based on past analyses of economic events by both economists and financial practitioners. These are discussed below.

The Inherent Tendency of Self-Interest to Generate Financial Exploitation

One of the axioms of democracy—and of most political science—is that all human beings are strongly motivated by self-interest. Self-interest is an inherent tendency to weight one's own welfare and the welfare of one's family and close associates more heavily than the welfare of other people when making behavioral decisions. The founding fathers of the United States, like many other political activists, believed that such a tendency is universal. Some observers argue that it is caused by original sin, a Christian doctrine; others believe it is a product of eons of survival-of-the-fittest evolution; still others think it arose from poor education and upbringing. Whatever the cause, almost all observers agree that the tendency toward self-interest has two central implications for democratic governance.

The first implication is negative: no one person or part of society should be given unchecked power over others, because those with such power will eventually use it to benefit themselves at the expense of the others. This is why the U.S. Constitution, written in 1787, rejected the idea of having a king or a nobility with greater powers and privileges than most people. This need to limit power was even more important within the government than within society generally, since the government normally had a monopoly on the use of force over its citizens. This skepticism of the founding fathers toward concentrated power was responsible for the U.S. Constitution's extensive use of checks and balances within the structure of the American government. The clearest example is that the people who run the government must be elected by the citizens it governs. A second example is that no legislation becomes law unless it is approved by both houses of Congress and signed by the president (unless Congress is overriding a presidential veto). A third example is the myriad of government regulations limiting the ability of private individuals or firms to undertake actions that unfairly exploit customers or others. This principle underlay the federal adoption of extensive regulations of financial markets after the Great Depression of the 1930s.

Unfortunately, because the people who are supposed to prevent too much power from being concentrated in one place are also human, they tend to overestimate their own powers. Hence they often become vulnerable to hubris or to believing the hype that surrounds them in society. As a result, they often fail to check excessive concentrations of power in others or in themselves.

The second crucial implication of self-interest is positive: the people who are governed are ultimately the best judges of what is in their best interest. Therefore, the governed should have the power of electing those who govern them and influencing what policies those governors adopt when in office. Moreover, the nation's economy should be run primarily by individuals pursuing their own self-interest rather than by the government acting for them. In fact, self-interest in private markets should be the principal driving force in operating the economy. As Adam Smith declared in two famous passages from *Wealth of Nations*:

> *Man has almost constant occasion for the help of his brethren, and it is in vain for him to expect if from their benevolence only. He will be more likely to prevail if he can interest their self-love in his favor, and show them that it is for their own advantage to do for him what he requires of them.*
> . . .
> *It is not from the benevolence of the butcher, the brewer, or the baker that we expect our dinner, but from their regard to their own interest. We address ourselves, not to their humanity but to their self-love, and never talk to them of our own necessities but of their advantages.*[6]

However, the adoption of laws and regulations designed to prevent exploitative behavior does not eliminate tendencies toward such behavior among all citizens, including those who operate the nation's financial system. Self-interest often leads to exploitative behavior if circumstances and laws allow individuals and groups to take advantage of others, as many mortgage brokers did in the credit crunch. I believe that experience over many centuries of human society proves that any arrangements that create such exploitative opportunities for a small group of individuals will sooner or later lead them to take advantage of those opportunities. When mortgage brokers can persuade potential homebuyers with low incomes and poor credit records to accept subprime mortgages that those homebuyers will be unable to support over time, at least some brokers will do that.

True, societies can protect themselves against some such excessive self-interest—often called greed—by adopting appropriate legal regulations, such as those recommended in chapter 7. But financial and most other government regulators are primarily reactive—responding to greedy or otherwise undesirable behavior that has already appeared. Regulators are much less successful at anticipating future, new greedy behavior and preventing it. In a complex and rapidly changing environment like that of the U.S. financial sector, where innovation is a constant, it is unlikely that regulators will be able to anticipate the greedy behavior that helps cause the next crisis. Regulations have a placebo-like effect: We feel better when we have taken them, even though they are not likely to succeed in preventing the next crisis. Therefore, I do not believe society can eliminate the negative externalities of self-interest as a key factor underlying financial instability. In fact, experience throughout the ages clearly demonstrates that people will constantly try to invent new means of using the powers available to them to exploit others. Practitioners in the world of finance often invent new financial instruments and tactics that create at least potential opportunities for such exploitation. Those opportunities are explicitly designed to evade regulations that were adopted to prevent just that eventuality.

Subprime mortgages are especially susceptible to exploitation. Each subprime mortgage not only has high initial interest rates but also often contains complex clauses that reset mortgage rates in the future in ways that are hard for borrowers to understand. After all, such mortgages were designed to serve households with poor credit ratings, many of whom have limited educations. But during the peak of the housing boom in the 2000s, many subprime loan borrowers were speculators seeking to flip the homes they bought. Financial derivatives provide many other examples of instruments that may have hard-to-anticipate consequences.

Self-interest also generates widespread behavioral tendencies in the financial world that can—and recently did—become exploitative or reckless. Many greedy mortgage lenders deliberately convinced low-income homebuyers—who really could not afford to purchase homes—that they should do so because rising home prices would overcome their inability to repay their initial mortgages. In fact, such brokers frequently reduced the requirements for buying homes beyond reasonable levels. They often cut downpayments to zero, accepted borrowers' own estimates of incomes without checking them, used interest-only loans and initially low "teaser" interest rates to reduce initial monthly payments, promoted types of loans that cut payments below levels necessary to cover interest, or used hard-to-understand mortgage documents. Subprime mortgages thus permitted multiple exploitations of others—both by unscrupulous brokers and by unscrupulous borrowers who lied about their incomes or about their intention to occupy the homes they bought.

As a result, the subprime mortgage market was a major generator of perverse incentives. It caused many actors to adopt behaviors that eventually subverted the market itself. Thus the promoters of subprime mortgages exploited capital suppliers as well as low-income borrowers. They did so by securitizing and selling high-interest-rate mortgages to bond market investors who were desperately seeking high yields in the low-interest-rate environment caused by the flood of lendable funds into real estate markets after 2000. Hence mortgage brokers were motivated to increase the volumes of subprime mortgages as much as possible and to sell them as fast as possible. Doing so enabled the brokers to shift the risk of default onto the investors who bought securitized mortgages.

Similarly, commercial banks were motivated to make risky loans because the banks could create fee income and then easily and profitably offload these loans into the securitized debt market. Banks could also sometimes borrow from the Federal Reserve or other banks at negative interest rates in real terms. Capital suppliers were motivated by self-interest to buy such mortgage securities because they wanted higher yields than were available on prime mortgages. Also, capital suppliers believed the high quality ratings on the securities they bought were accurate. Hence many security buyers thought they did not have to do much, if any, due diligence on the paper they bought. Yet in reality, the responsibility to ensure the quality of loans ultimately rests with the lenders themselves, even if they hire credit rating agencies as advisers. Moreover, the rating agencies—Moody's, Fitch, and Standard & Poor's—were required to work quickly and were motivated in part by the need to maintain client relationships; neither of these factors contributed to the soundness of their rating decisions.

Greed was also a key factor that generated excessive leveraging in financing business activities in general. The funds needed to finance a productive activity normally consist of both equity—money supplied by the owners—and debts—money borrowed from others. The profits from the activity are paid out as return on equity, as interest on and return of the principal of debts, and as taxes. If the interest rate on money borrowed is lower than the profit rate produced by the overall activity, borrowing a higher proportion of total funds will increase the rate of return on equity. For example, assume a one-year activity requires a total investment of $10 million, produces a net profit after taxes of $1 million (10 percent), and has to pay interest on borrowed funds at 5 percent. If the operator puts up $5 million in equity and borrows $5 million, he must pay back $5 million in principal and $250,000 in interest. That leaves him $750,000 in profit on $5 million of equity—a yield of 15 percent. But if the owner borrows $7 million, he must pay back $7 million in principal plus $350,000 interest, leaving him a profit of $650,000 on equity of only $3 million, or a yield of 21.67 percent. The operator thus has an incentive to increase his leverage as much as possible—as long as that does not jeopardize his ability to pay back both principal and interest. This incentive is encouraged by a steep yield curve that features very low interest rates on short-term credit and much higher ones on longer-term and riskier investments, as occurred in the United States from 2002 through 2004. But greater leverage also increases his problems if something goes wrong and he produces lower profits than expected or takes longer to produce planned profits. Thus, increasing leverage increases risks too.

The temptation to increase leverage becomes larger when the interest rate on borrowing is relatively low. Then the operator has to pay less interest and his risk of having his equity wiped out declines. Thus, whenever interest rates become unusually low and seem likely to remain low for a long time, borrowers become more strongly motivated to increase leverage. That is precisely what happened after 2000. And it is just what economist Hyman Minsky predicted would happen in any period of extended prosperity, as discussed in the next section. So the tendency for borrowers to shift into more leveraged financing in periods of steady prosperity and flat or falling interest rates is a direct result of the basic self-interest inherent in human nature.

In the real world, greed is an exaggerated form of self-interest. Greedy people overweight their own welfare relative to the welfare of others to an unusually great degree. Hence they become willing to harm others to increase their own benefits. In subprime housing deals, greed motivated all five key parties to these transactions—borrowers, banks, mortgage brokers, rating agencies, and mortgage-backed security buyers—to undertake risky behavior for which their actual rates of return were not adequate compensation. All of these key actors adopted perverse incentives that led them into excessively risky actions.

Minsky's Theory: Long Periods of Prosperity Motivate Investors to Become Overoptimistic and Use Too Much Leverage

Hyman P. Minsky was a critic of the "standard" theory of capitalism largely adopted by econo-mists after World War II. A professor of economics at Washington University in St. Louis, he was educated at the University of Chicago and in 1954 received a Ph.D. in economics from Harvard University. He critiqued standard economic theory, which asserted that a capitalistic economy tended automatically to seek an overall equilibrium in which supply and demand remained relatively balanced. Standard theory, he asserted, therefore claimed that the past ten-dency of the U.S. economy to experience periodic bursts of prosperity followed by recessions—a pattern especially dominant in the 19th century—was caused mainly by poor private economic decisions and bad government policies. The standard theory also claimed that financial markets themselves did not play a critical role in economic cycles, since money was only a "neutral veil" in the economy, not a primary driver of change. In contrast, Minsky believed that money and financial markets were critical factors that caused an inherent instability in capitalism.[2] That is partly because money is not just a "veil" disguising real objects but a vital lubricant that is more and more necessary as our economy becomes larger and more complex.

According to Minsky's theory, most private firms need to borrow money to carry out their normal activities, especially firms that produce investment goods (those used to produce other goods) rather than consumption goods. Minsky identified three types of borrowing done by private firms: hedged, speculative, and Ponzi. All three types use borrowed money to sup-port productive processes. Hedged firms create sufficient after-tax profits in every quarter to repay the debt services on their borrowed funds that were due that quarter. Firms that use speculative borrowing need borrowed funds too but do not produce enough after-tax profits to pay the resulting debt services in every quarter. So they often have to borrow more along the way. Firms with Ponzi borrowing never produce enough profits to pay their current debt services. Hence they have to continuously increase borrowing until the end of their productive process, when they have to sell assets at higher prices than prevailed at the outset, using the resulting profits to pay off their remaining debts.

At the beginning of every period of strong overall economic growth, most firms typically use hedged financing. But as the relatively tranquil period of growth continues, the tolerance of both productive borrowing firms and lenders toward increased use of borrowing tends to rise. This occurs because greater leverage with debt allows borrowers to get higher yields on equity and lenders to make greater profits by lending more. So both borrowers and lenders are motivated to accept higher degrees of leveraging. Such added borrowing causes more hedged firms to become speculative firms, and more speculative firms to become Ponzi firms.

Eventually, some type of unexpected short-term economic downswing occurs, and many lenders realized that their underwriting has become less stringent. So they raise interest rates sharply. This causes repayment crises among all Ponzi firms and many speculative firms. Their lenders press them for repayment, and those firms—strapped for liquidity—become distressed. Many such firms are driven into default. As a result, a downward movement takes place in financial markets as many borrowers scramble to raise money to pay off their debts, which exceed their profits. Left unchecked, this situation would lead to a sharp overall contraction in credit markets and then in economic activity generally as all those hard-pressed firms cut back their activities.

Minsky asserted that there was only one way to prevent a downward crisis under such circumstances. It was for the federal government to step in and push interest rates down and extend federal credit to banks that were unable to collect on their loans. This is normally done by the Federal Reserve Board, but such credit extensions generate a larger federal government deficit. If the deficit were large enough, a downward crash would be prevented. Then the whole cyclical process would begin again. Minsky argued that the severe downward crash in the Great Depression of the 1930s occurred because the federal government was then such a small part of the overall economy that it could not rapidly flood financial markets with enough money to prevent a major financial recession.

Evidence supporting the critical role of federal intervention under such circumstances is provided by World War II. The federal government's massive deficit spending generated by wartime preparation ended the long financial crises of the 1930s. That deficit spending and the absorption of millions of men into the military led to a long period of domestic prosperity with low unemployment. After World War II, several other financial crises began. But by then the federal government was large enough so it was always able to intervene with spending increases sufficient to prevent another massive depression or severe economic contraction.

Yet the cost of such repeated federal interventions was a long-run tendency toward rising inflation. Such inflation was caused by a combination of low interest rates and greater general liquidity, both stimulated by the Fed's responses to credit contractions. In the 1970s, the combined effects of these developments plus federal spending in Vietnam led to almost runaway inflation. Soaring prices were halted only after Paul Volcker at the Federal Reserve Board raised interest rates to record levels in the early 1980s. However, that threw the nation into a serious recession, though not nearly as bad as the Great Depression.

More recent empirical evidence supporting Minsky's theories has been provided by two researchers at the New York Federal Reserve Bank. In early 2008, Tobias Adrian and Hyun Song Shin published an article entitled "Liquidity, Monetary Policy, and Financial Cycles" in *Current Issues in Economics and Finance*.[3] They presented evidence that both commercial banks and investment banks tend to increase their financial leverage (defined as assets divided by equity) during economic booms and reduce that leverage during downturns. They raise leverage mainly by borrowing more in short-term collateralized security markets—mainly repurchase and reverse repurchase agreements—and decrease leverage by reducing their use of such agreements, which are liabilities on their books. In other words, banks and investment banks increase their liquidity in booms and reduce it during downturns. They do so by enlarging their balance sheets in booms and reducing their balance sheets in downturns. In booms, when asset prices tend to rise, these institutions increase their holdings of assets (loans they make) but they increase their liabilities (funds they borrow) even more, thereby increasing their leverage. The authors contend that this shows that bank behavior is pro-cyclical. That behavior tends to aggravate cyclical tendencies because banks buy more assets (that is, make more loans) when asset prices are rising but sell assets when asset prices are falling, or at least pay off more liabilities then.

Minsky argued that periodic instability was an endogenous trait of capitalism. It is caused by the inherent behavior of the financial system during periods of prosperity. Such instability does not result as much from flawed government policies as from the behavior of private borrowers and lenders in the financial system during booms. In essence, Minsky thought the excessive risk-taking and lack of prudence in response to long periods of prosperity was another trait of human nature, at least in modern developed societies. So this behavior pattern is just as inherent as self-interest itself and perhaps is a form of self-interest. Therefore, even regulators could not get rid of this tendency. The built-in tendency of lenders and borrowers to shift toward greater financial leveraging makes the economy susceptible to contractionary credit crises whenever some unexpected incident or international development causes a sudden rise in interest rates. Minsky believed that the only effective remedy for such situations was federal aid in the form of lower interest rates and more liquidity. But that remedy requires large-scale federal spending that eventually leads to strong inflationary pressures. Those pressures can be stopped only by deliberately causing a different type of financial crisis. This remedy for inflation consists of the strong contractionary actions by the Federal Reserve that generated recessions, as from 1980 to 1982.

I believe Minsky's analysis roughly fits American economic events since 2000. The immense flood of money into the economy after the stock market crash of 2000 generated low interest rates and easy availability of debt capital. After the stock market stopped falling in 2002, those two conditions led to great prosperity and increasing optimism in those sectors that could use such funds effectively—especially the real estate sector. This in turn led to very high degrees of debt leveraging throughout the real estate and financial sectors. For example, in housing markets after 2000, lenders steadily reduced the downpayments required of homebuyers, thereby increasing homebuyers' use of leverage. Many subprime mortgage brokers encouraged buyers to cut downpayments from the traditional 20 percent to 10 percent, then 3 percent, then 1 percent. The ultimate form of higher buyer leverage was when community-based organizations gave downpayment grants to homebuyers and then collected the funds for those downpayments from sellers of the homes concerned. This reduced actual buyer downpayments to zero. The experience of the Federal Housing Administration with buyers whose downpayments were financed by sellers indicates they were three times as likely to be foreclosed as buyers who financed their own downpayments.[4] These conditions meshed with the financing innovations discussed below to generate increased uncertainty about how well new financial derivatives would work under pressure. The excesses of lending in subprime mortgage markets then led to rising defaults that eventually exposed the whole overleveraged state of the financial sector, far beyond subprime markets themselves.

Minsky's analysis was indirectly confirmed by a recent study by the International Monetary Fund (IMF) entitled "The Changing Housing Cycle and the Implications for Monetary Policy."[5] The IMF's detailed study of changes in housing finance in many nations since 1970 showed that the nations which developed flexible and advanced systems of mortgage lending— including the United States—thereby encouraged homeowners to use greater leverage in their general consumption. Homeowners in such nations typically got mortgages with high loan-to-value ratios; that is, a lot of leverage. Then they collateralized those homes through home equity loans they used for general consumption, further increasing their leverage. This process strengthened the linkages between what happened in housing markets—part of the financial sector—and what happened to overall economic prosperity. It all fits in neatly with Minsky's theories about how the financial sector works.

The Complexity of Financial Innovations and the Tight Linkages of Financial Instruments

Financial innovations and the tight linkages of financial instruments create a potential for sudden downward spirals of adjustments—spirals that cannot be halted easily, or at all. Innovation has revolutionized how American financial markets operate through the invention of many security instruments or procedures that make markets much more efficient—when they work well. For example, portfolio insurance is a complex device invented by stock traders in the 1980s. It offsets declines in the market values of stocks in a portfolio by selling futures on those stocks in specific ways. In normal markets, this innovation protects an investor from losses when many stocks in his or her portfolio fall in value. The process of such "insurance" can be automated, so computers are programmed to carry out the required transactions whenever certain declines occur in stock prices. But if the use of portfolio insurance becomes widespread among investors and certain stocks they all hold start falling in value at the same time, that can automatically set in motion a massive process of selling stock futures. Such a huge sell-off may drive the entire market rapidly downward. In fact, this happened dramatically on October 19, 1987—"Black Monday"—causing a one-day fall in the Dow Jones Industrial Average of more than 508 points, or 22.6 percent.

In his 2007 book, *A Demon of Their Own Design*, hedge fund operator Richard Bookstaber argues that Wall Street is inherently susceptible to such "crashes."[7] The cause is a combination of complex financial innovations, a fundamental lack of transparency in many innovations, and a tight interlocking of financial instruments and computers in day-to-day trading. Any event unforeseen by the financial innovators may suddenly start an interlocked series of behavioral responses by computerized trading that causes a downward spiral of stock values. The result is a form of systemic risk inherent in the entire financial sector. Once such a downward wave begins, it may be difficult or impossible to stop if the trading procedures involved are both very widespread and built into automated computerized trading programs.

Bookstaber does not believe it is possible to eliminate either tight linkages or the great complexity of how financial instruments can interact, as long as unrestrained financial innovation is permitted. Most of the time, such innovation increases the effectiveness of the financial system—until a disaster occurs. Therefore, there is always a danger that some unexpected or random set of events might start a downward spiral that will precipitate a huge sell-off.

Moreover, as Minsky pointed out, the more successful a strategy or an innovation is, the more likely its users are to increase their use of leverage as time goes on. Greater leverage increases their ability to make profits. But more leverage also increases the chance that they will set off a downward spiral of prices when some unforeseen event requires them to raise capital to meet repayment demands. They then sell off some stocks to gain liquidity, but that selling drives down the prices on their remaining portfolio more than it raises cash.

Bookstaber believes the resulting tendency toward instability is inherent in modern financial innovations because of their complexity. No one can fully understand all the conceivable ways in which unforeseen events might set off such downward spirals. Yet he also believes that trying to make such outcomes impossible through regulation will not work. Such regulations would only increase the complexity of financial markets, thereby multiplying the possible and as yet unknown ways in which innovations may interact negatively. Moreover, financial innovations like interest rate swaps and futures contracts have greatly increased the effectiveness of financial markets—when they do not set off unforeseeable disasters. Therefore, he claims, regulations that inhibit financial innovations would make financial markets less efficient and less effective most of the time.

In his book *Traders, Guns & Money*, stock trader Satyajit Das describes many ingenious financial derivatives designed to get around stock trading regulations or save investors from paying legally required taxes. But many are so complex that it is not clear how they will behave under unusual market conditions. Yet the financial magnitudes involved can become enormous. In 2008, the total nominal value of outstanding CDSs exceeded $62 trillion. That was three times larger than the total value of all stocks on all American exchanges (about $21 trillion), 4.4 times larger than the U.S. annual GDP (about $14 trillion), and 1.67 times larger than the total amount of bonds outstanding in the world in 2003 ($37 trillion, according to McGraw Hill). Yet owners of those unregulated CDSs need not own or have any other legal connection to the underlying assets, payment on which the CDSs are designed to insure. Moreover, financial firms that were regulated—such as commercial banks—were permitted to enter this wide-open field and do whatever they wanted in it.

The Importance and Unpredictability of Random Events

Stock trader Nassim Nicholas Taleb argues in two recent books that many gains from trading in financial markets are due primarily to randomness, not to the skill of the traders involved. Pure chance will always allow some traders to do well over several consecutive years, just as many others will fall out of the game in those same years. However, those who do well—even if mainly from pure chance—will usually attribute their success to their personal skills or their methods of analysis, not to luck. Hence they will become more and more confident in their abilities.

Taleb illustrates the role of random chance with the following story:

Let us use a Monte Carlo generator [of random numbers] . . . and construct a population of 10,000 fictional investment managers. Assume that they each have a perfectly fair game; each one has a 50 percent probability of making $10,000 at the end of a year, and a 50 percent probability of losing $10,000. Let us introduce an additional restriction; once a manager has a single bad year, he is thrown out of the sample, good-bye and have a nice life. The Monte Carlo generator will toss a coin [for each remaining manager]; heads and the manager will make $10,000 over the year; tails and he will lose $10,000. We run it for the first year. At the end of the year, we expect 5,000 managers *to be up $10,000 each, and 5,000 to be down $10,000. Now we run the game a second year [with the remaining 5,000 winners from the first year]. Again, we can expect 2,500 managers to be up two years in a row; another year, 1,250; a fourth one, 625; a fifth, 313. We have now, simply in a fair game, 313 managers who made money for five years in a row. Out of pure luck.*

Meanwhile, if we throw one of these successful traders into the real world, we will get very interesting and helpful comments on his remarkable style, his incisive mind, and the influences that helped him achieve such success. Some analysts may attribute his achievement to precise elements among his childhood experiences. His biographer would dwell on the wonderful role models provided by his parents.[8]

In short, there is a widespread human desire to attribute success in markets where randomness plays a major role to the supposed skills of those who survive as winners over time, without recognizing the possible role played in their success by pure chance. Therefore

A population composed entirely of bad managers will produce a small amount of great track records [through pure chance]. As a matter of fact, assuming the [successful] manager shows up at your door, it will be practically impossible to figure out whether he is good or bad.[9]

As Minsky claimed, a high confidence of success, often generated purely by chance, always tends to make the successful operators start to use more leverage to increase their profits. As their success continues in a rising market, they become more and more exposed to adverse random events that they do not take into account. In fact, no one can successfully take into account all the random—and thus unpredictable—events that might affect financial markets in this dynamic and complicated modern world. That should be evident from human experience in the first eight years of the 21st century. The world has experienced rising terrorism around the globe, earthquakes and tidal waves that killed hundreds of thousands, the collapse of governments in many now stateless areas, and rebellious wars on many continents. Sooner or later, a random event of great adversity to many market participants is sure to appear, what Taleb calls a "black swan." (Taleb uses the term "black swan" because for centuries, bird experts in Europe said all swans were white, since they had never seen a black one. But in the 19th century, bird fanciers in Australia found a whole species of black swans. This discovery proved the former belief about the invariant color of swans to be false. It thus illustrated the potential error of assuming that repeated experiences of success in financial markets proves that no radically different and adverse experiences will ever occur.) Examples of unexpected events are the Russian default on international debts in 1998 and the terrorist attack on the United States in September 2001. Such unpredictable events cause big losses among many investors, who must liquidate their positions in order to pay off debts or regain capital. Because the other players in the market take their selling off as a signal, many also sell off the same types of assets or otherwise react in ways that aggravate the initial downward movement. Thus the interactive nature of the market tends to magnify any adverse trend that starts off small.

Taleb's recommended strategy for avoiding this outcome is always to make trades on the assumption that some large but unknown adversity may occur; therefore, one must be prepared to counteract it from the start. This means keeping a lot of assets in forms that are secure from random adversity (such as Treasury securities or money market funds) and making many bets with small positive payoffs, and perhaps a few small bets with large payoffs, in order to avoid one bet with a huge negative impact.

However, that strategy is not consistent with the inherent human tendencies to overestimate one's own abilities and to underestimate the likelihood of random but unexpected adverse events. Hence there is a tendency among successful investors to avoid the careful strategy they recommend whenever they have experienced relatively long periods of continuous success—even if their success has been caused mainly by chance. Such behavior closely conforms to what Minsky predicted. This means that long periods of prosperity for the entire market—such as in U.S. stock markets in most of the 1990s—increase the probability of financial excess and eventually financial crisis, especially if many parts of the market have become overleveraged.

Thus the tendency for financial markets to be unstable is built into the human natures of their trading participants plus the random—and therefore unpredictable—nature of significant adverse events. That instability cannot be fully avoided by planning or by any advanced trading techniques.

Does Market Participant Behavior Make Predicting Downward Movements Impossible?

George Soros, a highly successful trader and operator of hedge funds, recently wrote a book entitled *The New Paradigm for Financial Markets: The Credit Crisis of 2008 and What It Means*.[10] Soros argues that classical economics assumes that financial markets tend to operate in predictable behavior patterns. One reason is that economists assume all the key actors in such markets have perfect information about both what has happened in the past and what is happening now. Therefore, markets should not undergo periodic crises like the one we are in today. But in reality, markets do undergo such crises quite often.

Soros believes that financial crises arise from two flaws in classical economic theory. First, none of the participants in a market has perfect information about either the past or the present. All are subject to significant ignorance about past and current conditions, which naturally makes it much harder—in fact, impossible—for them to forecast future outcomes and therefore avoid actions that cause crises. Second, most market participants are trying to beat the game. They deliberately adopt behaviors that they think will provide much greater benefits to them personally than to all other market participants. Thus self-interested individualism can adversely affect future events that might be rather predictable if all market participants just followed the rules in investing. Each participant tries to anticipate what the others are doing or will do, and responds by adopting behaviors designed to take advantage of their likely actions. This tendency of many participants to outdo each other by highly individualistic actions makes it impossible to forecast how markets will behave. Soros calls this tendency "reflexivity" because it involves behavior patterns that turn back against normal trends to benefit individual actors.

Such unbridled individualism leads to a lack of broad leadership within the financial sector. True leadership requires well-known participants to raise warning signs when they see danger in their industry and seek ways to reduces dangerous industry activity. When all the sector's most successful leaders are focused solely on their own prosperity, none are analyzing what is happening overall and alerting the rest of the sector to possible calamities. Neither Wall Street nor the banking community showed much sense of social responsibility during the real estate lending and price run-up from 2000 to 2006. Few financial leaders were decrying what was happening or proposing ways to stop it before it inflicted severe pain upon the nation.

There is much truth in Soros' observations about reflexivity, but I think he overestimates the unpredictability of reflexive behavior upon market outcomes. Many types of behavior adopted by market participants to beat the game are themselves quite predictable from the basic nature of human beings. It is not hard to forecast that the lending community, freed from almost all regulations and given access to cheap capital, will indulge in behavior that will result in exploitation of others. That is certainly what many brokers did in subprime mortgage markets. Innovators who are allowed to invent almost any type of financial instrument will surely come up with some that are too complex for many to understand. Such instruments can easily interact with other instruments to cause downward credit spirals. That happened in the crash on Black Monday. Also, investors who are enjoying long-term success in markets will confidently engage in ever more leveraging, as Minsky predicted. Many people who achieve market success are actually heavily influenced by purely random events. Yet they will almost always assume that they have unusual personal talents and abilities, and therefore should keep repeating their seemingly successful behavior.

Thus, the existence of reflexivity—which I believe Soros has correctly identified—does not eliminate the ability of at least a few experienced and well-informed market observers to make accurate forecasts, including predicting credit crises. However, the absence of perfect information is the greater obstacle to accurate forecasting—one that cannot be fully overcome, even by high technology.

The Long-Term Cycle in American Politics

American historian Arthur Schlesinger, Sr., contended that American politics were influenced by long-term cycles between relatively liberal and relatively conservative groups within the nation. When the liberals won the presidency and dominated the government for most of several presidential terms in a row, they tended to emphasize the importance of government action and regulation as opposed to the unchecked operation of free markets. This has especially been the case since World War II, during which the size and power of the federal government expanded vastly. But after several decades in which government policies played critical roles in influencing economic activities, those policies tend to be marred by rising corruption, excessive influence by politically powerful groups, and decreasing economic efficiency in the private sector. Those adverse results cause the electorate to tire of liberal dominance and to elect conservatives. The newly elected conservatives typically reduce the power and influence of government and emphasize the relatively free operation of market forces with fewer government regulations. But as more conservative policies are applied over time, they generate greater economic inequality, including continued widespread poverty, and often end in economic recessions with significant economic suffering. So the electorate eventually tires of that approach too. It then shifts its support back to more liberal policies, emphasizing a greater role of government in the operation of the economy.

Schlesinger opined that such a cyclical tendency in politics is not precisely regular but tends to generate a switch from one approach to the other roughly every 15 years. The specific timing of each basic switch was heavily influenced by other factors like external wars, industrialization, immigration, and many others.

Thus, in the 20th century Franklin Roosevelt's New Deal, which greatly increased the role of the federal government in economic affairs, and World War II, which increased it even more, dominated federal actions toward the economy from 1932 through 1952. Then the more conservative Dwight Eisenhower was elected president. In 1960, centrist John F. Kennedy was elected. Then Lyndon Johnson defeated conservative Barry Goldwater by a landslide and pushed the nation to adopt civil rights reform and strong antipoverty policies as well as to continue fighting in Vietnam. Although Richard Nixon was elected as a conservative in 1968, he continued policies that emphasized a strong federal role in the economy by abandoning the gold standard and supporting serious antipoverty policies. This emphasis was continued by Jimmy Carter.

But the election of Ronald Reagan in 1980 signaled a shift back toward more conservative policies. Reagan reduced the role of government in the operation of the American economy and put greater emphasis on relatively free-market capitalism. However, he failed to cut government spending much and therefore generated rising federal deficits. George H.W. Bush continued this emphasis after being elected in 1988, and so did William Clinton. Clinton balanced the federal budget (partly because of high federal revenues generated by the high-tech stock bubble) and pushed through the North American Free Trade Agreement against the desires of his labor union supporters. George W. Bush further emphasized free markets in the American economy by cutting taxes and even more fully deregulating markets of all types—including financial markets. But he also started the Iraq war, vastly expanded the federal deficit, and encouraged greater economic inequality—actions that were highly unpopular.

The credit crunch and financial crisis that appeared in the last two years of George W. Bush's presidency launched the nation into a recession in 2008. Consequently, the American electorate was ready to change directions, toward federal policies that more closely regulated the financial markets that had clearly generated both the recession and striking economic inequalities. As Charles Morris pointed out in his insightful book, *The Trillion Dollar Meltdown*, this long-run cyclical reversal was sure to influence what policies the newly elected president and Congress would adopt toward the American economy and federal regulations concerning its operation.[11] A long period of almost fully deregulated freedom of action in financial markets was certain to be changed by greater federal "interference" with the market forces that had so recklessly plunged the nation into a major financial crisis.

If Schlesinger's long-term cyclical analysis is correct, as I believe it is, then financial markets are subject to periodic shifts in their basic degree of government regulation. When relatively conservative governments are holding sway, financial markets will be relatively free from intensive government regulation and allowed to innovate as they desire. When relatively liberal governments are in power, financial markets will be more intensively regulated and their powers checked by government regulation and oversight. Shifts from one of these regimens to the other tend to occur roughly every 15 to 17 years in American politics, usually related to the type of financial crisis the economy experiences. However, the tenure of one view may sometimes be considerably longer. Such policy shifts create a certain amount of instability in how American financial markets operate.

A long-range consequence of this cyclical nature of market regulation is that more and more government regulations concerning financial markets are built up over time, though some are periodically dismantled in conservative cycles. As the number of surviving regulations increases, they become less and less effective at preventing the next partly new and different financial crisis. That is partly because regulators are overwhelmingly reactive rather than proactive; that is, they adopt regulations that are designed to prevent the last crisis rather than to anticipate the next one, which is extremely difficult, if not impossible, to foresee. Thus, the desire to do something in response to the credit crunch of 2007 and 2008 will improve some aspects of financial markets, but it will probably not prevent some new form of crisis from appearing in the not-too-distant future.

Linking the Financial Crisis to Globalization

British economist Graham Turner has advanced another source of instability in financial markets by claiming that the current financial crisis is closely linked to the globalization of world trade. In his recent book, *The Credit Crunch*, Turner argues that the underlying cause of the credit crunch was the desire of large multinational corporations to increase their profits by outsourcing their production to developing Asian and Eastern European nations that have very low wage rates.[12] This shift of jobs overseas—especially in manufacturing—caused wage rates in wealthier developed nations to stagnate because of competition from much poorer workers abroad. Although wage stagnation has occurred to some extent in many developed nations, most American economists believe its main cause is technological improvements in production processes, not competition from low-wage foreign workers. However, low-wage foreign competition surely has had a strong impact both on world wage rates and on holding down the rate of inflation throughout the world, as I pointed out in *Niagara of Capital* and Greenspan stated in *The Age of Turbulence*. The entry of many millions of low-wage workers into competitive markets caused by the end of communistic control over production in Eastern Europe and China, and by the development of other Asian nations, has had a profound impact upon world trade everywhere.

Turner claims that the explosion of debt in America, the United Kingdom, and other developed nations was a direct result of central bank policy responses to wage stagnation caused by the outsourcing of manufacturing and other jobs overseas. When the dot-com bubble in stock markets burst in 2000, central banks were fearful that a deflationary recession might occur, partly because wages were being held so low by competition from developing nations. Greenspan publicly stated that he feared possible deflationary impacts from the stock market crash. According to Turner, central banks responded by deliberately slashing interest rates and flooding their economies with financial liquidity in order to encourage the maximum use of borrowing by consumers to underwrite an asset boom in housing. Making credit more easily available to consumers would offset the negative effect upon consumption of stagnant wages and keep economic growth from faltering. Turner provides no convincing evidence that central bankers cleverly schemed to stimulate a housing price bubble. But he is certainly correct that a major effect of their action—plus a flood of capital into developed nations from developing ones—was a sharp rise in both housing prices and debt throughout the developed world, except in Germany and Japan.

Turner further argues that the flood of capital from developing nations into the housing markets in developed nations was also at least partly a result of the outsourcing of jobs from the latter into the former. Multinational corporations and investors in developed nations poured capital into China and other low-wage nations both to build manufacturing facilities and to pay for the imports to the United States that they produced there. That caused large trade surpluses in developing nations that would have raised the value of currencies in developing nations to restore a greater balance of trade. But many developing nations—especially China—did not allow their currencies to rise in value for two reasons. They wanted to keep expanding their exports so as to provide what were, for their populations, well-paying jobs as thousands of poor rural residents poured into their cities. And they wanted to build up currency reserves to avoid having an economic crisis if currency speculators suddenly shifted focus elsewhere, as happened in Asia in 1987.

So these nations offset pressure on their currencies to rise by using local currency to buy dollars and keep the demand for dollars high. But then they had a lot of excess dollars to spend, which they sent to the United States to invest in financial assets there—including many mortgage-backed securities being issued by American lenders. Thus, the flood of capital from abroad into developed nations was at least indirectly caused by the outsourcing of jobs by multinational firms located in developed nations. But that flood was also caused by very low savings rates in America and the United Kingdom. That contributed to the large trade deficits both nations ran as they imported more and more low-cost goods produced in developing nations.

Turner's argument that the source of foreign funds flooding financial markets in America and other developed nations was the outsourcing by American firms of jobs ignores the fact that savings rates in many developing nations have long been very high. One reason is that governments in those nations do not provide safety nets for their populations, such as Medicare, Medicaid, and Social Security. Hence households have to accumulate large savings to cope with health care and retirement costs. Moreover, as Turner admits, oil-exporting nations have accumulated large savings surpluses because of the skyrocketing price of petroleum in the past few years, and they contributed heavily to capital inflows into developed nations. So outsourcing of jobs may have led to more capital flows into developed nations, but it was certainly not the only source of those flows that constituted the Niagara of capital.

I believe Turner's argument that the credit crunch was caused primarily by multinational firms outsourcing jobs to developing nations is greatly exaggerated. However, such outsourcing was at least a partial cause of the large flow of capital into developed nations that stimulated rising housing prices. Moreover, that massive inflow of capital seeking real estate generated the intense competition among investors that led them to abandon prudent underwriting in their lending and buying practices. But the outsourcing of jobs by multinational firms did not cause the abandonment of good sense by investors, the greed that led mortgage brokers and lenders to make subprime loans to people who could never repay them, the excessive pursuit of profits that led homebuilders to build too many new houses, and the additional greed that caused securitizers to sell bonds based on poor-quality mortgages both at home and abroad. Rather, all those actions were caused by bad behavioral choices made by Americans swept away by the greedy motives described in earlier chapters.

In short, there is some linkage between the outsourcing of jobs inherent in the globalization of world trade and the current credit crunch. That linkage does partly explain why so much capital flowed into developed nations after the stock market crash of 2000. And that linkage may still operate when the credit crunch is over, at least until rising wages in developing nations eventually improve the living standards of all the remaining poor residents of those nations. As Greenspan points out in *The Age of Turbulence*, the deflationary pressure on the world's economies caused by low foreign wages is going to last for at least several more decades before the vast majority of poor rural residents in developing nations also enter into competitive world markets at better wages. Hence there may be future occasions during which large amounts of foreign capital flood into the U.S. financial sector. However, that seems highly unlikely for a considerable time until investors regain confidence in the desirability of investing in that sector.

But the credit crunch itself was caused primarily by the adverse behavior patterns that American financial markets and their participants adopted in response to large capital inflows, not solely by the capital inflows themselves. As long as the financial sector continues to exhibit such adverse incentives and behaviors, that sector will remain basically unstable and susceptible to future financial crises. Therefore, it is up to the financial sector and the regulators who watch over it to prevent those behaviors from happening again, even if there are future floods of capital into that sector.

Restricting the Behavior of Financial Firms through Reserve Requirements

Back in the 1950s, when demand for housing was strong—in response to 15 years of low levels of building, owing to the Great Depression and World War II—methods of financing new housing were much different from those used in the 2000s. Homebuyers borrowed money from banks and savings and loan associations in their local communities. Those financial institutions in turn got their funds from deposits that were made mainly by local residents and businesses. The mortgages made by those depository institutions were held by them until maturity or until the home involved was sold. All such institutions were required by law to hold a certain amount of capital in reserve against the total amount of loans they had made. In addition, commercial banks could not sell financial securities, as many had done in the Great Depression of the 1930s.

These arrangements placed definite limits on the abilities of lending institutions to originate mortgage loans. They could not lend more than the deposits they garnered from local residents and firms. Once they had made a loan, they had to hold capital in reserve against it. Even though they in essence created money when they made a new loan, they could not lend the same money over and over because each loan had to have its own capital reserve. The interest rates they could pay on deposits were limited by federal rules (Regulation Q). They could make new mortgages only on properties within 25 miles of their main offices. That was a locally focused system of finance.

In that system, four basic anchors prevented excessive lending and building:

- Lending institutions could not generate more loanable funds by raising deposits from far-off locations, especially since they were limited by what rates of interest they could pay.
- They had to set reserves aside for every loan they made.
- They could not sell their loans to get more capital to lend.
- They could not originate or sell financial securities.

These rules prevented the kind of explosion of mortgage lending that occurred after 2000. Yet the same rules made it difficult for borrowers to get loans in localities where savings were low, even if those borrowers had great ideas with great economic prospects. This cut down on the national efficiency of the banking system.

All these conditions had radically changed by 2000. Banks were able to raise money from anywhere by mail or over the Internet by advertising for it and bidding high interest rates on the funds they got. They were permitted to set up holding companies that could own subsidiaries which were not deposit takers and could make loans without holding reserves against them. They could pay any interest they desired to attract deposits, and they could take deposits from anywhere. They were allowed to put into a pool a bunch of loans they had made or purchased, issue securities against that pool, and sell those securities to investors anywhere. This allowed them to get those loans off their books, free up the reserves against them that they had been holding, and use the proceeds to make a whole new set of loans. They could also lend money to their own subsidiaries, which lent the money without holding reserves against the loans involved and then gave the loans back to the banks to use in securitization.

In short, all the restraints that prevented runaway lending in the 1950s had been abolished. This had occurred gradually in response to changing conditions and events that made each restraint seem unreasonable and unworkable. For example, in the 1960s and 1970s, California was growing much faster than other states and therefore needed to build much more housing than could be financed by savings from local residents. So California thrifts developed "loan participation" arrangements that, in essence, sold half of a mortgage to other thrifts in Iowa where residents were saving and depositing more than local housing markets could absorb. That increased efficiency at both ends of such transactions, so it seemed like a good idea to end the 25-mile limitation.

Could the United States bring back all the restraints on excessive lending that existed in the 1950s, in order to prevent future financial instabilities? Not really. Why not? Because the whole nature of finance has become more globalized today than it was then. Banks now operate all over the nation and the world, not just within 25 miles of home. This has enormously beneficial impacts on the availability of finance. Capital can be raised from anywhere and invested anywhere. That freedom allows capitalists to pursue the most attractive investment possibilities they can find. Furthermore, it permits reallocation of excess savings from one region to others that have excess demands for funds. It also causes investors to be interested in possible uses of funds that are so distant they cannot by themselves analyze the soundness of those opportunities. Instead, they must have some other means of determining soundness, such as trusted credit rating agencies or legal requirements that force the creators of such opportunities to have a lot of their own capital involved. Thus, any attempt to completely recapture the sound conditions of the 1950s would enormously limit the flexibility and efficiency of the capital investment systems of today. That would impose a huge cost on financial systems and citizen borrowers and savers everywhere.

However, one principle can be retained from those older days and put to use under modern conditions. In fact, it is a form of self-interest. If the persons offering an investment opportunity are compelled to have a sizable amount of their own resources at stake in that opportunity, their own self-interest will motivate them to ensure that it is a sound opportunity. Of course, that is the idea behind capital reserves in banking. But the share of the total resources in any opportunity that the originator is required to provide must be large enough to give that originator a very strong incentive to make that opportunity work well. That means reserve requirements must be much larger than the 3 percent share some investment banks were recently putting behind opportunities they were offering other investors, which amounted to a 33 to 1 ratio (or greater) on their own behalf. A minimum self-supplied reserve or coinvestment of something like 10 to 20 percent should be required of all purveyors of investment opportunities to ensure that those people are truly interested in making their deals successful.

Could a financial system based upon such universal minimum reserve requirements in all parts of the system overcome the instability described in chapter 5? I believe that such an approach is the best possible way to put more stability back into the system. However, I am by no means sure that it would fully eliminate the kinds of crises we have seen in American finance during the past 20 years. Rather than claiming that such instabilities would disappear, I prefer to say that this would be the best way to minimize both the frequency and the severity of their occurrences. But with human nature in all its complex forms being what it is, in a world filled with uncertainties and unpredictable events, I think some elements of instability would at least occasionally break into even a well-reserved financial system.

Conclusion

In my opinion, trading in American financial markets is motivated by the inherent self-interest of human nature, involves the trading behavior and random events described by Taleb, occurs in the same complex and tightly linked conditions analyzed by Bookstaber, almost always leads to the process of increasing financial leveraging and deterioration as claimed by Minsky, occurs in a financial regulatory environment heavily influenced by the political cycles posited by Schlesinger, and is partially linked to the whole process of globalization, as contended by Turner. As a result, American financial markets are bound to run into periodic, massive deleveraging or debt-liquidating periods because of the confluence of random and unpredictable events. That is why financial markets in modern capitalist societies are inherently unstable and likely to generate periodic periods of debt crises. How to offset these deficiencies is discussed in chapter 7.

NOTES

1. Satyajit Das, *Traders, Guns & Money: Knowns and Unknowns in the Dazzling World of Derivatives* (Harlow, U.K.: Prentice Hall, 2006), pages 165–66. I have reworded some of the details from his original listings and omitted two. Incidentally, this book does not contain one word about guns, despite its title.

2. For an explanation of Minsky's views, see Hyman P. Minsky, *Can "It" Happen Again? Essays on Instability and Finance* (Armonk, New York: M.E. Sharpe, 1982).

3. Tobias Adrian and Hyun Song Shin, "Liquidity, Monetary Policy, and Financial Cycles," *Current Issues in Economics and Finance* (Volume 14, Number 1—January/February 2008).

4. Dina ElBoghdady, "Congress Is Set to Limit Downpayment Assistance," *Washington Post*, July 22, 2008, page D-1.

5. *World Economic Outlook: Housing and the Business Cycle*, International Monetary Fund, April 2008, Chapter 3.

6. Adam Smith, *An Inquiry into the Nature and Causes of the Wealth of Nations* (New York: The Modern Library, 1937), page 14.

7. Richard Bookstaber, *A Demon of Our Own Design* (New York: John Wiley & Sons Inc., 2007).

8. Nassim Nicholas Taleb, *Fooled by Randomness—The Hidden Role of Chance in Life and In the Markets* (New York: Random House, 2005), pages 152–53.

9. Taleb, page 154.

10. George Soros, *The New Paradigm for Financial Markets: The Credit Crisis of 2008 and What It Means* (New York: Public Affairs, 2008).

11. Charles Morris, *The Trillion Dollar Meltdown* (New York: Public Affairs, 2008).

12. Graham Turner, *The Credit Crunch: Housing Bubbles, Globalisation, and the Worldwide Economic Crisis* (London: Pluto Press, 2008).

Chapter Six

Public Policy Responses to the Financial Crisis

WRITING ABOUT PUBLIC POLICY RESPONSES to the U.S. financial crisis is both difficult and complicated for several reasons. First, there are many levels of responders: the federal government, state governments, local governments, professional organizations, and international agencies. This chapter will focus mainly on policy responses already undertaken or recommended by the U.S. federal government but will occasionally discuss responses by other public bodies. The next chapter will set forth additional proposals concerning public policies that I believe ought to be undertaken in order to restructure the entire U.S. financial sector and other parts of our economy.

Second, the financial crisis was caused in part by public policies, or lack thereof, at several levels of government that existed in 2000 or occurred thereafter. Some were policies related to housing and lending that were in place before the financial crisis occurred, such as the deregulation of bank lending actions and the provision of large federal income tax benefits to homeowners, especially wealthy ones. Others included lack of oversight or regulation of subprime lending and securitized mortgage markets.

Consequently, it is necessary to examine possible public policies at all government levels. That is the best way to recommend policies that are most likely both to remedy current difficulties caused by the financial crisis and to prevent such difficulties from occurring in the future.

However, it is more fruitful to organize discussions of possible public policies in terms of specific problems emerging from the financial crisis, rather than by the levels of policies described above. This seems especially desirable because remedies to specific problems often involve policy responses at two or more levels of government. For example, consider one such problem: burgeoning foreclosures of recent home purchasers. These foreclosures are injuring millions of households and damaging hundreds of urban neighborhoods across the nation. This directly affects the financial situation of thousands of local governments, as well as the level of national prosperity. Another example is harmful behavior by banks, mortgage brokers, and others involved in mortgage lending. Such behavior is the single most important direct cause of the current financial crisis.

Therefore, many parts of this chapter and the next are organized around discussions of possible public policy responses to specific difficulties that have emerged from the financial crisis. Within each such discussion, I often present possible remedies that need action at two or more of the basic levels of government set forth above. If this seems overly complex, blame the nature of reality. However, before exploring specific recommendations for public policies, I discuss a weakening in the Federal Reserve Board's general ability to use public policies to influence financial markets—a weakening that preceded the financial crisis.[1]

The Role of the Federal Reserve in the Financial Crisis

For a long time, the Fed has strongly influenced the money supply in the United States in two ways. One is by affecting the interest rates used by banks and other financial institutions. The other is by supplying liquidity to the same organizations by making loans to them or even by printing money, if necessary. However, recent events connected with the massive inflow of a "Niagara of capital" into U.S. real estate markets after 2000 and the subsequent credit crunch starting in 2007 have weakened the Fed's ability to influence U.S. financial conditions.

Since the end of World War II, the Fed has adopted two major goals for monetary policy. One is to keep the overall rate of inflation low, preferably below 2.5 percent per year as measured by the Consumer Price Index. The other is to help stimulate the growth of the American economy, as measured by the unemployment rate and the annual percentage change in the nation's real GDP. (In contrast, the European Central Bank focuses almost entirely on the first goal of keeping inflation in check.) By pursuing these two goals, the Fed sometimes creates policy tensions within monetary policy. Hence the Fed is often required to exercise rather subjective judgments about how to weight each goal in determining the proper monetary policy.

The Fed's main weapon for influencing interest rates is the federal funds rate (hereafter called the FFR). It is the rate of interest that private banks and other depository institutions are required to use in lending money to each other at the Fed, mainly on an overnight basis. Such interbank lending is quite common in the everyday transactions that commercial banks carry out in order to meet short-term demands for different amounts of funds. Those demands often vary considerably, because each depository institution is required by law to keep a certain amount of cash reserves against its loans. So whenever such an institution increases or decreases its loan portfolio, it may have to acquire or rent capital to balance its reserve requirements. Since the FFR is used primarily for overnight lending, it is a very short-term interest rate. It can influence longer-term rates only indirectly, by raising or lowering the cost to banks of acquiring funds from other banks.

The FFR is set by the Federal Open Market Committee, mainly by buying or selling federal securities on the open market. The committee raises the FFR if it wants the interest rates used for lending by banks and other financial institutions to increase and lowers the FFR if it wants those interest rates to decrease. The Fed also controls the rate at which it will lend capital to individual banks, called the discount rate, which is generally somewhat higher than the FFR. The Fed follows the same general behavior concerning the discount rate when trying to influence longer-term interest rates.

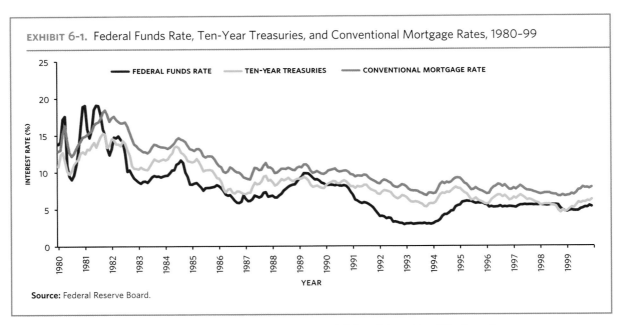

EXHIBIT 6-1. Federal Funds Rate, Ten-Year Treasuries, and Conventional Mortgage Rates, 1980–99

Source: Federal Reserve Board.

Why the Fed's Ability to Influence Financial Conditions Has Weakened

Ironically, the great credit freeze of 2007–09 began with a condition in financial markets that was the exact opposite of a credit shortage. It was the huge flow of money from both domestic and foreign sources into U.S. real estate and other financial markets, especially after the stock market crash of 2000. Much of this capital flood came from foreign sources that were not subject to direct regulation by the Fed. So the Fed actually had less power to influence U.S. interest rates during the initial years of this capital flood than it had traditionally enjoyed.

This deterioration in Fed effectiveness can be seen by comparing the movements of different interest rates in relation to movements of the FFR in two time periods: from 1980 to 1999 (before the stock market crash) and from 2000 to 2008 (after that crash), when so much foreign capital flooded into the United States. Exhibits 6-1, 6-2, and 6-3 compare monthly movements of the FFR with monthly movements of interest rates on ten-year Treasury bonds and conventional mortgages. The data underlying these illustrations is from the Federal Reserve Board's website. Movements of the FFR rate are shown on the graphs. They are almost always at lower levels than the other two types of interest rates—the ten-year treasury rate and the conventional mortgage rate.

I have conducted a simple statistical analysis of the monthly movements of these three interest rates in 14 time periods between 1980 and May 2008. The results are shown in exhibit 6-3. Two of those 14 periods were the overall periods covered by exhibits 6-1 and 6-2: from January 1980 to December 1999 and from January 2000 to May 2008. The other 12 periods were shorter ones, in each of which the Fed was using the FFR to influence other interest rates—either downward by moving the FFR downward or upward by moving the FFR upward.

I tested the effectiveness of the Fed's use of the FFR as a lever by measuring how much other interest rates moved during the periods when the Fed was either pushing the FFR

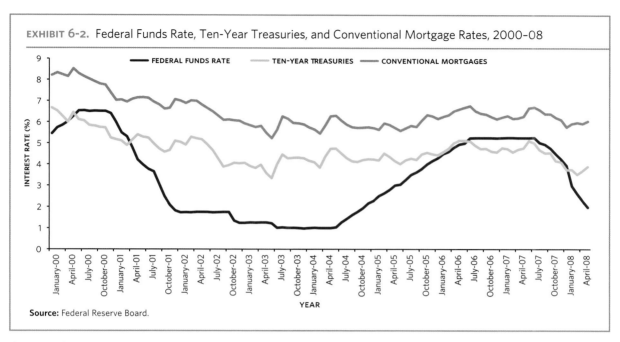

EXHIBIT 6-2. Federal Funds Rate, Ten-Year Treasuries, and Conventional Mortgage Rates, 2000–08

Source: Federal Reserve Board.

downward or raising it. The analysis deals with two other interest rates: the ten-year Treasury bond rate and a measure of conventional mortgage interest rates. I have focused on the impact of the FFR on the conventional mortgage rate, because it is an interest rate in the private sector and vital in housing markets. The upper part of exhibit 6-3 covers interest rate movements from 1980 through 1999, before the "Niagara of capital" really started flowing in full force. The lower part covers interest rate movements from 2000 through May 2008, after it was flowing at full blast—including the beginnings of the credit crunch in 2007 and 2008.[2]

In exhibit 6-2, there is a long period from July 2004 to July 2006 in which the FFR rose steadily because the Fed kept increasing it at each meeting of the Open Market Committee. The Fed was clearly trying to increase private interest rates in order to slow down the acceleration of housing markets. This period is the last one shown in exhibit 6-3. At the start of this period, the FFR was at 1.26 percent and the conventional mortgage rate was 6.06 percent. At the end of the period, the FFR was 5.24 percent and the conventional mortgage rate was 6.76 percent. Thus, the FFR had risen 315.9 percent and the conventional mortgage rate had risen only 11.6 percent. To put it another way, the FFR rose by 3.98 percentage points, while the conventional mortgage rate rose by 0.70 percentage points. This occurred over a period of 25 months. This shows that the Fed's ability to influence mortgage rates in this period was relatively weak. As a result, the statistical correlation—covering all 25 months—between the values of these two rates over that period was a low 0.07884.

These results are in strong contrast to the earlier period shown in exhibit 6-1, when the Fed was also trying to raise interest rates by increasing the FFR. This is the period from February 1983 to August 1984. At the outset of that period, the FFR was 8.51 percent and the conventional mortgage rate was 13.04 percent. At the end of this period, the FFR was 11.64 and the conventional

ANALYSIS OF SPECIFIC INFLUENCE OF FEDERAL FUNDS RATE ON OTHER INTEREST RATES, 1980–95

Period Description from 1980 through 1995	Fed's Directional Intention	Start of Period	Initial FFR	Initial 10-year Treasury Rate	Initial Convent. Mortgage Rate	End of Period	Ending FFR	Ending Treasury Rate
July 1981 to Feb. 1983	Lowering rates	Jul. 1981	19.04	14.28	16.83	Feb. 1983	8.51	10.72
Aug. 1984 to Feb. 1987	Lowering rates	Aug. 1984	11.64	12.72	14.35	Feb. 1987	6.1	7.25
Mar. 1989 to Dec. 1993	Lowering rates	Mar. 1989	9.85	9.36	11.03	Dec. 1993	2.96	5.77
—Lowering averages								
July 1980 to July 1981	Raising rates	Jul. 1980	9.03	10.25	12.19	Jul. 1981	19.04	14.28
Feb. 1983 to Aug. 1984	Raising rates	Feb. 1983	8.51	10.82	13.04	Aug. 1984	11.64	12.72
Feb. 1987 to Mar. 1989	Raising rates	Feb. 1987	6.1	7.25	9.08	Mar. 1989	9.85	9.36
Dec. 1993 to Apr. 1995	Raising rates	Dec. 1993	2.96	5.77	7.17	Apr. 1995	6.05	7.06
—Raising averages								

ANALYSIS OF SPECIFIC INFLUENCE OF FEDERAL FUNDS RATE ON OTHER INTEREST RATES, 2000–08

Period Description from 1980 through 1995	Fed's Directional Intention	Start of Period	Initial FFR	Initial 10-year Treasury Rate	Initial Convent. Mortgage Rate	End of Period	Ending FFR	Ending Treasury Rate
Jan 2000 through May 2008 (Entire period)	Lowering and raising rates	Jan. 2000	5.45	6.66	8.21	May 2008	1.98	3.98
Dec. 2000 to Jan. 2002	Lowering rates	Dec. 2000	6.4	5.24	7.38	Jan. 2002	1.73	5.04
Oct. 2002 to Jun 2004	Lowering rates	Oct. 2002	1.75	3.94	6.11	Jun. 2004	1.03	4.73
July 2007 to May 2008	Lowering rates	Jul. 2007	5.26	5	6.7	May 2008	1.98	3.88
—Lowering averages								
Jan. 2000 to July 2000	Raising rates	Jan. 2000	5.45	6.66	8.21	Jul. 2000	6.54	6.05
July 2004 to July 2006	Raising rates	Jul. 2004	1.26	4.5	6.06	Jul. 2006	5.24	5.09
—Raising averages								

mortgage rate was 14.47 percent. Thus, the FFR went up by 38.78 percent, but the conventional mortgage rate went up 10.87 percent over those 13 months. So the conventional mortgage rate went up three-tenths as much as the FFR—a lot more than in the later period. And the correlation of the monthly series of those two rates over those 13 months was a high 0.92928.

Four tentative conclusions can be drawn from this comparison and from the other cases analyzed in the exhibit:

■ The Fed's ability to move the conventional mortgage rate upward by raising the FFR is limited in all cases. The mortgage rate always moves up much less than the FFR in either percentage or absolute terms. This conclusion is borne out by the results in every other period charted.

■ The Fed's ability to influence the conventional mortgage rate upward was much weaker after 2000 than before then. The massive inflows of funds after 2000, including many funds from outside the United States, seem to have reduced the Fed's ability to influence mortgage rates.

Ending Convent. Mort. Rate	No. Months	PERCENT CHANGES EACH PERIOD			RATIOS TO FFR RATE OF CHANGE			Correlations between FFR and Mort. Rates
		FFR	Treasury Rate	Convent. Mort. Rate	FFR	Treasury Rate	Convent. Mort. Rate	
13.04	21	(55.30)	(24.93)	(22.52)	1	0.45	0.41	
9.04	31	(47.59)	(43.00)	(37.00)	1	0.90	0.78	(0.76)
7.17	57	(69.95)	(38.35)	(35.00)	1	0.55	0.50	0.88
		(57.62)	(35.43)	(31.51)	1	0.63	0.56	0.94
16.83	58	110.85	39.32	38.06	1	0.35	0.34	0.35
14.47	13	36.78	17.56	10.97	1	0.48	0.30	0.88
11.03	26	61.48	29.10	21.48	1	0.47	0.35	0.93
8.32	17	104.39	22.36	16.04	1	0.21	0.15	0.56
		78.38	27.08	21.64	1	0.38	0.29	0.78

Ending Convent. Mort. Rate	No. Months	PERCENT CHANGES EACH PERIOD			RATIOS TO FFR RATE OF CHANGE			Correlations between FFR and Mort. Rates
		FFR	Treasury Rate	Convent. Mort. Rate	FFR	Treasury Rate	Convent. Mort. Rate	
6.04	101	(63.67)	(40.24)	(26.43)	1	0.63	0.42	0.78
7	14	(72.97)	(3.82)	(5.15)	1	0.05	0.07	0.65
6.29	21	(41.14)	20.05	2.95	1	(0.49)	(0.07)	0.57
6.04	11	(62.36)	(22.40)	(9.85)	1	0.36	0.16	0.03
		(58.82)	(2.06)	(4.02)	1	(0.03)	0.05	0.76
8.15	7	20.00	(9.16)	(0.73)	1	(0.46)	(0.04)	0.45
6.76	25	315.87	13.11	11.55	1	0.04	0.04	0.10
		167.94	1.98	5.41	1	(0.21)	0.00	0.28

■ The responsiveness of the conventional mortgage rate to Fed movements of the FFR is not greatly influenced by the length of the period during which the Fed moves the FFR. Thus, the responsiveness was much greater in a 13-month period during the 1980s than it was in a 25-month period in the 2000s. This conclusion is less clearly borne out by examining the other periods. In particular, very short periods (in months) seem to show less responsiveness to FFR movements than much longer periods, if the periods concerned are both within either the 1980–99 period or the 2000–08 period.

■ In both periods, the Fed was better able to use the FFR to influence other interest rates downward than upward. The average ratios of downward percentage movements of the conventional mortgage rate to similar movements of the FFR were 0.56 to 1.00 for 1980–99 and only 0.05 to 1.00 for 2000–08. But the average ratios for upward movements were 0.29 to 1.00 for 1980–99 and 0.00 to 1.00 for 2000–08. These data also confirm the

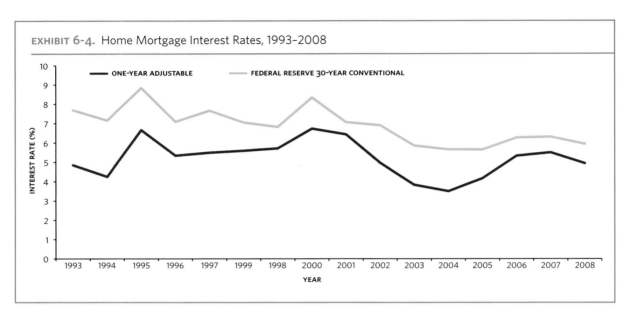

EXHIBIT 6-4. Home Mortgage Interest Rates, 1993–2008

greater ability of the Fed to influence other interest rates during 1980–99 than during 2000–08.

Was the Fed Mainly Responsible for the Very Low Interest Rates after 2000?

Some critics have argued that Chairman Alan Greenspan and the Federal Reserve Board should bear major responsibility for driving mortgage and other interest rates very low after 2000. The low interest rates that appeared then helped stimulate "excessive" housing price and construction booms shortly thereafter. It is certainly evident from exhibit 6-2 that the Fed did push the FFR to very low levels after the stock market crash of 2000. The FFR dropped from 6.54 percent in July 2000 to a plateau of about 1.75 percent from January 2002 to October 2002, then declined to another plateau of 1.00 percent from July 2003 to June 2004. Only after those plunges did the Fed shift its policy to increasing the FFR steadily, which it did from July 2004 to July 2006, then stabilizing the rate at 5.25 percent until August 2007.

Home mortgage rates during much of the period covered by the two exhibits are shown in exhibit 6-4. This chart also shows that interest rates for one-year, adjustable-rate mortgages were notably lower than those for 30-year, fixed-rate mortgages, with the one-year rates hitting their low points in 2004. The lowest rate for such mortgages at any time reported by the source involved was 3.36 percent in March 2004. Thus, the Fed's pushing the FFR to very low levels of 1 percent in 2004 did seem to help many homebuyers to get very low initial rates on adjustable-rate mortgages.

However, I do not believe the low home mortgage rates in this period were caused mainly by Federal Reserve policy or by the low level of the FFR. Rather, just the massive flow of financial capital into U.S. real estate markets after 2000 would have driven interest rates down close to the levels that were actually reached. That probably would have happened even if the Fed had not encouraged such low rates by cutting the FFR to 1 percent in 2004. Credit was so easily available from many sources that the Fed probably would have been unable to prevent home mortgage rates and other interest rates from dropping to such low levels. There was too much intensive competition among suppliers of capital to meet the needs of borrowers. This conclusion is partly confirmed by the high levels of mortgage financing that occurred in the United States. Such financing peaked in 2003 when over $4 trillion of home mortgages were originated, mostly to refinance existing homes. However, by keeping the FFR so low for so long, Greenspan intensified the impacts of this flood of capital on the easy availability of low-cost credit.

Greenspan himself arrived at the same conclusion in his book *The Age of Turbulence*, in discussing the impact of massive global savings on U.S. interest rates. He argued that

During the past five years, developing country growth has been twice that of developed countries. Their savings rates, led by China, rose from 24 percent in 2001 to 32 percent in 2006. . . World intended savings has exceeded intended investment in recent years, as evidence by the worldwide decline in long-term interest rates . . . adjusted for inflation expectations. . . . It was the spillover of developing country savings that drove real interest rates lower. . . . I doubt that we had the resources to counter the downward pressure on real long-term interest rates, which were becoming increasingly global.[3]

Journalist Martin Wolf of the *Financial Times* came to the same conclusion in his recent book *Fixing Global Finance*:

As a result of the emerging market financial crises of the 1990s, the bursting of the Japanese economic bubble in 1990, the bursting of the U.S. and European stock market bubbles in 2000, the determination of China to pursue export-led growth and eliminate any risk of financial crisis, and finally the soaring oil prices of the 2000s . . . a significant surplus of desired savings over investment emerged in the early 2000s. . . . One result of this situation has been the low long-term real interest rates that have become a feature of the world economy.[4]

Did the Fed Fail to Check Flagrant Abuses of Lending Procedures Involving Subprime Loans?
A much stronger case can be made that the Fed failed in its responsibility to supervise the behavior of mortgage lenders. That failure consisted of permitting such lenders to use abusive policies and procedures unchecked. In 2000 and again in 2002, Edward M. "Ned" Gramlich, then a member of the Federal Reserve Board, sent messages to Greenspan warning that abusive behavior was widespread in subprime lending practices. He requested that the Fed chairman take strong action to prevent continuation of what he thought were practices injurious to the welfare of many homebuyers and potentially to the entire housing market. Greenspan did not accept this advice. Instead, he refused to intervene to stop such practices or even to investigate to see whether they were widespread.

It turned out that Gramlich's observations were correct. Consequently, Greenspan's refusal to pay much attention to them allowed many abusive practices to contaminate subprime lending markets and securities based upon them. Many practitioners in subprime mortgage markets were engaging in nefarious practices that eventually led to widespread defaults among subprime borrowers. This was a key factor in precipitating the worldwide financial crisis of 2007–09. Greenspan and the Fed should have reacted much more effectively to this warning by conducting an official investigation of subprime lending practices and then calling for greater regulation of those practices. I believe this failure was far more important in generating the financial crisis than was the Fed's pushing the FFR to very low levels in 2004. The decline of mortgage rates in general would have happened anyway, because of the huge flow of financial capital into home financing markets, although the Fed's policy probably somewhat prolonged the period of very low interest rates. In his testimony before Congress in late October 2008, Greenspan admitted that his failure to promote more regulation of both subprime lending and the explosion of financial derivatives and debt securitization was a mistake that helped cause the financial crisis and the subsequent financial crisis.[5]

Policy Responses to Burgeoning Home Foreclosures

As discussed in chapter 3, the number of homes being foreclosed upon annually across the entire nation has escalated rapidly. According to RealtyTrac, the number of foreclosures filed each year shot up from 657,000 in 2005 to 3.158 million in all of 2008. (That 2008 total included all filings; the number of actual foreclosures was significantly smaller.)

Many economists and housing experts have declared that the financial crisis cannot be ended until housing prices stop declining in U.S. housing markets. Further price declines cause potential homebuyers to refrain from purchasing homes because they think prices will fall lower and they will be able to get better bargains. That weakens overall housing demand and prevents homebuilders from expanding construction efforts. Housing price declines also discourage lenders from putting up money for home mortgages because they believe such loans would become riskier as home prices fall, raising the loan-to-value percentages involved.

The adverse effects of so many foreclosures were discussed in detail in chapter 3. To avoid these harmful outcomes and help stop home prices from falling farther, it would be desirable to limit the number of home foreclosures in future years, especially in 2009. The U.S. Congress grappled with possible legislation aimed at this goal for several months in early 2008. It eventually produced the Housing and Economic Recovery Act of 2008, which was adopted in late July 2008 and signed by President Bush. Several additional approaches to reducing future foreclosures have been suggested by various experts, both within and outside the federal government. These approaches are discussed in detail below.

Renegotiating Mortgages Under the Housing and Economic Recovery Act of 2008

The Act provides for many policies aimed at improving housing market conditions, including the following means specifically designed to reduce future foreclosures:

■ It provides up to $300 billion in federal funds to help homeowners in danger of foreclosure renegotiate their mortgages with their original lenders. Those lenders must voluntarily reduce the amounts that the borrowers owe to no more than 87 percent of the original amounts. The federal government will then guarantee repayment of the new mortgage to the original lender. This would reduce the monthly payments required of those homeowners.

The $300 billion would be part of a new federal housing trust fund that also would fund other activities related to affordable housing.

- How many lenders will voluntarily accept such terms is not clear. According to the *Wall Street Journal*,[6] the Congressional Budget Office estimated that this provision would help 500,000 homeowners and would cost the government about $85 billion. However, the number of foreclosures filed in 2008 exceeded 3.2 million. Hence this provision may not eliminate major downward pressure on housing prices from further foreclosures. Fortunately, not all filings result in actual foreclosures. But the rate of filing in all of 2008 almost guarantees that more than 600,000 actual foreclosures will have occurred that year.

- It permits the U.S. Treasury to advance unlimited amounts of federal credit to Fannie Mae and Freddie Mac if they face insolvency, compared with the $2.25 billion limit originally in effect for such advances. It also raises the national debt limit of the U.S. government by $800 billion to $10.6 trillion, to cover the possibility that the government would have to take over the government-sponsored enterprises and their large debts, which it has since done. These two entities plus the Federal Housing Administration are vital to the functioning of the U.S. housing market. Together, they accounted for 90 percent of the home mortgages initiated in the second quarter of 2008—up 49 percent from one year earlier. Their importance to the housing industry is shown by the fact that in 2008 they owned or guaranteed about $5.4 trillion of the nation's $12 trillion in home mortgages outstanding.

- It provides $4.6 billion for tax credits of up to $7,500 per household for relatively low-income, first-time homebuyers to help stimulate the purchase of homes in the existing inventory of homes for sale, including foreclosed homes. The tax credit must be repaid to the government without interest within 15 years.

- It grants states and local governments up to $3.9 billion to buy foreclosed homes and provides $210 million to pay for counseling for homeowners being foreclosed.

Altogether, this is one of the largest and most comprehensive housing bills ever passed by Congress. Yet, with the number of foreclosure filings during 2008 exceeding three million, it is not clear whether the Act, despite its multipronged approach, will help slow the rate of housing price decreases. In fact, as of December 2008, it had not been very effective at persuading lenders to participate in this program. As a result, the head of the FDIC has called for the development of other methods of slowing down foreclosure rates.

Direct Federal Purchases of Subprime Mortgages

The Congressional Budget Office has examined several other approaches to achieving the same goal. It concluded that the one most likely to exert the maximum effect would be for the federal government to buy subprime mortgages directly.[7] However, this approach has two serious drawbacks. The first concerns the federal government's experience in managing the resale of any large number of repossessed assets to the public. It received such experience when the Resolution Trust Corporation helped liquidate assets from failed savings and loan associations in the early 1990s. That process was plagued by political considerations concerning who would get such assets and how much they would have to pay. Those considerations are likely to increase greatly the ultimate costs to taxpayers of disposing of any mortgages or homes purchased by the federal government. The second objection is that, even with the best management, directly buying enough subprime mortgages to stop home prices from falling any farther would be enormously expensive to taxpayers. Perhaps that is why Congress did not seriously consider this approach. But Congress or the Treasury may reconsider it in the future.

Federal Purchase of Equity Stock in Banks Short of Capital

This approach was suggested by British financial authorities and also by Brookings economist Douglas Elmendorf. It was put into practice by then Treasury Secretary Henry Paulson and Federal Reserve Bank Chairman Ben Bernanke when they met with the executives of nine large U.S. banks on October 14, 2008. The federal government would purchase equity stock, in the form of preferred stock, in banks suffering from severe shortages of "clean" capital, thereby expanding the capital those banks could use as reserves to support new lending. The Treasury and the Federal Reserve have already put this tactic into practice for those banks and are extending it to many smaller banks. The hope is that this expansion of banking capital will free banks to begin lending to all types of customers. Eventually, after the financial system recovers, the government could sell its stock at a profit. This is a more direct way to recapitalize banks. However, it might still be necessary to remove at least some of the toxic assets from such banks in order to free enough capital to support large-scale new lending. Hence this approach might require a mixed program in which the government would buy both toxic assets and equity stock in weakened banks.

Federal Purchases of Foreclosed Homes

One possibility suggested by Robert Litan of the Brookings Institution is for the government to buy the homes of defaulting households from their lenders, essentially by purchasing the mortgages involved. The government would probably pay less than their book values and could then rent those homes to the occupant households on five-year leases at relatively low rents. Then those households would not have to move, at least until the initial leases ran out. If this happened on a large enough scale, it might put a floor under home values and stop them from falling farther. That in turn would create enough stability in the economy to encourage banks to start making normal loans again, including home mortgage loans. It is not clear to me whether this could be done under the Act's current legal language or would require passage of another similar bill to allow the purchase of homes rather than toxic assets held by banks. Moreover, this approach could be very expensive for the federal government, especially because many lenders who could afford to go through foreclosure would prefer to sell their properties to the government at better prices than they would get from foreclosures. That might balloon the total cost of such an approach.

Federal Mortgages for Defaulting Homeowners

A similar possibility was suggested by Professor Martin Feldstein of Harvard University, as follows:

> The federal government would offer any homeowner with a mortgage an opportunity to replace
> 20 percent of the mortgage with a low-interest loan from the government, subject to a maximum

of $80,000. This would be available to new buyers as well as those with mortgages. The interest on the loan would reflect the government's low cost of funds and could be as low as 2 percent. The loan would not be secured by the house but would be a loan with full recourse, allowing the government to take other property or income in the unlikely event that the individual does not pay. It would by law be senior to other debt and not eligible for relief in bankruptcy.

The individual could repay the loan at any time or could refinance the remaining loan on more favorable terms as long as the principal did not increase. A 30-year amortization of the government loan would make the payments low, and a life insurance policy would protect taxpayers if the borrower dies before the loan is repaid. If the homeowner chooses to accept the loan, creditors would have to accept the 20 percent repayment, reducing the monthly payment of the principal and interest by 20 percent.

Although the total size of the mortgage loan program might be as much as $1 trillion, this program would not be comparable to other government spending or to a swap of government bonds for impaired assets. The government would instead have a fully offsetting claim on individuals who could be counted on to repay their low-interest government loans. The cash that the banks and other creditors would receive from the government to replace the existing mortgages would be available to finance new loans. . . .

The recent financial recovery plan that Congress enacted will not rebuild lending and credit flows. Doing so requires a program to stop a downward overshooting of housing prices and the resulting mortgage defaults. The mortgage-replacement loan program may be the best way to achieve that.[8]

This approach—or something very like it—was endorsed by Senator John McCain in the candidates' debate held on October 7, 2008. He estimated the total gross cost as about $300 billion, in addition to the funds authorized in the Recovery Act. His opponent, Senator Barack Obama, apparently agreed with at least giving serious consideration to such a program.

The Obama Administration's Federal Housing Recovery Plan (FHRP)

In mid-March 2009, the U.S. Treasury Department announced a new three-part program to help two sets of homeowners. The first group consisted of those who were current on their monthly payments, but had homes of lower market value than the mortgages on them because of the national decline in home prices. Many such households cannot sell their homes at market prices without taking losses when they repay the larger mortgages involved. Mortgage rates in March 2009 had fallen to lower levels than earlier, but these households were not eligible to refinance to get smaller monthly payments because their homes are worth less than the mortgages on them. Under the new program, both Freddie Mac and Fannie Mae are willing to refinance such mortgages with smaller ones that would better position the homeowners for long-term ownership of their homes. Those two agencies would buy the mortgages from their lenders for 62 cents on the dollar. Thus, the holders of loans already existing on such homes would have to accept a "haircut" on their mortgages in return for being relieved of the problems associated with foreclosure. FHRP representatives would negotiate the mortgage payment terms with each homeowner at a monthly amount the homeowner could afford. The original mortgage would be back-figured to a first lien mortgage. The difference between the original and new mortgages would be held as an FHRP Bond for up to 15 years with no interest due, recorded as a second lien on the property. That lien would be required to be paid off when the home was sold or refinanced prior to the maturity date. This assumes that the market value of the home will rise in 15 years significantly above where it is now. This part of the program would aid households whose homes have fallen in value below the mortgages on them to reduce their monthly payments.

A second part of the FHRP is for homeowners with adjustable rate mortgages who find themselves unable to keep paying new higher rates after a rate reset. The plan would be limited to resident households, excluding speculators. Households current on their payments would be eligible to participate, as would those behind on their payments. The goal is to bring monthly payments down to no more than 31 percent of the borrowers' income. Lenders would receive up-front fees as an incentive to initiate loan modification with eligible borrowers. If a lender agrees to modify a mortgage to a lower level but the borrower defaults, the lender will have insurance funds in compensation. As an incentive to remain current, borrowers will receive a $1,000 principal reduction of their mortgage for each year current up to five years. Except for such reductions, the total amount of the loan is not reduced, but the monthly payments are significantly lowered.

The third part of this program is providing an additional $200 billion in federal funds to Fannie Mae and Freddie Mac so they can participate in the first two parts. They will buy more mortgage-backed securities and increase the size of their portfolio limits.

The complexity of this program, and many of the others described earlier, shows how difficult it is to design an approach to slowing down foreclosures that will (1) work for hard-pressed homeowners, (2) be acceptable to lenders, and (3) actually reduce the number of foreclosures each year. This program is too new to provide any evidence of whether it will work better than others tried before it.

Suing the Mortgage Companies That Originated "Predatory" Subprime Loans

This approach has been adopted by California Attorney General Edmund G. (Jerry) Brown, who—along with several other state attorneys general—successfully sued Countrywide Home Loans and reached a settlement "expected to provide up to $8.68 billion of home loan and foreclosure relief nationally, including $3.5 billion to California borrowers."[9] Countrywide is now owned by the Bank of America. Brown's press release also states,

> *This settlement will enable eligible subprime and pay-option mortgage borrowers to avoid foreclosure by obtaining a modified and affordable loan. The loans covered by the settlement are among the riskiest and highest-defaulting loans at the center of America's foreclosure crisis. Assuming every eligible borrower and investor participates, this loan modification program will provide up to $3.5 billion to California borrowers.*

This result will occur by suspending foreclosures pending loan modification, waiving late fees, waiving prepayment penalties, and making payments for borrowers who are late or who cannot make future payments as scheduled. Presumably, other attorneys general could launch similar suits in other parts of the nation against mortgage originators who used predatory tactics. However, this approach assumes that such mortgage originators still have enough assets to make such settlement payments, which is questionable considering how many have already gone out of business.

Modifying the Mortgages of Defaulting Homeowners
The mortgage loans of defaulting homeowners can be modified so as to cut their payments to levels that they can afford to pay from their verified incomes, thereby allowing them to remain in those homes. This program protects lenders by providing them with a revised loan that is more profitable (or less costly) than undergoing foreclosure on the homes concerned. This program was designed and espoused by the FDIC and its chairperson, Sheila C. Bair. It is based on the following principles[10]:

- Eligible households are those that are 60 days or more delinquent, are not in bankruptcy, have not been through Section 7 bankruptcy, are living in the home as a primary residence, and are not facing imminent foreclosure.
- The loan servicing organization calculates a monthly payment that is feasible for the homeowner, which is from 31 to 38 percent of the owner's verified income (the payment includes principal and interest, real estate taxes, home insurance, leasehold estate payments, and homeowners association dues), reduces the monthly payment by 10 percent or more, is based on an interest rate no less than 3 percent, and is extended over an amortization period of up to 40 years. The resulting reduced interest rate is retained for five years, after which it gradually rises to a maximum of the Freddie Mac weekly survey rate.
- The loan servicer includes a partial forbearance of loan principal, if necessary, to get the monthly payment down to where the owner can afford it.
- The loan servicer calculates the cost to the lender of using the modified mortgage agreement to the estimated cost of putting the same home through foreclosure and proceeds only if the latter exceeds the former. This is done through a traditional financial calculation of net present value.
- The entire process is marketed through a bulk mailing and the use of an automated loan-level underwriting process to minimize administrative costs.

The FDIC worked out this procedure with many delinquent loans it took over when it seized the Indymac Bank in California. The Treasury Department borrowed several elements of this program for the new Federal Housing Recovery Plan described above.

Neighborhood Home Price Reductions Leading to Mortgage Renegotiations
Luigi Zingales of the University of Chicago suggests that a 20 percent decline in the average price of homes in a neighborhood from the time that their owners bought those homes should automatically trigger an option to alter the terms of the mortgage loans involved. Lenders of those loans would be forced to write off a chunk of the original loan, shrinking its value in proportion to the fall in the neighborhood's home prices. In return, the lenders would receive a share of future home price increases.[11]

Using Fannie Mae and Freddie Mac to Provide "Normal" Mortgages

Fannie Mae and Freddie Mac could be used to provide mortgages at 5.25 percent for 30 years, as though mortgage markets were working normally. Glenn Hubbard and Chris Mayer of Columbia University suggest that the government use the GSEs to provide home loans to new and existing borrowers on terms that would be available if markets were working properly. That would mean a 5.25 percent, 30-year, fixed-rate loan, but households with negative equity would not be eligible, because their new mortgages would be too small to pay off the old ones. However, both Fannie Mae and Freddie Mac sustained large losses from delinquent payments and defaults as housing prices slid lower in late 2008. They would need large federal capital infusions in order to carry out the strategy proposed by Hubbard and Mayer.

Moratorium on Additional Foreclosures

Several others have suggested a national moratorium on home foreclosures for one to several months while the government designs a program to attack this problem. That would keep present homeowners in their homes and prevent those homes from becoming vacant, becoming deteriorated, and driving down surrounding home prices. However, it would impose a significant cost on lenders if the homeowners stopped making their monthly payments.

The Need to Reduce the Stated Amount of Mortgages to Avoid Foreclosure

Many households unable to keep making their monthly mortgage payments simply have incomes too low to cope with the high interest rates their adjustable loans have assumed, especially after being reset upwards. In many cases, they bought homes beyond their ability to finance; in other cases, rising unemployment has drastically reduced their monthly incomes. As professor Nouriel Rubini of New York University said on a recent interview program hosted by Charlie Rose:

> My fear is that unless you have a significant reduction in the face value, in the principal of the mortgages, most of the people are not going to be able to afford the mortgage, even if you cut for a while their payments on a monthly basis. So we're going to try this approach [the Federal Housing Rescue Plan], we'll see whether it works. I feel that maybe six months from now, a year from now, we'll have to do something more radical . . . something like across-the-board reductions in the principal value of the mortgages. . . . We're not ready to do that yet.[12]

Any such across the board reduction in mortgage amounts raises huge questions about the sanctity of contracts, since it would impose large losses on lenders and investors. Yet Professor Roubini may be right that there is no other effective way to prevent a continuation of many thousands of home foreclosures. Time will tell.

Criteria for Choosing among Tactics

How should federal authorities choose among the possible means of reducing future foreclosures described in the preceding section? I believe the authorities should use specific criteria of desirability to evaluate the tactics suggested above for halting further home price declines in order to determine which would be more effective. My suggested criteria are set forth below:

1. Does the tactic focus on aiding those homeowners most likely to be foreclosed?
2. How difficult is it to administer to a single eligible homeowner?
3. How much money would it cost the federal government per household aided?
4. How difficult is it to carry out on a large scale?
5. Is it susceptible to being used by households who really do not need it but think they could gain from it?
6. How many households would qualify for it?
7. Would lenders be willing to participate voluntarily in it, or would they have to be coerced or given expensive incentives?
8. How much would it cost the federal government overall to apply it on a large scale?
9. Would the parties involved in it have enough funds to make the program work at a national scale?
10. Would the tactic be likely to stop national housing prices from declining farther?

Public Policy Responses by the Federal Reserve and Treasury Department

Despite the Federal Reserve Board's generally weakened ability to influence financial markets, it reacted with unprecedented speed and forcefulness to the financial crisis during 2008. The Federal Reserve Board and the U.S. Treasury carried out the following major actions in the latter part of 2008:

■ The Federal Reserve Board forced investment banking firm Bear Stearns to sell out to JPMorgan Chase when it became impossible for Bear Stearns to keep raising enough capital in private markets to meet its debt obligations. This impossibility arose because of the major losses from subprime mortgage lending that subsidiaries of Bear Stearns had incurred and the damage to Bear Stearns' reputation for financial solvency that ensued. Bear Stearns had earned a profit of more than $1 billion for the quarter when the Federal Reserve forced it to sell out. So it was not lack of profitability that caused the Fed to react but lack of liquidity to meet its debts and capital needs.

■ As part of that forced transaction, the Federal Reserve advanced billions of dollars in aid to JPMorgan Chase to help that firm cope with some of the illiquid and perhaps overvalued assets of Bear Stearns. This was in violation of its longtime policy of refusing to advance federal credit to private investment banks as it often did to commercial banks.

■ The Federal Reserve Board also opened its lending window for at least a short time to other investment banks and other financial firms that were having trouble raising enough money to remain solvent. This was also a change in its longtime policy of refusing to advance federal credit to private investment banks.

■ The Federal Reserve also indicated that it would financially support both Fannie Mae and Freddie Mac if they encountered difficulty in raising enough capital to continue their operations as secondary-market operators in residential mortgage markets. This offer was incorporated into the housing bill passed by Congress in July 2008, as described above. However, on September 7, the U.S. Treasury seized legal control of both Fannie Mae and Freddie Mac. Treasury Secretary Paulson stated that such nationalization was necessary in order to prevent these two huge mortgage-securitizing agencies from any chance of bankruptcy, which would have caused serious financial crises for many central banks and other banking firms that held large amounts of bonds guaranteed by the two agencies. Shortly thereafter, the Treasury removed the chief executive officers of both GSEs and replaced them with its own appointees.

- The Federal Reserve Board and the U.S. Treasury were crucial participants in helping to draft and gain passage of the Housing and Economic Recovery Act of 2008.

- On October 3, 2008, the House of Representatives passed the second version of a bill already defeated by the House on September 29 and then passed by the Senate on October 1. Passage in the House occurred after the bill had been expanded with more than $100 billion in special earmarks designed to increase legislative support. This bill—the Troubled Assets Relief Program, or TARP—authorized the Treasury and the Federal Reserve to spend up to $700 billion to buy toxic securities from U.S. banks and take other steps to defrost the credit freeze that was slowing economic activity throughout the U.S. economy. The bill was immediately signed into law by President Bush.

- On October 14, 2008, then Treasury Secretary Paulson convened a meeting of the senior executives of nine major U.S. banks in Washington. He told them that he wanted the government to provide them with a total of $125 billion in federal funds in return for preferred stock in their banks, so as to help rebuild their capital to help them start making commercial loans again. They all finally agreed to accept such capital. The preferred stock will be paid a 5 percent dividend for the first five years and 9 percent thereafter. The stock can be redeemed after three years if the banks raise private capital to replace that stock. Paulson also said the federal government was prepared to supply another $125 billion to smaller banks in need of more capital, their identity as yet to be determined. This tactic was modeled after policies already adopted by the Bank of England. It constituted another weapon in the federal government's use of the $700 billion authorized in the TARP bill.

- On various dates in September and October 2008, the Treasury and the Federal Reserve and the FDIC announced that they would extend the deposit insurance over individual bank accounts to larger amounts, up from $100,000 to $250,000 for individuals, and would stand behind the credit extended by money market and commercial paper funds in order to encourage more use of such short-term means of providing more credit.

- The Federal Reserve Board announced that it would provide credit to money market funds to prevent depositors in those funds from withdrawing all their funds in fear of default, which would shut down the market for very short-term loans needed by businesses to stay operating.

- On March 19, 2009, the Federal Reserve Board set forth a new program to aid the economic recovery by spending $1 trillion in buying Treasury bonds (including long-term bonds) and mortgage-backed securities. Among the goals of this action were reducing mortgage interest rates and stimulating more spending by private firms and households.

- On March 23, 2009, the Treasury and the Federal Deposit Insurance Corporation announced a new public/private program to help remove toxic assets—now called legacy assets—from banks' books. The government would use a combination of TARP funds co-invested with private funds to generate from $500 billion up to $1 trillion to buy legacy assets that banks have indicated they are willing to sell. The government would bear most of the risk of the assets declining in value and would also subsidize the entry of private investors into such joint purchases. Private investors competing with each other to participate would set the prices to be paid for the legacy assets. Both legacy loans and legacy securities will be sought. The Treasury would provide half the equity capital for each fund, but private managers would maintain control of the money. The government would also share in any profits earned from selling such assets. On the day this program was announced, many private investors said they would participate, and the Dow Jones Industrial Average rose more than 400 points.

Restructuring Federal Financial Entities and Oversight

In addition to the policies that the Federal Reserve Board and the Treasury Department have already adopted, leaders in these agencies and others have recommended numerous other actions and policies to improve financial oversight, agency coordination, and the functioning of the financial system, including the following:

- Because of the multiple and duplicative nature of the many federal agencies charged with overseeing financial institutions, those agencies should be reorganized and the responsibilities for financial oversight should be realigned among them. Secretary Paulson had already initiated a study aimed at that objective before the credit crunch began to appear serious. His ideas were contained in a document entitled "Blueprint for Financial Regulatory Reform," released on March 31, 2008.[13]

- Among the specific recommendations in Paulson's document are the following (presented in highly abbreviated form):
  - Enhanced interagency coordination through a larger version of the President's Working Group on Financial Markets (PWG), which was established in 1987. Heads of more federal oversight agencies would be added to this group, and its mandates would be expanded to "mitigating systemic risk to the financial system, enhancing financial market integrity, promoting consumer and investor protection, and supporting capital markets' efficiency and competitiveness."
  - Forming a new Mortgage Origination Commission from members of several existing regulatory organizations at state and federal levels. It would "oversee uniform minimum licensing qualification standards for state mortgage market participants."
  - Formalizing ways in which nondepository institutions could gain access to the Federal Reserve's discount window to access added capital.
  - Creating a dual state-federal regulatory system for regulating the insurance industry by establishing an optional federal insurance charter and an Office of Insurance Oversight. This is aimed at concentrating the regulation of the insurance industry in one federal agency rather than having it scattered in 51 state and district agencies, in order to standardize insurance regulations and rules.
  - Merging the SEC and the Commodity Futures Trading Commission, to provide uniform oversight of the futures and commodity securities industries.
  - Rationalizing the regulation of broker-dealer and investment advisers.
  - Abolishing the Office of Thrift Supervision and shifting its functions (over savings and loan associations) to the Office of the Comptroller of the Currency.

- Placing examination authority over state-chartered banks with either the Federal Reserve Board or the FDIC, but not both.
- Establishing a federal charter for "systematically important" payment and settlement systems and giving the Federal Reserve Board primary oversight responsibility.
- Establishing an "optimal regulatory framework" that reflects an objectives-based approach like those used in Australia and the Netherlands. This would include
  – Empowering three regulatory agencies to assume responsibility for the entire financial sector. They would be the Federal Reserve Board and two new agencies—a Prudential Financial Regulatory Authority and a Business Conduct Regulatory Authority.
  – Creating a Federal Insurance Guarantee Fund and a Corporate Finance Regulatory Authority.
  – Requiring all financial institutions to hold one of three federal "charters." Those institutions would include banks, insurance companies, broker-dealers, hedge funds, private equity funds, venture capital funds, mutual funds, and investment banks. The three charters would be for all depository institutions with federal deposit insurance, all insurance companies involving products with some type of federal guarantee, and all other financial firms of any type.
- Many additional policies already included in the housing bill that Congress passed in summer 2008.

It is clear that the adoption of these policies would involve a major restructuring of the federal government's agencies to interact with the nation's financial sector. Along with other public policies discussed earlier in this chapter, these changes would amount to making the federal government a central player in the financial sector itself, not just a regulator of activities that occur there. Billions of federal dollars would become involved in the normal operation of the nation's financial institutions and activities.

Altogether, such restructuring would be a major departure from the past roles of the federal government in the operations of the American economy's financial sector. The concept that the federal government should remain separate from the financial sector, except in its role as a regulator of activities in that sector, would be radically changed. Instead, the federal government would become the single largest active player in that sector, while also regulating the behavior of all the other players. Although that would be a far cry from socialism, in which the government completely controlled the financial sector, it would mark a fundamental change in the structure of the American government, as compared with its previous role in that crucial sector.

NOTES

1. Credit Suisse has developed a list of 16 U.S. government program responses to the current credit crunch. Ten are essentially Federal Reserve programs to lend money to banks and other financial institutions, and six others are programs to be carried out by the Treasury and the FDIC. This chapter deals with many but not all of these specific programs. Credit Suisse, "Government Polity Initiatives: U.S. and European Interest Rate Strategy, October 2008," slide show presented to Invesco in 2008.

2. Data from Mortgage-X, Mortgage Information Services, http//mortgage-x.com/x/ratesweekly.asp. Data for the Federal Reserve Measure of conventional mortgage rates taken from the Federal Reserve Board Website, Interest rates.

3. Alan Greenspan, *The Age of Turbulence* (New York: The Penguin Press, 2007), pages 388–91.

4. Martin Wolf, *Fixing Global Finance* (Baltimore: Johns Hopkins University Press, 2008), pages 107–08.

5. Kara Scannell and Sudeep Reddy, "Greenspan Admits Errors to Hostile House Panel," *Wall Street Journal*, October 24, 2008, pages 1, 15.

6. Damian Paletta and James R. Hagerty, "Housing Bill Will Extend Federal Role in Markets," *Wall Street Journal*, July 24, 2008, page A16.

7. Statement of Peter R. Orszag, Director of the Congressional Budget Office, "Options for Responding to Short-Term Economic Weakness," before the Committee on Finance, United States Senate, January 22, 2008, page 37.

8. Martin Feldstein, "The Problem Is Still Falling House Prices," *Wall Street Journal*, October 4, 2008.

9. Office of the Attorney General, State of California, "Attorney General Brown Announces Landmark $8.68 Billion Settlement with Countryside," http://ag.ca.gov/newsalerts/print_release.php?id=1618.

10. Federal Deposit Insurance Corporation, FDIC Loan Modification Program (Washington, D.C., November 2008), www.fdic.gov.

11. Description of these alternatives was taken from *The Economist*, October 25, 2008, page 92.

12. Nouriel Roubini on Charlie Rose's *Conversation* program, on the Internet at www.CharlieRose.com, accessed on March 16, 2009.

13. A summary of this document has been compiled by the law firm of Davis, Polk, and Wardwell and is available on the Internet. See Davis, Polk, and Wardwell, "Paulson Proposes Financial Regulatory Overhaul," March 31, 2008, http://www.dpw.com/1485409/pdfs/03.31.08.blueprint.pdf.

Chapter
Seven

New Public Policies for Improving the Financial System

THE PREVIOUS CHAPTER DISCUSSED PUBLIC POLICY responses to the credit crunch and financial crisis that have already been carried out or proposed by the Congress, the U.S. Treasury, or the Federal Reserve Board. This chapter sets forth additional proposed public policies for the federal government, other levels of government, and the private sector to implement so as to improve the future operations of the U.S. financial system and our whole economy. The policies proposed in this chapter are based in part on ideas garnered from many economists and financial specialists from all over the world. All embody the underlying belief that the entire financial sector of the U.S. economy needs major restructuring and regulatory reform.

If such reforms are to work over the long run, they must be supplemented by changes in many other parts of American society. Those parts include our systems of education and our immigration policies, and even our patterns of residential settlement. I believe the economic crisis generated by the credit crunch and the ensuing recession represent an unusual opportunity for Americans to reconsider how certain basic parts of the economic and political systems work and to undertake some key reforms we have long been postponing. Some of those reforms suggested in this chapter and in others represent my own thinking, but others have been developed by many other persons concerned with America's future. Most of the policy suggestions in this chapter and the remainder of the book focus on reforming the financial sector.

Mortgage Lending and Securitization

Excessive behavior, often reckless and sometimes illegal, by major participants in the home mortgage industry was a key factor that caused the credit crunch in American housing markets. Therefore, some policy changes are necessary to limit the ability of these participants to engage in such destructive behavior. Those changes should consist mostly of tighter regulations concerning how legal mortgage lending must be carried out.

Mortgage Lending Rules and Regulations

In July 2008, the Federal Reserve Board passed "A Final Rule Amending Home Mortgage Provisions of Regulation Z (Truth in Lending)," which becomes applicable for all mortgages made on or after October 1, 2009. This rule includes the following provisions for "higher-priced loans," which include subprime loans:

- Mortgage lenders must obtain information about homebuyers' incomes from certified sources, such as employers or tax forms; they cannot rely solely on buyers' estimates or declarations.

- Homebuyers should not be allowed to take out mortgages that would raise their total monthly payments, including other debt like credit card payments, to more than some maximum fraction of their monthly incomes, such as 28 or 31 percent, unless the mortgage would be repayable from the borrower's other assets.

- There must be no prepayment penalties if the monthly payment can change during the initial four years. For other high-priced loans, a prepayment penalty cannot last for more than two years.

- The lender must establish an escrow account for the payment of property taxes and homeowner insurance for first-lien loans. The lender can offer to cancel the escrow account for the borrower after one year.

The following provisions apply to all closed-end mortgages secured by a borrower's main dwelling:

- Certain servicing provisions are prohibited, such as not crediting a payment to a consumer's account on the date the payment is received and "pyramiding" late fees.

- A creditor or broker is prohibited from coercing or encouraging an appraiser to misrepresent the value of a home.

- Creditors must provide a good-faith estimate of the total loan costs, including a schedule of payments, within three days after a consumer applies for any mortgage that is secured by the consumer's principal dwelling, including home improvement or refinancing loans.

This provision applies to all mortgages:

- All advertising must contain additional information about rates, monthly payments, and other loan features. Moreover, seven deceptive or misleading practices are prohibited, including any representation that a payment is fixed when it can change.

In addition, I recommend adoption of the following regulations for all mortgages:

- Homebuyers must provide downpayments from their own funds amounting to at least 10 percent of the full cost of buying the homes concerned. No assisted downpayments using funds provided by the sellers or by local community organizations should be permitted.

- No mortgages should be permitted in which monthly payments do not cover the entire minimum costs of interest (if interest only) or interest and principal (if amortized), so the amounts by which monthly payments fall short of those minimum amounts are added to the total amount owed. Such "option mortgages" or any mortgages in which the total mortgage amount exceeds the market price of the home should be illegal.

- In every mortgage transaction, the borrower should be required to get a three-day waiting period after the mortgage is agreed upon, but before the closing, in which the borrower can reject the entire mortgage and the entire transaction without loss of income or deposit.
- In advance of finalizing any mortgage, every mortgage broker should be required to show the borrower a complete schedule of interest rates, future increases in such rates and when they would occur, and the impacts upon monthly payments. They should be required to have the borrower sign a document acknowledging that he or she has seen that schedule and has been given a written copy of it.
- The fees charged by mortgage brokers and originators and any other participants in the mortgage origination process should be limited through a schedule worked out by the mortgage industry and the federal government. Every borrower should be given a complete written copy and explanation of those fees as part of any mortgage negotiation.
- A schedule of maximum interest rates chargeable by mortgage lenders and lenders of all types, including credit card lenders and automobile lenders, should be worked out by the federal government and private agencies representing lenders and borrowers. That schedule should be widely promulgated. Lenders should be required to provide written copies of that schedule to any borrower as part of the loan negotiation process. Any lenders who violate this schedule by charging interest rates in excess of the maximum permissible amounts should be subject to having to repay that excess to all the borrowers involved and facing fines and possible jail sentences. Complete deregulation of interest charges has been in force in the United States for many years, since the abolition of usury laws. But one result has been exploitation of borrowers by lenders that use excessive rates, particularly to take advantage of ignorant consumers. A return to the use of maximum interest rules should be seriously considered, especially in such fundamentally important and universal procedures as making home mortgages.

One of the most difficult aspects of mortgage regulation reform during periods of rising home prices is preventing speculators from buying homes for the purpose of quickly flipping them and collecting a profit, rather than living in them. On the one hand, people in a free-enterprise economy should be able to do such things as part of their freedom of action. On the other, when many speculators buy homes while pretending to be future occupants, that inflates the number of homes being built beyond society's true needs. That can in turn lead to overbuilding and foreclosures on vacant homes. In fact, that happened in many American neighborhoods from 2003 to 2007. Moreover, speculators who do not occupy the homes they buy do not have the supposed virtues of homeowners for which Congress has created special subsidies to encourage owner occupancy. Therefore, it would be socially desirable to make it extremely difficult for speculators to act in that way. But doing that is not easy and seems to go against the principles of a free-enterprise system. It would be possible to pass a severe law fining any home purchaser who does not occupy a home he or she has bought within a certain period after the sale, without unusual extenuating circumstances. I believe Congress should at least consider such a law, but I recognize that it is morally ambivalent in our supposedly free-enterprise society.

Currently Unregulated Actors in Mortgage Markets

Another aspect of mortgage markets that has been prominent in the credit crunch is the extensive participation in such markets of actors that are not closely regulated by any public agencies. Many mortgage brokers, in particular, were not legally attached to commercial or investment banks. Therefore, those brokers were not legally prohibited from undertaking behavior that was injurious to both borrowers and society as a whole. An example: brokers persuading people who could afford to take out prime mortgages to take out subprime mortgages instead, even though such mortgages were much more expensive to the borrowers, because such mortgages provided the brokers with higher fees. Other brokers persuaded first-time buyers to take out mortgages that had very low initial interest rates—hence low monthly payments—without the buyers fully realizing that their monthly payments would rise substantially after the passage of a certain time.

In order to limit such harmful behavior by participants in the mortgage-making process, I recommend that the following public policies be adopted:

- All individuals or firms participating at any stage of the mortgage process should be required to register with a public agency in the state or states involved or be legally prohibited from such participation. It would be more efficient to have one federal agency involved for the entire nation rather than 50 state agencies with varying rules. I am not recommending any educational or even financial requirements for such registration. Such specific requirements can easily be manipulated by established participants to block the entry of potential competitors. However, those who register should be required to provide accurate information about their education and experience, and that information should be available to any lenders or borrowers who wish to see it.

- Commercial banks that have been originating, securitizing, or selling mortgages through branch agencies that fall under holding companies that also own the banks themselves should be required to consolidate their annual income statements and balance sheets along with those of such branch agencies. In that manner, such agencies would have to conform to the reserve requirements that are applicable to the banks themselves.

- The federal government could continue to operate Fannie Mae and Freddie Mac roughly as they are, as parts of the government itself. Or it could sell their portfolios of mortgages, break them up into smaller organizations, and privatize them. However, for reasons set forth in Chapter 9, I believe the government should—and will—retain ownership of these organizations and use them as major securitizers of home mortgages. Whether or not it merges them into one organization remains to be seen.

Unregulated Parts of the "Shadow Banking System"

As Nobel Prize–winning economist Paul Krugman points out in his recent book, *The Return of Depression Economics and the Crisis of 2008*, one of the most serious elements in the current credit crisis and recession in the United States is the virtual collapse of what he calls "the shadow banking system."[1] By that term, he means all the organizations that actually engage in banking-like activities but have not been regulated by the government. In fact, most of these entities came into existence precisely to escape the regulations and precautionary structures that commercial banks had to endure from the 1930s until the deregulation of many of their activities in the 1980s and 1990s. Examples of such entities include all the unregulated mortgage lenders and brokers discussed in the preceding section, commercial paper markets, hedge funds, private equity funds, auction-rate security markets, money market funds, and investment banks. All these entities essentially create credit and make loans but are not subject to the intense regulation, supervision, and regular inspections endured by commercial banks. These entities are not protected by the various arrangements enjoyed by commercial banks, such as deposit insurance, requirements for reserve funds, ability to borrow from the Federal Reserve Banks, and frequent reviews of their books.

Yet it was the behavior of many of these entities, as much as of commercial banks, that created much of the overleveraging that is now being dismantled, to the distress of credit markets worldwide. Therefore, the fundamental long-range strategy toward such entities is to bring them into the orbit of legal financial regulation by the government. True, the people who originated these entities will claim that the freedom to act that they enjoyed was a key factor underlying the financial growth of the U.S. economy in the 2000s. But the negative side of that overexpansion should be obvious to everyone by now. Exactly what regulatory arrangements should be adopted will vary for different types of entities; hence they cannot be analyzed in detail here. But they should be forced to exhibit much more responsibility for the long-run consequences of their behavior than they have been in the past.

Inadequate Due Diligence

The failure of loan originators to perform adequate due diligence arose in part because those originators did not retain enough ownership of the securities involved to have sufficient skin in the game. Hence the originators were not vitally concerned about how well those securities would perform. That led to another deficiency: loan originators were able to shift risk assessment about the borrowers' ability to repay to third-party credit rating agencies. But those agencies were much less familiar with the borrowers involved than were the banks who had long had those borrowers as customers.

A 2008 study by the staff of the SEC examined and analyzed the procedures and behavior of the three major credit rating agencies in the United States. Some of its findings were as follows:

> *Each rating agency publicly disclosed that it did not engage in any due diligence or otherwise seek to verify the accuracy or quality of the loan data underlying residential mortgage-backed security (RMBS) pools they rated. . . . The rating agencies each relied on the information provided to them by the sponsor of the RMBS. . . . They also did not seek representation from sponsors that due diligence was performed.*[2]

Therefore, credit rating agencies had to develop statistical methods for evaluating borrower creditworthiness, rather than relying on knowledge of those borrowers' past activities. Such statistical models are always based on data taken from the past performance of earlier borrowers. Yet in 2000 and shortly thereafter, there was almost no real experience with how subprime borrowers would react to various economic circumstances. Hence the models used by credit rating agencies were often outdated and ineffectual.

Another problem for credit rating agencies was that their staffs became somewhat overwhelmed by the volume of securities they were asked to rate, especially in 2006 and 2007, years of very high subprime mortgage and CDO originations. The one major credit rating agency that did the most business in those years saw its total revenues from rating RMBSs rise about 200 percent above its 2002 level in 2005 and 240 percent above that level in 2006. But its staff grew only 140 percent above the 2002 level in 2005 and 160 percent above that level in 2006. These comparisons were even worse for CDO ratings. The number of CDO deals that the agency rated rose more than 300 percent above the 2002 level in 2005, more than 900 percent above that level 2006, and more than 700 percent above that level in 2007. But its staff assigned to such deals expanded only about 100 percent above the 2002 level in 2005, 130 percent in 2006, and 150 percent in 2007. (These data came from the SEC analysis of credit rating agencies mentioned above.)

Even more important, the very nature of many subprime mortgage loans tended to reduce the ability of borrowers to repay as time passed, because the initial low interest rates were later reset to much higher rates. Although borrowers could qualify to make initial low monthly payments, it was very likely that many could not make such payments after their interest rates were reset to higher levels. This possibility was not sufficiently taken into account by those assessing the riskiness of the loans concerned, especially since they often assumed that housing prices would keep rising to help offset higher interest rates.

Unfortunately, these shortcomings weakened and then ultimately destroyed the trust that investors had in the agencies that were originating securities and the credit rating agencies that were giving them high ratings. Once such trust has been undermined, it is extremely difficult to restore it. One of the major advantages of securitization is that it enables investors all over the world to participate in lending that is carried out in locations far from them with borrowers about whom they know almost nothing. This is possible only because they trust those who are originating such loans and giving them credit ratings. The globalization of financial markets cannot be maintained if that trust is destroyed.

Ultimately, there are only three ways for such trust to be restored. One is to increase the transparency of all parts of the financial sector so that investors can know clearly in advance exactly what they are buying or lending against before they carry out any such transaction. Such transparency would have to apply to both the financial reports and the balance sheets of all financial firms, and also to the nature of all securities they produce—including mortgage-backed securities—and of the properties underlying them. It would further involve ending the practice of putting key activities by banks and other financial firms off their balance sheets, where investors and regulators cannot perceive what was really going on. Although there are some ways to make the transparency of financial dealings much greater than it has been during the past decade, I do not know of any foolproof ways to make it 100 percent clear. Moreover, enforcing transparency regulations would be very difficult because only those people working in each firm would have a clear and accurate idea of what was going on there.

The second way to restore at least some trust is to require the originators of securitized instruments to retain at least a 10 to 20 percent share of those instruments, preferably either from the lowest ranking tranche or from all tranches so they have an incentive to be sure that the debts involved will be repaid. Since the lowest-ranking tranche normally receives payments only after all the other tranches have been paid their designated interest returns, this arrangement provides a maximum incentive for the originators to perform careful due diligence about the borrowers' ability to repay.

The third way to restore trust is to let enough time pass so that investors can see that current actions by loan originators and credit rating agencies are succeeding. That is likely to take several years, especially for investors distant from major financial markets, such as many in Asia and parts of Europe. As Minsky said in his analysis of financial problems, the mere passage of time when economies are performing well tends to make all the participants in them gain more confidence that those economies will continue to perform well. That in turn makes many of those participants more confident—and often more reckless—about making economic decisions. It also encourages them to use more and more debt to leverage their own activities, thereby raising their rates of return on equity.

Improving Mortgage Securitization

The process of securitizing mortgage loans has become central to the entire operation of housing and commercial real property finance in the United States. Securitization provides enormous benefits to major financial institutions, including commercial banks and savings and loans, and to homebuying households. One such benefit is that securitization has greatly broadened the sources of capital for commercial real estate and housing markets. The resulting increase in funding sources for mortgage markets helped lower interest rates and saved homebuyers huge amounts of money. But the manner in which securitization was carried out prior to and during the recent credit crunch revealed several problems that need to be addressed.

Two major deficiencies were critical causes of the credit crunch. One was the failure of loan originators or credit rating agencies to perform adequate due diligence on the creditworthiness of persons, households, or firms borrowing money. The other was the difficulty of renegotiating mortgage repayment schedules with borrowers who were unable to repay as initially planned.

Renegotiated Repayment Schedules

A major deficiency in securitization or mortgages is that it makes it very difficult for borrowers who encounter trouble repaying their loans to work out alternative payment schedules with those who lent them the money. To whom should such borrowers turn? The originators no longer own much, if any, of the loans concerned. In fact, such ownership has been split up into hundreds or thousands of pieces and resold to new investors, each of whom may own a small piece of a given loan to a particular borrower. Those investors do not want to be bothered by having to work out new repayment schemes for a tiny piece of some security they bought. So they turn over workout problems to special servicers appointed to handle such problems.

But those servicers do not know the borrowers or their special circumstances. In many cases these special servicers have limited options for working out loan problems, as they must abide by pooling and servicing agreements that govern the distribution of loan proceeds and losses to bond-holders. Moreover, servicers can also become overwhelmed by the number of delinquent borrowers who want to work out revised deals when their subprime mortgages become too burdensome. It can be very costly in time and money to carry out such renegotiations, especially because the special servicers have no strong incentive to renegotiate rather than pressing forward to foreclosures. As yet, no one has come up with an effective method to overcome this inherent weakness of securitization. Providing incentives for servicers to renegotiate loans is one option that could be considered.

Overhauling Mortgage Securitization

Mortgage securitization can and should be overhauled and improved so that it can again become a viable and trusted segment of the real estate financial market. Several actions can be undertaken to achieve these reforms, including the following:

- Originators of mortgage loans, such as mortgage brokers, should not be paid their full fees at the time of origination but should be paid over time in relation to the mortgage payments made by the borrowers. That is how life insurance salespeople are rewarded; they collect over time as the insured person pays the premiums. This would give originators, as well as securitizers, a stake in creating only mortgages that are likely to be paid successfully in the long run. In other words, it would give mortgage originators skin in the game long after the initial transaction was over.
- The fees that securitizers can charge for packaging, tranching, and selling securities should be limited by regulators in some manner, and those fees should be promulgated to all parties that are considering buying the securitized issues.
- Credit rating agencies should be required to review the degree of due diligence carried out by the arrangers of securitizations and to take the results into consideration in rating the securities involved.
- Credit rating agencies should also be required to create stronger firewalls between those of their staffs who solicit business from securitizers and those who rate the credit quality of securities brought to the agencies.
- At present, credit rating agencies do not systematically follow up with surveillance reviews of their original ratings or even have detailed documentation about how such reviews are supposed to be conducted, and whether and how they have been conducted. Regulations concerning such agencies should insist that these deficiencies be remedied.
- Credit rating agencies should not be paid by the firms that originated the securities to be rated, but by the potential buyers of those securities. Some arrangement should be made that adds a small fee to every security sold by the originators—a fee that is paid to the credit rating agencies involved. This would eliminate the temptation for credit rating agencies to provide more favorable ratings to security issues than are appropriate in order to capture the business of rating those issues from the firms originating them.

Financial Derivatives

Another important form of security involved in, or related to, mortgage markets consists of various types of financial derivatives bought or sold by organizations participating in those markets. The most common forms are credit default swaps (CDSs), interest rate swaps, and interest rate futures. The overall derivative market is huge, with some estimating the total nominal size of the market at about $668 trillion. These derivatives are often created and interchanged among parties over the counter; that is, outside any formal exchanges that have been designed to facilitate security or derivative trading. As a result, there is no complete registration of how many financial derivatives have been created, who owns them, who the counterparties are, and what types of trading relations the derivatives contain. This could lead to massive difficulties if large numbers of such derivatives become involved in defaults. Such difficulties could have dire adverse effects on key financial actors like major commercial banks. In fact, such a possibility was one of the Federal Reserve Board's main concerns when it forced the liquidation of Bear Stearns in 2008.

In order to bring greater order and more transparency to the use of financial derivatives, I believe the following regulations should be adopted or at least given serious consideration:

■ All forms of financial derivatives should be legally considered as securities. Therefore, they should be regulated in the ways described below and subject to the same transparency and integrity rules that apply to all other forms of securities traded on markets. Such treatment for financial derivatives was proposed in the 1990s by Brooksley Born, head of the Commodity Futures Trading Commission, who testified in favor of such a requirement before various Congressional committees numerous times. However, treating derivatives as securities was rejected by Alan Greenspan, chairman of the Federal Reserve; by Robert Rubin, secretary of the Treasury in the Clinton Administration; and by Arthur Levitt of the SEC. They claimed that the Commodity Futures Trading Commission had no jurisdiction over derivatives (no one did!) and that such regulation would diminish the effectiveness of the financial sector. This lack of regulation opened the door to risky and sometimes nefarious use of such derivatives as synthetic CDOs, many of which had no direct ownership of, or other legal relationship with, actual assets.

■ All parties who enter into financial derivative arrangements with others should be required to register the size and nature of their transactions with a licensed exchange for trading in such instruments. This registration should take place within a short period after the transaction is closed. It should include identification of all parties involved, the nature of the derivative relationships they have created, and the amounts of money at stake. This information should be available to all regulatory authorities working with the exchanges involved and to such other parties as those regulatory authorities and the exchanges concerned agree to give access to this information. Periodic summaries of financial derivative activities should be published by all the exchanges involved without identifying the parties concerned.

■ All persons or firms who act as counterparties in financial derivative arrangements (the buyer or the seller of services) should be required to state what financial resources they have available to cover their responsibilities in case such action is required by their contracts. This information should be part of the information included in their derivative registrations. It should be kept confidential within the exchanges involved, except that the direct counterparties of participants should have access to this information. This information is necessary to produce reasonable transparency in derivative markets.

- All persons or firms who are parties in financial derivatives should not be allowed to sell or assign their interests in such transactions to other parties without notifying their original counterparties concerning to whom such transfers have been made. Those new participants in such transfers should also be required to register with established exchanges, as described above.

- Any person or firm who proposes to initiate the use of some newly defined financial derivatives should be required to register the nature of those new forms with the exchange where they will register those derivatives. Those exchanges should keep records of all the different types of financial derivatives being used by those patronizing or registering with the exchanges.

- Some financial regulatory agencies of the federal government should be appointed as regulators of exchanges where financial derivatives are registered or traded. These regulators should have the authority to question the viability or legality of any new derivative arrangements being proposed. If such questions are raised, the initiators of the new derivatives should have an opportunity to defend their use of them. Unless specific violations of existing laws are involved or there is some clear and present danger of massive credit problems arising from the use of these instruments, the originators should be allowed to use them.

Commercial Banks

In both developed and emerging nations, access to financial credit is critical for the day-to-day operation of all parts of every economy. Almost every business firm, large or small, needs to borrow money to finance its daily operations. Similarly, many households need to borrow money on credit cards to buy the normal necessities of life—and especially for any extra spending. Without relatively easy access to such credit, no modern economy can survive very long—at least, it certainly cannot prosper.

Both commercial banks and shadow banking entities are the sources of such credit in nearly all economies. In America, commercial banks were for a long time the main source of normal lending for most businesses and households. Every bank uses the same basic principles: it takes in financial deposits from many firms and households, uses a large fraction of those deposits to lend money to others, and holds a certain fraction of the deposits in reserve. Banking works successfully most of the time because only a few depositors want to withdraw their funds on any one day. Thus, banking is built on the principle of borrowing short—through deposits that can be immediately withdrawn—and lending long—through loans that take much longer to mature. This principle works as long as the majority of depositors have confidence that they could withdraw their funds immediately if they wanted to. If many lose that confidence and start withdrawing their funds simultaneously, this creates a run on the bank. That endangers the bank's liquidity, because the bank cannot turn its long-term loans into short-term cash instantly. After many financial crises in which such runs occurred, the Federal Reserve was created in 1913 to help lend money to banks experiencing such runs. Then when a run on the entire banking system occurred in the 1930s, the government invented federal deposit insurance to give depositors confidence that they would not lose their funds if a run on any one bank started.

Banks and the Credit Crunch

In the credit crunch of 2008, however, the problem was not depositors who tried to withdraw funds from banks, but bankers who stopped making loans at terms potential borrowers could accept. Bankers stopped making loans for five reasons:

- Banks were suffering huge losses of capital from defaulting loans and other poor investments they had made, so they did not have enough uncommitted and valid capital to make many new loans. There were too many toxic assets on their books that they could neither lend nor use as reserves for lending.

- Bankers decided to charge much higher interest rates and spreads than they had been charging from 2000 to 2007 because those earlier rates did not cover the risks they had been taking. But most borrowers could not afford the banks' new terms. This inability was made worse because banks also reduced their loan-to-value ratios and the asset values they placed on individual properties after mid-2007. Those terms greatly increased the equity that borrowers would have to pay to roll over their existing loans. Many borrowers were unwilling or unable to raise this additional equity capital.

- Banks also had used too much leveraging in making loans from 2000 through early 2007. That is, they had based too many dollars worth of loans on a small amount of reserve capital by repeatedly recycling their loan capital through the "originate and distribute" model discussed earlier. Once they had pooled a lot of mortgages repurchased from mortgage brokers, created several tranches of securities on that pool, and sold those securities, they no longer had to hold reserves against those mortgages or their loans to the brokers who had made the mortgages, since they had in essence been repaid for those loans. So the banks could start the whole process again, using the same reserves they did the first time. This greatly increased the amount of lending they could create from a limited supply of reserve capital. Hence, in 2008 and thereafter they had to greatly reduce the amount of loans they could support from a given amount of sound reserve capital, since they could not keep repeating the process of "originate and distribute" because so few people would buy their mortgage-backed securities. This problem was immensely exacerbated by their losses of sound reserve capital through defaults and other forms of toxic assets on their books. So banks were doubly required to reduce the amount of lending they could support, both by "deleveraging" in general and by cutting their total lending to match the greatly diminished sound capital they possessed. This means that banks could not simply roll over loans that came due; they had to reduce drastically the total amount of such loans they could carry on their books.

- Banks were uncertain of the true market values of the collateral they would have to accept in making new loans because of worldwide uncertainty about real estate values in particular. This uncertainty was greatly reinforced by dramatic declines in both stock prices and REIT shares from September 2008 well into 2009. So bankers refused to make loans against collateral of unknown value, especially collateral that might decline in value even more in the future.

- Banks were uncertain of the quality of assets held by most other banks. So they stopped making interbank loans because of the lack of transparency about what other banks' assets were worth.

These actions resulted in a virtual strike against lending by most banks in the United States. Yet without clear and easy access to credit, most firms and even households cannot sustain their operations for very long. Hence consumer spending fell dramatically, investment funding dried up, and thousands of firms with debts coming due could not pay them on time, if at all. Business production dropped greatly and the nation plunged into a severe recession.

This situation was worsened by the simultaneous failure of the nation's shadow banking system—that is, nonbank institutions that were not regulated by federal authorities but provided credit to millions of households and especially businesses. These institutions included investment banks, money market funds, auction-rate security organizers, commercial paper dealers, and the like. They stopped operating because the investors on whom they had relied to supply the capital which they lent became plagued by the same uncertainties about asset values as commercial bankers had. So those investors simply stopped putting their funds into these entities, many of which promptly disappeared because they had no money to lend.

The "Mark to Market" Problem

Many banks have complained that accounting rules force them to reduce the book value of many of their holdings and securities to the latest actual price of those holdings and securities on open markets—but because of the financial crisis and the credit squeeze, there are no active markets for many such holdings. As a result, the banks are forced to carry such assets on their books at very low values—even values of zero—even though those holdings may well be worth more, especially if they are held until markets recover. Enforcing this "mark to market" rule thus pushes down the overall value of assets held by the banks, moving them closer to insolvency or perhaps actually into insolvency. Therefore, such banks want to be free to carry these assets on their books at some value above zero, though perhaps less than when they were acquired. Hence they have requested that the SEC allow them to suspend the mark to market rule for such securities.

The accounting profession recognizes this problem but its authorities believe there is no clear way to reliably estimate the true value of such securities. Therefore, most banks faced with this difficulty are likely to overestimate the values of such securities, thus providing readers of their balance sheets with false and misleading information. When this chapter was written, the SEC had provided no resolution of this conflict, thereby leaving the mark to market rule in effect.

The Transparency Problem in Banking

A major reason why the banking system is not making credit available under normal procedures is each bank's fear that if it lends money to another bank, that other bank will go broke and not repay the loan. This fear arises because no bank is sure exactly what type of assets any other bank actually has on its books, even if it has a copy of the other bank's balance sheet. There is a reasonable probability that a bank has many toxic assets on its books within established asset categories (such as mortgage loans) or in subsidiaries that are not on the balance sheet. But the existence of such bad loans cannot be detected by simply looking at that bank's balance sheet. If there were some way to compel every bank to make public—at least to other banks and to bank regulators—exactly what types of assets it was holding on or off its formal balance sheet and whether they were toxic or not, then much of the uncertainty caused by this lack of transparency would be alleviated and banks might again begin lending to each other in normal fashion.

Therefore, federal bank regulators should immediately begin requiring all the banks they regulate to classify their assets in each major category as "normal" or "impaired in value" and to report the results to the regulators, along with estimates of the extent of such impairments. The regulators should establish severe fines for failing to identify such impaired assets. True, it will be difficult for banks to accurately measure the amount by which each bad asset is impaired, given the current absence of functioning markets for impaired assets. Nevertheless, establishing strong national pressure on all banks to provide such reports might greatly improve the volume of interbank lending, which needs to be restored to pre–credit crunch levels.

Federal Efforts to Address Bank Problems

When the U.S. Treasury and the Federal Reserve realized what was happening, they decided to leap into action to try to restore bank lending to the economic system before that system collapsed. But how should they do it? There were several options and they tried most of them, as follows:

- The Federal Reserve attempted to reduce interest rates, especially on home mortgage loans. But banks raised their effective interest rates on most commercial loans and increased the stringency of other terms in those loans—for example, by reducing loan-to-value ratios and asset value estimates. Although home mortgage interest rates have stayed low, rates on commercial real estate have moved upward notably, at least as best can be observed from the few transactions that have occurred.

- The federal government decided to buy up some of the defaulted toxic assets cluttering banks' books and remove such assets from those books in hopes that the banks would then start making more loans. This was hard to do because no one knew what those toxic assets were really worth and thus how much the federal government should pay for them. In addition, the amount of such assets was much larger than the federal government originally realized. Therefore, this tactic was not carried out on a very large scale.

- Then the federal government tried injecting federal funds into the equity accounts of the banks to improve the quality and amount of bank capital. However, federal officials did not initially put any requirements upon bankers that received such funds concerning what they should do, or not do, with them. Hence most bankers used the money to shore up their own balance sheets or for their own profit, not for making more loans or making easier credit available to borrowers.

- Federal officials also encouraged relatively solvent banks to merge with much less solvent ones to prevent the latter from failing altogether. This required large injections of federal funds into the solvent banks to help them bear the costs of the toxic assets held by the less solvent ones. The most prominent example is that of Bank of America, which absorbed Merrill Lynch but needed added capital to stay afloat itself. Again, no clear increases in lending resulted.

■ One other tactic the federal government used was nationalizing certain banking institutions and having them run by federal officials. This was done with Fannie Mae and Freddie Mac, both with substantial infusions of federal money.

Despite large injections of federal funds into commercial banks, lending by those banks had not increased significantly by early 2009, but their losses of capital through defaults had gone up. Hence these uses of federal capital appear to have become a bottomless pit that has produced few positive results for the nation's economy.

In summary, three fundamental problems have frozen the banking system. The first is great uncertainty in the minds of American bankers. They are not willing to put at risk either their positions in their banks or the interests of stockholders by making loans in the current environment of immense uncertainty. The second is banks' need to deleverage their overall loan positions by reducing the total amount of loans on their books to more reasonably match the amount of sound capital they have both for loans and reserves. The third is lack of sound capital on banks' books. Their assets are too heavily weighted by toxic securities and bad loans to enable them to increase lending and still have adequate reserves against new loans. Moreover, few private investors will buy stock in banks loaded with toxic assets. These three problems are closely interrelated and tend to intensify each other.

Strategies to Address Bank Problems

The first step toward a solution is to isolate the impacts of the banks' toxic assets on their overall operations. Initially, the federal government sought to buy and hold those assets but could not establish reasonable prices. If that tactic had worked, the federal government would have had to manage all those assets. Several alternative approaches have been suggested by financial experts and observers both within and outside the federal government. These are briefly described below.

Multiple Small "Bad Banks" within Individual Banks

One alternative would be to identify the classes of assets considered toxic, then federally guarantee the values at which banks had those assets on their books, but leave the assets within the banks—in "small bad banks within each bank," so to speak. Any further declines in the values of those assets would be borne by the federal government. But the government would also receive 50 percent of any future increases in the values of those assets. The banks would pay the overhead and personnel costs of managing their internal "bad banks" as their contribution to the solution.

This approach would enable private investors to buy stock in banks without fear of having their investments tainted by those toxic assets. But it would also prevent the federal government from having to buy those assets and manage them. However, this approach does not overcome the banks' need to deleverage their lending—that is, to shrink the total amount of loans they have on their books because they don't have enough sound capital to reserve against their present amount of loans. That problem could be tackled by temporarily reducing the reserve requirements by a significant amount, say 50 percent, for several years. U.S. commercial banks containing over $44.4 million in loans must hold reserves of $1.023 million plus 10 percent of amounts over $44.4 million, according to the Federal Reserve Board. If this reserve requirement were reduced to 5 percent, that would in effect double the lending power of each such bank. This policy change, plus the isolation of toxic assets within the bank, would counteract the need for much of the deleveraging mentioned above. It would also encourage private parties to invest in the stock of such banks, because any future losses in their toxic assets would be borne by the federal government.

True, bankers' uncertainties about the future values of possible collateral they would obtain in making loans might still inhibit them from making more loans. Therefore, such a program directed at banks should have two important traits: first, it should be done for all banks in the nation simultaneously, and second, it should occur in accompaniment with the major economic stimulus and rescue program being proposed by the Obama Administration and Congress. If that program has enough positive impacts, it might reduce the degree of general uncertainty in the U.S. economy facing bankers who are considering making loans. That is the outcome that the federal government should aim for in carrying out these suggested policies toward the banking system.

Nationalization of All Banks

Many observers have called for full federal nationalization of the banking system instead of the approach described above. That alternative would have the advantage of removing present banking officials from their offices and financially wiping out bank shareholders. Those changes would presumably eliminate the current refusal of banks to lend because of fear of jeopardizing stockholder interests or the positions of top banking officials. Putting toxic bank assets into one national "bad bank" would be similar to what the government did in coping with the failure of the savings and loan industry in the 1980s and 1990s. In one version of this approach, the government would not pay the banks to take over the assets that the banks themselves designated as toxic. But if that happened, after removing such toxic assets, many banks might be insolvent—that is, their liabilities would exceed their assets, even with generous estimates of what those assets were really worth. Then they would be unable to increase their lending without much more capital inputs from somewhere—presumably the federal government in some way. True, the government would gain from any profits it made by later selling those assets to investors, but it might also lose by just running such a "bad bank."

Another form of the bad bank would be to pay the banks for the toxic assets taken off their books so they would have some capital with which to lend. But how could anyone determine how much the government should pay? No one knows, though this is discussed further below.

However, bank nationalization has several major drawbacks. First, the federal government would have to take over management of all the banking system's toxic assets, rather than leaving them isolated within each bank and managed by bankers. Second, the federal government would have to find, train, and hire new people to run each of the nation's nationalized banks—a huge undertaking. Third, the federal government would eventually have to sell those banks back into the private sector. Fourth, the undesirable possibility that political considerations would influence how those banks were run and eventually sold would certainly arise in some cases.

Finally, nationalization would wipe out the equity held in all banks by their shareholders. But banks' shares—at least of the ten largest U.S. banks—are owned mainly by financial institutions, including pension funds, mutual funds, etc. Those institutions also hold many savings and retirement accounts of individuals and households; so the part of their accounts that included bank shares would be wiped out altogether. This would be devastating to the individuals and households who had put their 401(k) and other accounts into the institutions concerned. Hence it would be politically unacceptable to Congress and most other elected officials.

Temporary Nationalization of Some Big Banks
Simon Johnson, former chief economist for the International Monetary Fund (IMF) and now at the Massachusetts Institute of Technology, argues for temporary nationalization of some of America's largest banks.[3] As of 2008, the ten largest banks in the United States in terms of total assets held about two-thirds of the total assets of all 8,451 Federal Deposit Insurance Corporation–covered institutions, and the four largest banks held over half of all those assets. Many of these big banks have been receiving huge infusions of taxpayer dollars to keep them operating.

In nations where the IMF has helped restructure the banking system, Johnson thinks the basic problem was a political coalition of the biggest banks and the national government. He calls it the "financial oligarchy." Bankers did not want to give up their equity and lose management control, even if their banks were in fact insolvent. Bankers kept stalling and seeking more government support. The financially unstable governments involved would not tackle those politically powerful executives until the IMF required them to do so in order to qualify for IMF funding.

A comparable situation now exists in the United States, even though it is a much richer nation than most IMF client states. Johnson suggests temporarily nationalizing some of the big American banks. That means firing their top management, eliminating shareholder interests, and transferring toxic assets to a federally mandated "bad bank" similar to the Resolution Trust Corporation established during the savings and loan crisis. Then private investors could put capital into those banks, and the healthy banks could be reprivatized. Johnson also believes the largest banks should be broken up so that no banks are "too big to fail," a view that I share.

Until now, the political and economic strength of America's financial oligarchy—aided by well-funded lobbyists and highly placed government officials—has successfully blocked even temporary nationalization of big banks. Former members of the financial elite now lead the U.S. Treasury and serve as economic advisers in the White House. Because the United States does not seek aid from the IMF, the IMF cannot threaten to withhold aid in order to cause big banks to reform. U.S. elected leaders—the president and Congress—must buck the political power of the financial oligarchy by halting big banks' strategy to extract billions of American taxpayer dollars without resuming lending. As long the government regards any banks as too big to fail and those banks refuse to start lending again, we will not get out of the current lending freeze, and the recession will likely get worse.

Providing Financial Capital by Investing in Troubled Banks
One of the first tactics that the Federal Reserve and the Treasury tried was investing federal funds into troubled banks in order to increase their supplies of nontoxic capital. This was done

by having the banks sell the federal government preferred stock with significant dividend rates. But this tactic in itself did not get rid of the toxic assets in those banks. Moreover, the worse off a bank was, the more capital the federal government had to invest in it to keep it going. After a while, the federal share of the bank's total equity value became close to a controlling interest in the bank's equity structure. This nearly happened in the case of the CitiGroup Bank when the federal stake in its ownership reached about 40 percent in February 2009. Hence this tactic did not really solve the basic problem, which was getting enough toxic assets off a bank's balance sheet so that the bank would have enough good quality capital to begin lending again. At the limit, this became almost a form of nationalizing the banks concerned.

Letting the Banks Take Care of Themselves—Even If They Fail

Many conservative economists believe that banks in trouble ought to take care of their own problems, even if that causes them to become insolvent and fail. After all, it is supposed to be a free enterprise system in which you can either win big or lose big. The banks in big trouble got that way because of their own foolish and greedy decision-making and behavior. So if they fail, let them fail. Let their stockholders get wiped out—as many of them have already been. The largest bank in the nation—Citigroup—has already had a 95 percent fall in its common stock price since mid-2007.

However, if the ten largest U.S. banks, which so far have suffered the biggest stock value losses, all failed, that would wipe out almost two-thirds of all the assets held by all the commercial banks and savings and loans in the United States. Most of the stock of those banks is held by financial institutions rather than individuals, though those institutions hold many individual investment accounts. As noted above, millions of those accounts were owned by individual investors who had put their 401(k) savings into such banks or into other financial institutions that owned stock in the biggest banks. Even just the four largest banks hold over half of all U.S. bank assets. If all those assets were wiped out, who would be left to restore credit in the American economy? And how would individual owners of 401(k) money in those bankrupted banks ever recover any of their life savings when the economy recovered in the future? Even though many American and foreign investors might eventually step forward to buy new stock in those banks, that would not happen very fast. Meanwhile, the credit freeze would continue and the nation's economy would plunge deeper into recession. That is not a prospect that thrills many. And the destruction of all those individual savings vehicles holding stock in the bankrupted banks makes this approach politically unacceptable to Congress and the president.

What Strategies to Use in Reviving the Banking System

In my opinion, temporary nationalization of some of the largest banks or some version of the federal government's offer to take toxic assets off their balance sheets would probably be the best course of action. Nationalizing and breaking up the biggest banks has the advantage of neutralizing the political power of Wall Street's financial oligarchy to continue absorbing taxpayer dollars without improving their lending behavior. We must do something rapidly to prevent the credit freeze from driving the U.S. economy even deeper into recession.

A Shrinking Financial Sector

At the outset of chapter 5, I pointed out that the financial sector of the U.S. economy had grown steadily until it became the largest single sector in the U.S. GDP. Moreover, a high share of all business profits was being earned in the financial sector, even though it generated only about 21 percent of real GDP. The flood of financial capital into that sector from 2000 to 2007 further expanded its size and influence in the overall economy.

However, the events of 2007–09 have revealed that the financial sector expanded too far. It did so by feasting on a seemingly inexhaustible supply of low-cost debt, provided by capital sources both within and outside the United States. Too many firms and households borrowed too much money in relation to the resources they themselves contributed to their own activities.

When it came time for borrowers to repay much of their debt, much of the financial system was stretched beyond its means of repayment. Hence it froze into a standoff between capital suppliers and capital users. Transaction activity virtually vanished within less than a year. One of the long-range actions necessary to return financial activity to more normal levels will be shrinking the overall size of the financial sector—in particular, the total amount of debt generated through too much borrowing. So a massive process of deleveraging has been launched throughout the sector all over the world. Deleveraging is merely a sophisticated name for repaying debt and thereby reducing the amount of debt in the system in relation to the amount of equity.

This shrinkage process has taken several forms. One is the bankruptcy of many financial institutions, such as Lehman Brothers and other investment banks, commercial banks, and mortgage lending and origination firms. Another form is the consolidation of many firms through takeovers aimed at avoiding outright bankruptcies, such as the acquisition of Merrill Lynch by Bank of America and of Wachovia by Wells Fargo. In those takeovers, many employees are discharged and many bad assets are written off. Another is the seizure of private financial firms by the federal government, such as Fannie Mae and Freddie Mac.

Another form of shrinkage is reducing the amount of debt carried by financial firms, especially commercial banks—both absolutely and relative to their equity. In fact, many banks have decided they have too many real estate–related assets and they want to cut back severely on such holdings. Insofar as they can, those firms are paying down debts, selling assets, floating more equity to outside investors, creating preferred equity shares and selling them to investors, and so on. Writing off bad loans as losses is another version of this form of shrinkage, and it has accounted for a large-scale disappearance of financial capital from the entire sector.

A shrinking financial sector necessarily means a reduction in the total amount of financial capital in that sector available to finance the nation's future activities of all types—including real estate. Another implication of this analysis is that upward pressures on stock prices—and the prices of real estate and other tradable assets—will be weaker in the next decade than they were in either the 1990s or the 2000s. The fantastic bull stock market of the 1990s—even including the crash in 2000 to 2002—is not likely to repeat itself in the 2010s or perhaps even in the 2020s, though that is too far away for any reliable forecasting.

There will be only two major offsetting factors to this reduction in upward pressures on asset prices. One will be the continued economic growth of the less developed portions of the world. At first, continued low wages of more rural workers there being drawn into urban areas and into modern production activities will keep world prices from rising much. But the high saving rates in those societies—which will gradually decline as they become more consumer-oriented—will still generate funds that will be available for investment outside their borders.

Eventually, as developing nations draw most of their poor rural workers into urban areas where productivity is higher, real wages will begin to rise in those nations and their savings will become more focused on their own domestic investments. Then, as Greenspan noted in *The Age of Turbulence*, inflationary pressures are likely to rise around the entire world, because neither the gold standard nor low foreign wages will still hold down the world's price structures. That may result in another huge future expansion of America's financial sector and similar sectors in other nations.

The second factor likely to influence the future of the financial sector will be an increased role of federal funds in providing credit, to make up for the shrinkage of private debt and private lending. The federal government has already stepped up its role in the financial sector by providing federal funds to back all types of credit guarantees, ranging from temporarily insuring the safety of bank accounts to new high levels ($250,000 for single-person accounts) to providing direct federal capital infusions to many key banks in the financial system. The government is motivated to expand its credit-enhancing role not only by the need to shrink private debt, as discussed above, but also by the need to offset the economy's entry into a major economic recession in 2008 and 2009. To counteract the decline in employment, which fell by more than 2.7 million jobs in 2008, the Obama Administration launched a large-scale program of infrastructure construction and repair across the entire nation in early 2009. This antirecession goal has greatly expanded what the federal government will try to do in response to the credit crunch and the worsening recession. As a result, a major restructuring of the financial system was well underway in 2008 and 2009, with the U.S. government becoming a newly dominant and active part of that system. It is too early even to estimate the extent to which increased federal involvement and spending will offset the shrinkage of the private financial sector in the next few years.

However, I believe that in the near future America will be influenced more by net financial sector shrinkage than by inflationary pressures, unless the rescue efforts described in the next chapter generate too much government spending. In the long run, the United States needs to reduce consumption to what Americans can pay for without borrowing from abroad, to raise federal revenues to meet expanding retirement and health care entitlement costs, to increase savings by both households and the federal government, and to increase infrastructure spending to cut petroleum costs and maintain our mobility. Yet in the short run, the government is trying to stimulate more consumption to help offset the drop in activity throughout the economy by launching many large federal spending programs. Reconciling those directly conflicting needs will challenge political leaders, because the vast majority of Americans today have no idea of what economic pressures will soon be placed on them by meeting those needs—though they are beginning to grasp the difficulties facing them. Nor do most Americans have much desire to confront such realities.

One thing that helped cause the credit crunch is a lack of effective political leadership concerning the costs incurred by Americans during this decade as the obverse of their big increases in housing and other consumption. Political leaders in both parties, Congress, and the White House kept saying the economy was strong and in great shape right until the last minute before the financial meltdown in September and October 2008. As M.I.T. economist Simon Johnson humorously put it at a Brookings Institution seminar in early October 2008:

Talk about lack of transparency! America's political leaders kept telling us we were in strong economic shape until one September morning Secretary of Treasury Henry Paulson showed up at the doors of Congress. He handed them a three-page note asking them to put $700 billion in a paper bag in small unmarked bills, to be turned over to him with no strings attached, or else the entire nation would almost immediately have an economic catastrophe!

True, the action Paulson requested was an act of political leadership. But as the nation moves toward the full retirement of the baby boom generation and all that means for federal outlays for Social Security, Medicare, and Medicaid, most political leaders are again ignoring the realities that the nation must face in the next decade. However, President Barack Obama seems to be aware of the immense challenges confronting us and is willing to talk about them openly—at least some of the time. Let us hope that he and our other new political and economic leaders will be more farsighted and more willing to discuss hard realities with the people than were our former federal and private officials during this financial crisis.

Redirecting Key Housing Policies

One of the possible causes contributing to the tremendous upward surge in home prices after 2000 was the federal government's longstanding policy of encouraging maximum amounts of homeownership among American households but providing much less help to renters. This biased policy had at least three components:

- The large-scale federal tax benefits of homeownership are not available in any form to renters. The most important such benefits are the deductibility of interest payments on one's home and second home from federally taxable income, the deductibility of property tax payments on one's home and second home from federally taxable income, and the exclusion of the benefits of occupying one's home rent-free from any federal tax liability (in contrast to the taxes a landlord must pay on income earned from renting a home to others).

  The interest deductibility benefit is heavily skewed toward high-income homeowners. Every dollar of tax deduction provided them with larger tax savings than the same number of dollars deducted by someone in a lower income tax bracket. The Urban Institute stated

The President's Advisory Panel on Federal Tax Reform (2005) divided tax return filers into six income groups and showed the average value of the [mortgage interest] deduction for each group. Those in the highest income group—individuals making more than $200,000 per year—received more than eight times the benefit as those in the third income group—people making between $50,000 and $75,000 per year.[4]

- Promoting homeownership through public pronouncements favoring "an ownership society," made by President Bush and many other federal officials, all praising the American dream of owning one's own home as vastly superior to renting. This behavior helped persuade many renter households that they should buy a home by whatever means possible, even if their resources were very limited.
- Providing much smaller federal expenditures to aid renter households than those for owner-occupant households (including tax losses from homeowner tax benefits as federal expenditures). The difference in magnitude between these sources of assistance to households is much larger than their relative proportion among all households (just about two-thirds are homeowners and just about one-third are renters).

These heavily promoted benefits of homeownership—both absolute and relative to renting—are further emphasized to the public by many private firms that gain from households becoming homeowners. These firms include homebuilders, Realtors, mortgage bankers, commercial bankers, Fannie Mae and Freddie Mac, some investment banks engaged in mortgage lending, and insurance companies that sell homeowners policies. Promotional efforts by all these firms continuously strengthen the concept of the American dream of homeownership in the minds of millions of Americans.

One way in which the federal government could more fairly distribute its aid to housing occupants would be to change the present mortgage interest deduction to a tax credit. Then each dollar of interest deducted from taxable income would provide the same tax benefit to a taxpayer, regardless of his or her total income. At present, taxpayers in high income brackets get much larger tax benefits per dollar of interest deducted than taxpayers in lower brackets who deduct the same dollar amount of interest. True, a tax credit arrangement would still favor wealthier households. They typically have larger homes and thus larger mortgages, so their savings would still be greater per household—but far smaller than they are now.

This policy suggestion has been made repeatedly by federal tax advisory and housing advisory committees for many decades. But it is vehemently opposed by real estate agents, homebuilders, mortgage brokers, construction unions, many homeowners, and other interest groups that benefit from building or selling the most expensive housing they can. Surprisingly, President Obama's new federal budget announced in February 2009 included a form of this policy as a means of providing fairer treatment of the tax system to homeowners with different incomes. Since I have been advocating using a homeowners' tax credit instead of a tax deduction for over 30 years, I applaud this suggestion. Even so, I doubt that Congress will adopt this provision in view of the extensive opposition to it.

I believe it is proper and legitimate for the federal government to promote homeownership to some extent, because homeowners as a group exhibit some important qualities of citizenship not exhibited as fully by renters. But the extent to which homeownership has been extolled over renting during the past two decades has been far out of proportion to the true relative superiority of homeownership. Moreover, most poor households—the ones who need economic assistance the most—are renters, not owners. Therefore, I believe the federal government should strive to strike a more even balance between aiding renters and aiding homeowners—both financially, in its promotional efforts, and in its recognition of the importance of both groups to the nation's welfare.

Another established public policy that benefits homeowners more than renters is the use of local zoning powers to exclude low-income housing, especially rental apartments, from most suburban local communities. This policy comes from local governments, not the federal government, but the federal government has not done much to offset it. Because local elected officials have to respond to strong pressure from a majority of their constituents in order to be reelected, those officials often adopt regulations that prohibit or restrict low-cost housing. I believe this is the single most important reason why so little low-cost housing is built in the United States and why not much will ever be built as long as such local opposition remains strong.

The federal government cannot directly change local housing-related ordinances, but it could adopt incentives for state and local governments to oppose exclusionary zoning. In theory, the federal government could make the receipt of some of its financial aid to states and localities contingent upon their conducting intensive reviews of their housing laws and eliminating those that prevent the construction of low-cost or rental housing, or the conversion of other housing or structures to low-cost or rental units. At present, very few states require local governments to conduct such reviews or make such changes in their housing-related ordinances. But if state receipt of federal transportation aid or community development block grants or educational assistance were contingent upon states requiring localities to conduct such reviews and follow up on them, that might cause a notable reduction in exclusionary zoning and other exclusionary laws.

Local resistance to the creation of lower-cost ownership or all rental housing within most suburbs is one reason that so many renter households had to stretch their financial resources to the limit—and often beyond it—to buy homes for themselves. Until more low-cost ownership housing and rental housing is available to low-income households, they will continue to feel pressure to stretch their resources to gain the benefits of homeownership. That situation makes them vulnerable to pressure from mortgage brokers and real estate agents to buy homes they really cannot afford—a key factor in the subprime mortgage difficulties that helped precipitate the financial crisis.

The Need for a Global Approach

The underlying cause of the global financial crisis involved both one set of nations that borrowed and spent too much money—including the United States—and another set of nations that ran large trade surpluses and saved too much money rather than spending it on their own economies—such as China, Saudi Arabia, and many others. The second set of nations provided massive amounts of capital to the first set of nations that were crucial to generating the financial crisis gripping the world in 2008 and 2009. Preventing any repetition of such global financial crises requires changing the past behavior of both types of nations, not just of the excessive borrowers and spenders. That in turn requires getting many nations to agree upon some set of policies concerning how to handle international trade and capital flows among nations.

Although many of the most important nations involved in these processes have met together in a few short gatherings, there has been no widespread formulation or agreement on what specific international trade and capital flow regulations should be adopted across the globe. I am not expert enough concerning this subject to formulate such rules, but I am convinced doing so should be an integral part of future policies by the United States and other nations if we are to avoid future repetitions of this crisis.

Considering Financial Policy Options

The recommendations made in this chapter constitute a huge menu of suggested changes to the way that American financial markets are now regulated and operated. In order to give full consideration to these suggestions, it would be necessary for Congress to hold public hearings on them so that the trade organizations and firms in the financial sector would have chances to express their views. If this were done, it would take many months and even years of deliberation and intense political wrangling before most of the changes suggested here could even be reasonably considered, let alone adopted. That is because the policies proposed would constitute a complete reorganization and reregulation of the U.S. financial sector.

Hence the probability that all or even most of these recommendations will be seriously considered must be regarded as quite low. Too many organizations of all types would have to give up some of their long-established policy turf, or even be abolished and replaced, to expect this process to result in the major overhaul that the financial sector clearly needs. Nevertheless, the seriousness of the financial difficulties that have been generated for the entire nation by the credit crunch make it necessary for objective observers to lay out a complete menu of changes that ought to be made in the currently unstable U.S. financial markets, as I have tried to do.

Many participants in U.S. financial markets will object to some or all of these policy recommendations. Those objectors will claim that the recommendations limit the freedom of private persons and firms to carry out whatever financial transactions they believe are in their own best interest. This claim is certainly correct. In fact, limiting such freedom is precisely the intention of most of the recommendations in this book. Any reasonable observer of the behavior of financial markets from 2000 onward must agree that allowing financial market participants to do whatever they want has been an unsuccessful—even disastrous—strategy. That strategy of extreme deregulation resulted in outcomes that were terribly harmful to the markets themselves and to millions of people, households, and firms affected by them. In light of what has happened in financial markets from 2006 through 2009, only a complete fool or an anarchist could conclude that it would be socially undesirable to limit individual freedom of action in those markets through better regulations.

A more subtle attack on these recommendations would be to claim that their enactment would greatly reduce the efficiency of financial market operations under normal conditions. Opponents of these recommendations could argue that, yes, some bad behaviors took place in those markets from 2000 to 2008. But those behaviors are just the price that society must pay for enjoying what—most of the time—is the most innovative and efficient financial market system in the world. My answer to that argument was set forth in chapter 5, on why U.S. financial markets are inherently unstable. Allowing an inherently unstable system to operate without conscious attempts to counteract or offset its instabilities seems socially irresponsible. I believe this is especially the case in light of the millions of households who have suffered from housing foreclosures; financial losses; the insolvencies of mortgage bankers, investment banks, and commercial banks; and a large decline in financial and other stock prices. Even the major federal financial regulators themselves, such as the chairman of the Federal Reserve Board and the secretary of the Treasury, stated near the beginning of the credit crunch that the overall financial system did not need much more stringent regulation, only a rearrangement of the regulatory agencies that now exist. However, they seem to have changed their minds since then, judging from their more recent aggressive and extensive actions and recommendations seeking to alter both the past and present behavior of the financial sector. Certainly the financial system should not be subjected to regulations so stringent that all its innovative and flexible capacities would be destroyed. But neither can its present, totally permissive attitudes toward flagrant excesses and even fraud be tolerated without major changes. That is why I have set forth the often controversial recommendations presented in this chapter.

Nonetheless, I do not believe these recommendations are sacrosanct. On the contrary, I believe all should be reviewed by both public and private authorities in financial markets and perhaps substantially modified or even rejected for good reasons. But not to consider them seriously would be a serious mistake that would perpetuate the perverse incentives that arose during the financial crisis of 2007–09 and would increase the probability of similar disasters occurring in the future.

NOTES

1. Paul Krugman, *The Return of Depression Economics and the Crisis of 2008* (New York: W.W. Norton, 2009).
2. Staff of the Office of Compliance Inspections and Examinations, Division of Trading and Markets, and Office of Economic Analysis of the United States Securities and Exchange Commission, "Summary Report of Issues Identified in the Commission Staff's Examinations of Select Credit Rating Agencies," July 2008, p. 18.
3. Simon Johnson, "The Quiet Coup," *The Atlantic*, May 2009, on the Internet at http://www.theatlantic.com/doc/200905/imf-advice.
4. William G. Gale, Jonathan Gruber, and Seth Stevens-Davidowitz, "Encouraging Homeownership Through the Tax Code," *Tax Notes*, June 18, 2007, page 1178.

Critical Near-Term Financial Questions and Scenarios

THE MOST DIFFICULT QUESTIONS concerning the financial crisis in real estate and finance are, how bad will it get, how long will it last, how will it end, and what will happen next? This chapter tackles those issues by developing several scenarios involving different possible answers. Before describing those scenarios, it is necessary to place the task of ending the financial crisis in the context of even larger forces affecting the American economy and society.

Basic Problems: Savings, Consumption, and Deficits

The U.S. economy is facing several critical long-run challenges that will influence how long the current financial crisis will last and how the nation might recover from it. The most fundamental challenge is that, for at least a full decade, the American people have been consuming far more than they have been producing or saving. They are financing that excess consumption by both borrowing from abroad and running large fiscal deficits in the federal government. This behavior has led to massive foreign account deficits on top of major federal budget deficits. The impact of this imbalance is going to be aggravated in the next decade by rising federal expenditures for both Social Security and health care as the baby boom generation retires from active employment.

Unfortunately, American political leaders have shown little willingness to confront either the nation's current fiscal imbalance or the much larger imbalances lurking not far down the road. Neither candidate in the 2008 presidential race even indicated much awareness of the dire fiscal challenges facing the nation. Both promised either to cut taxes or to spend more without describing how they would pay for the resulting greater federal deficits. Neither seriously discussed the even greater fiscal deficits that all economists are foreseeing for the next decade and longer. President Obama has shown more awareness of these issues since being elected, but no clear strategy has emerged for dealing with them.

From 1946 to 1985, personal consumption constituted an average of 62.8 percent of real GDP. But that average rose to 66.7 percent from 1986 to 2000 and to 70.3 percent from 2001 to 2007, reaching a high of 71.6 percent in 2007. In contrast, net exports of goods and services (exports minus imports) fell from an average of 0.3 percent of GDP from 1946 to 1985 to –1.8 percent of GDP from 1986 to 2000 and to –5.1 percent from 2001 to 2007. Thus, 91.7 percent of the rise in personal consumption spending from 2001 to 2007 consisted of greater net imports of goods and services, thereby contributing to our rising balance-of-payments deficit. Clearly, Americans have been consuming more than they produced themselves and paying for this behavior by borrowing from foreigners. In 2007, our balance-of-payments deficit was 6.7 percent of GDP.

One reason for this outcome has been the low levels of savings by American households compared with households in some of the nations that are running trade surpluses with the United States. According to the Bureau of Economic Analysis in the U.S. Department of Commerce, personal savings as a percentage of American personal disposable income fell to 0.4 percent in 2005, 0.7 percent in 2006, and 0.6 percent in 2007. The Department of Commerce does not consider increases in home equity among private households as savings. Yet most American households definitely count such equity gains as their own savings. During the housing price run-up from 2000 to 2006, millions of them drew on their gains in home equity to finance additional personal consumption, often unrelated to housing. That was a key factor driving personal consumption spending to postwar record-high percentages of GDP.

However, this excessive spending on consumption has been drastically changed by the financial crisis and the onset of a serious recession in America in 2008. Most American households can no longer draw cash out of the excess equity in their homes because the market value of those homes has been falling across much of the nation. Furthermore, Americans had already borrowed heavily against their homes, through taking out either mortgages at high ratios to the purchase prices of homes or home equity loans after the homes were purchased. Moreover, according to the Bureau of Labor Statistics, over 2.7 million Americans employed in December 2007, at the beginning of the current recession, had lost their jobs as the unemployment rate rose to 7.2 percent in December 2008. This decline in jobs reduced the ability of several million American households to continue high-level consumption.

Finally, the stock market declined sharply in value during 2008. That both eliminated a large share of the financial assets accumulated by American households and cut into the pension funds previously saved by both individual households and in corporate and other pension plans. From January 2 to December 5, 2008, the Dow Jones Industrial Average fell 33.8 percent and the S&P 500 index declined 39.36 percent. This wiped out trillions of dollars of wealth in the United States and around the world.

In contrast, savings rates are very high in many Asian nations that now run big surpluses in trade with the United States. China provides a striking example. A main reason why Chinese citizens and firms save so much is that the Chinese government does not provide any significant safety nets for its population comparable to Social Security or Medicare and Medicaid. Therefore, Chinese households have to provide for their own old-age incomes and health care by setting aside savings from their current incomes. In 2005, China's national savings rate—including savings by business firms—was 47 percent of income and its household savings rate was 25 percent of household income, according to an article recently published by the Federal Reserve Bank of St. Louis.[1]

These high rates of savings generate a saving surplus in China, which most savers deposit in Chinese banks that are run by the government. Then the government draws upon those savings to finance export surpluses to the United States. That enables Chinese firms to create more jobs for millions of poor Chinese peasants moving to big cities—a critical policy objective of China's communist government. That government needs to provide means for millions of poor peasants to improve their living standards by moving from impoverished rural areas into higher-paying industrial jobs. If that effort fails, the Chinese government faces the likely prospect of many thousands of protests in both its big cities and its rural areas. Similarly, Indian households save about 22 percent of their disposable incomes, according to a McKinsey consulting analysis. The resulting surpluses of savings in these and other Asian nations creates pressures on their governments to keep running export-based trade surpluses with the United States. But Americans can do little to change the saving behavior of Asians. Instead, they need to change their own saving behavior to reduce the trade and fiscal deficits the United States is now experiencing.

The sharp decline in American household spending on consumption during 2008 caused by falling home prices and rising unemployment has been a major contributor to the onset of the recession across the nation. Sales reported by retailers have declined markedly compared with levels one year earlier, causing many retail firms to lay off more workers or reduce their normal Christmas season hiring. Firms supplying consumer goods, including automobiles, have also had major declines in sales, falling profits, and shrinking labor forces. Thus, the downward spiral in financial activity has led directly to a matching downward spiral in economic production generally.

This situation has motivated federal government officials to focus on increasing American household consumption and employment in order to slow down the recession's negative impacts on the economy. Thus a direct conflict has emerged between the long-run need to reduce American consumption below its excessive levels through 1997 and the short-run need to increase America's currently declining consumption to stop the recession from worsening. One compromise approach is to create a federally financed investment program in infrastructure improvements to provide large numbers of jobs to presently unemployed workers, who would then have enough income to maintain reasonable consumption levels. This is an element of President Obama's program to combat the recession. And there is little doubt that any elected president would consider stopping the declining activity caused by the current recession as the nation's top priority, compared with reducing consumption levels to solve longer-range problems. Nevertheless, the need to reduce consumption below its mid-2000s levels remains an important goal over the longer run.

These observations are relevant to how long the present financial crisis will last. Future national policy should not only restore confidence to investors about property values but also help reverse the U.S. trend toward ever-rising trade deficits and fiscal deficits. Therefore, just having the federal government spend more money to stabilize financial markets would be unwise, because it would aggravate already large federal deficit spending. Instead, government policy toward the financial crisis should be designed to contribute to reducing both trade and fiscal deficits, rather than either sustaining or increasing them. Such deficit reduction would have to involve

- Lower rates of consumption among American households,
- Greater incentives for savings by both households and the federal government, and
- Greater investment in improving American infrastructure.

These elements combined would amount to a significant reduction in living standards for a majority of Americans for at least several years. The last element is necessary both because U.S.

infrastructure is now being underfinanced and because cutting personal consumption would reduce the nation's overall growth rates unless doing so was offset by greater investment. But it is extremely difficult—if even possible—to devise policies that would simultaneously cut consumption, cut government spending, raise savings, and increase domestic investment. This is especially true in the current American political environment of vehement popular resistance to having households bear any more costs than they are now encountering, even to pay for benefits they want to enjoy—such as Social Security, health care aid, and improved infrastructure.

Critical Economic and Financial Questions

The financial crisis has now affected so many parts of the American economy that how it will play out in the future will be affected by numerous specific factors. These include the following:

- How far and how fast will American home prices fall in the future?
- What will happen to the large inventory of homes for sale, which creates downward pressure on home prices?
- Regarding the current recession, which began in late 2007, how bad will it be, how long will it last, and how much unemployment will it generate?
- How much will economies outside the United States continue to grow in the near future? The stronger their growth, the more they will stimulate U.S. economic growth through greater demands for goods and services produced in the United States.
- How much new housing production will there be in each of the next few years?
- How fast will the confidence of investors and lenders concerning what real properties and real estate securities are actually worth be restored? How will that restoration of confidence be accomplished?
- How long will the current market standoff last between capital suppliers—who want higher yields—and property owners and borrowers—who do not want to pay higher interest rates or accept lower prices?
- What policies designed to end the financial crisis will the federal government and private firms adopt? How well will those policies work?
- How effective will so-called bailout bills be in both enabling and motivating the nation's banks to resume something like normal lending so as to permit future economic growth?

No one has a crystal ball clear enough to answer all those questions decisively and accurately. Therefore, it would not be wise to describe a single course of events as most likely to occur. A more prudent approach is to describe several scenarios showing how different possible courses of action might play out. But even to do that, it is first necessary to discuss the key factors named above in detail to understand their implications for the future of the financial crisis.

Economic Stability

According to the Bureau of Economic Analysis, real GDP increased 3.3 percent in the second quarter of 2008, after increasing only 0.9 percent in the first quarter. Then it fell 0.3 percent in the third quarter. In 2008 as a whole, real GDP increased by only 1.1 percent. In 2007 real

GDP grew 2.0 percent, down from 2.8 percent in 2006, 2.9 percent in 2005, and 3.6 percent in 2004. So the economy has been on a gradually slowing track, pointing to a significant decline in real GDP in 2009. The National Bureau of Economic Research, which normally defines the timing of economic recessions, declared in late 2008 that the U.S. economy has been in a recession since the last quarter of 2007. What happens to real GDP is important for other key variables affecting the financial crisis. It is especially crucial for employment, which directly affects consumer incomes, consumption spending, and the demand for housing. When real GDP stays out of negative territory, jobs do not decline as much as they would if a recession occurs. (A recession is usually defined as two consecutive quarters of negative real GDP.) Except for five months in mid-2003, the national unemployment rate was at or below 6.0 percent from 1994 until October 2008, when it reached 6.5 percent—that is, for 13 years not counting 2008. It was below 5 percent in six of the 11 years from 1998 through 2008. Total nonfarm employment increased by an annual average of 2.162 million jobs in the ten years from 1990 to 2000, but by an average of only 832,000 jobs per year from 2001 to 2007. Total employment declined in both 2002 and 2003, even though real GDP increased slightly in both years. In all of 2008, nonfarm payroll employment fell by 2.6 million, according to the Bureau of Labor Statistics. This raised the unemployment rate to 7.2 percent in December 2008.

In the 64 years since 1944, the U.S. economy has experienced three notable downturns: a three-year recession right after World War II in 1945–47, a two-year recession in 1974–75, and two years of recessionary conditions in 1980 and 1982 (but not 1981). Exhibit 8-1 shows all those recessions except the postwar one. Since 1982, the United States has experienced only one year of negative real GDP growth. That was in 1991, when real GDP fell by 0.2 percent, partly owing to the real estate market collapse in 1990. Aside from that small setback, the U.S. economy has grown steadily from 1983 to 2007—a period of 23 years (excluding 1991)—at an average annual gain of 3.54 percent in real GDP.

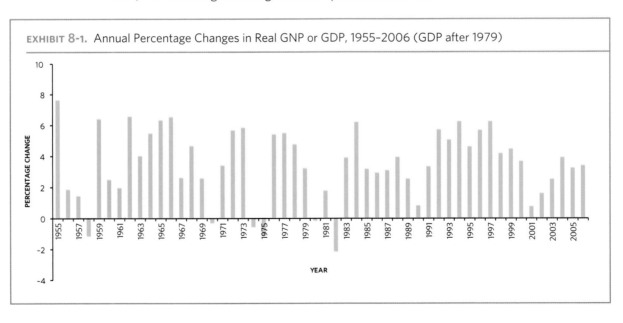

EXHIBIT 8-1. Annual Percentage Changes in Real GNP or GDP, 1955–2006 (GDP after 1979)

Five factors have strongly contributed to the recession of 2008-09:

- The world price of petroleum rose more than 100 percent from 2005 to mid-2008 and more than 339 percent since 2003, and this rapid increase contributed greatly to the economic slowdown that ensued. Although oil prices have moved down sharply from their recent peak, which will help the economy going forward, there are no signs that they will stay down in the long run. It is true that in a worldwide recession, which is now well underway, demand for oil will fall and therefore oil prices will fall too. But once world prosperity reappears, oil prices are likely to move upward again.

- Excesses in the U.S. homebuilding and home mortgage sectors—and the subsequent homebuilding recession that began in 2006—are principal reasons behind the current world recession. Homebuilding is not likely to return to prosperous levels of activity until the large inventory of existing homes for sale is worked off. But foreclosures are likely to rise in late 2008 and well into 2009 because of resetting interest rates among subprime mortgage holders. Therefore, housing starts will remain low in 2009 and may start to recover slowly only in 2010. Yet housing has long been a key factor in starting economic recoveries from U.S. recessions.

- The federal government is facing record deficits in 2008 and will probably have larger ones in 2009. This will inhibit federal spending as a force large enough to reverse a recession rapidly.

- The finance industry—the largest sector in the U.S. economy—was in a dire condition as of early 2009. It will not rapidly recover without new sources of capital and time to heal. Although there is still a lot of capital in the world looking for someplace sound to invest, its owners will probably not be in a hurry to invest in the U.S. financial sector, given its recent adverse experiences.

- Prices of commodities other than oil have been rising because of increased demand from developing nations, especially China and India, though that has started declining again in late 2008. These high prices were contributing factors to economic slowing. The growth rates in China and India are slowing as the world moves toward recession, but they will expand again when prosperity returns. That means their commodity needs will remain high in the long run. Their competition for resources drives up prices that U.S. firms and households must pay for those resources.

Whatever happens to the U.S. economy, another important question is, how fast will other economies around the world grow during the next five years or so? The faster they grow, the less serious a U.S. recession is likely to be, because its negative impacts would be partly offset by expansion in other nations. Until very recently, most economists thought that both the European Union and Asian developing nations would continue expanding faster than the U.S. economy, as has been occurring in the past few years. The IMF estimates of annual real GDP growth rates for selected nations are shown in exhibit 8-2. All the other nations shown (other than Japan) had faster real GDP growth rates in 2007 than the United States, and the other two Asian nations grew much faster. In fact, the same is true for the average growth rates of those nations from 1999 to 2009, which incorporate the IMF estimates for 2008 and 2009.

Widespread signs of slowing growth in early 2009, both in Europe and among Asian developing nations, seem to have weakened the amount of help that the U.S. economy can expect

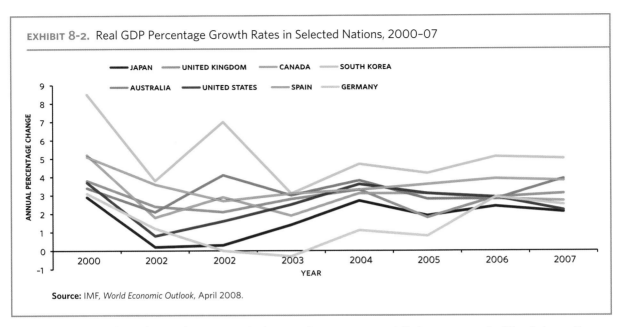

EXHIBIT 8-2. Real GDP Percentage Growth Rates in Selected Nations, 2000–07

Source: IMF, *World Economic Outlook,* April 2008.

from these other nations in the next few years, especially because most of the Asian nations shown have much smaller GDPs than does the United States. Even so, it is likely that the growth of other major nations—especially emerging nations—will remain faster than growth within the United States. That should offset some of the negative impacts of a recession on the recovery from the financial crisis, especially through expanding exports.

Housing Stabilization

Several key issues in the housing industry must play out and be resolved before the financial crisis can end. These relate to when and at what level home prices stabilize, when home foreclosures and home inventories are reduced, and when the homebuilding industry ultimately stabilizes and begins to recover.

Home Prices in the Near Future

Just how far will the national median home prices decline in the future, and when will they stabilize? Many housing experts believe this is a critical factor that will influence how long the financial crisis in general will last. I have adopted several approaches to grappling with this question.

Past Examples of Regional Declines in Home Prices. The national median price of single-family homes, as tracked by the NAR since 1968, never declined year to year until 2006. Its first decline was from 2006 to 2007, a fall of 1.31 percent. However, during that same 38-year period, home prices fell sharply within different regions of the United States when negative conditions prevailed there. For example, in Houston, Texas, when oil prices collapsed in the mid-1980s, the oil-based state economy was hit hard by a general recession. As a result, almost every major bank and savings and loan in the state went bankrupt in the 1980s. That drastically restricted the supply of mortgage funds for housing markets. Median prices of single-family homes in the Houston metropolitan area had been rising in the early 1980s but peaked in 1983 at $79,900. They stayed close to that level until 1985, then began falling to their lowest level of the decade—$61,800—in 1988. That was a drop of 22.7 percent from their 1983 peak, but it took five years for that drop to occur. Subsequently, the median price of housing in the Houston area did not recover to its 1983 peak until 1992—nine years later.

Similarly, in Southern California, the regional recession of the early 1990s caused a significant fall in home prices. Median single-family home prices for California as a whole declined by 11.3 percent from 1991 to 1996. However, Southern California was hit harder by that recession than the state as a whole. The median price of existing single-family homes sold in Los Angeles County—by far the most populous county in the state—fell from $218,520 in 1991 to $172,886 in 1996, a decline of 20.9 percent. It took five years for the median price in Los Angeles County to decline from its peak in 1991 to its low point in 1996. Then it took another five years for that median price to regain and surpass its 1991 level. The other main Southern California counties also had notable home price declines in the same period, but they were smaller than those in Los Angeles County.[2]

During the 23 years from 1977 through 2000, the ratio of national median home prices to national median household income (both in current dollars) varied within a narrow range from a low of 3.16 to 1 to a high of 3.57 to 1, averaging 3.27 to 1. So movements in home prices were closely related to movements in household incomes. Then after 2000, median housing prices started increasing much faster than household incomes. By 2006, the national median home price was 4.79 times as high as national median household income. In 2006, the national median price of housing measured by the NAR was $221,900, the highest in history to that time. In order for the ratio of median housing price to median household income to return to about 3.2 to 1 (if median incomes did not increase), the median housing price would have had to fall to $154,200—a drop of 30.48 percent. If median incomes rose just 2 percent per year—half their increase from 2005 to 2006—then by 2008, the median income would be $50,148 in current dollars. At that point, housing prices would have to have fallen by 27.7 percent from their 2006 level to create a ratio of 3.20 to 1. I believe that about 30 percent is an outer limit for how much national home prices will fall as a result of this financial crisis, unless the U.S. economy falls into an unusually deep recession. However, home price declines will be much larger in a few specific regions, especially those where median home prices rose the most from 2000 to 2006 and those where the percentage of homes being sold because of foreclosures is much higher than the national average.

The Unique Character of Home Price Movements since 2000. Home price movements from 2000 to 2007 showed a very different pattern from those in preceding decades. In the first part of that period, from 2000 to 2006, home prices soared to record levels. In the nation as a whole, the NAR's median home price measure rose 59 percent, peaking in the third quarter of 2005. In California, the median single-family home price for the entire state skyrocketed 163 percent in six years. In Florida, it shot up 113 percent during the same six years.

Then home prices in some regions went into a nose dive. True, the NAR median for the entire nation in the second quarter of 2008 was only 7.6 percent lower than it had been one year earlier. (That price was actually slightly higher in the second quarter of 2008 than in the first quarter.) But in California, the statewide median price of single-family homes sold plunged 38.0 percent in 13 months, from the peak in May 2007 to June 2008. In Florida, the median price dropped 16.8 percent in two quarters in 2008. According to NAR data, the median price in the entire West region in the second quarter of 2008 was down 17.4 percent from one year earlier. That was more than twice as big a drop as in the entire nation and 81 percent more than the fall in the second most hard-hit region, the Northeast. One reason for the large price declines in California and Florida was that many of the homes being sold there were foreclosed by banks and resold at bargain prices; in fact, those two states had the highest foreclosure rates in the nation after Nevada.

In order to identify any key patterns about which metropolitan areas were experiencing the largest home price declines, I ranked home price data for the 157 metropolitan areas used by the NAR in three ways. First, I ranked them by the percentage increases in median home prices from 2000 to the peak—usually in 2006. Then I ranked them by the highest peak price from 2000 to 2007—usually in 2005 and 2006. Then I ranked them by the percentage decline in median price from its peak price to the first quarter of 2008. After each ranking, I divided the areas that had the data necessary for that ranking into five quintiles, so that the areas in each quintile had roughly the same total population as those in the other four.[3]

The ranking based on the largest percentage increases in home prices from 2000 to 2006 showed that 12 of the 16 metropolitan areas with the greatest percentage gains in home prices were in either California or Florida, with the highest gain of 204 percent in the Riverside–San Bernardino area of California. The average population of areas in the top quintile was three million—much larger than the average populations of areas in the other four quintiles. This ranking indicates that home prices tended to rise more in larger metropolitan areas than in smaller ones and much more in coastal areas in the West and Northeast than in inland areas, especially those in the Midwest.

The ranking based on the highest median prices does not indicate that large metropolitan areas tend to have higher prices than smaller ones. However, it does show that coastal areas have higher prices than inland areas, other things being equal: 15 of the 26 highest-priced areas are coastal. Conversely, only two of the 58 areas in the quintile with the lowest median prices were coastal. Also, the areas with the highest peak prices tended to have much larger dollar declines in prices after 2006 than did areas that had lower peak prices.

The third ranking involved the percentage by which home prices fell from their peak in each area up to the first quarter of 2008. It shows that there is a tendency for those areas that had the biggest percentage increases from 2000 to their peaks also to have the largest percentage price declines after their peaks. There does not seem to be any tendency for areas with the largest percentage price declines to have a different average population size than others.

Factors and Scenarios. The following tentative conclusions can be drawn from the preceding observations:

- The degree to which home prices have fallen varies enormously across the nation. It seems to be greatest in those areas that had the highest price run-ups from 2000 on, including many coastal areas, and in those areas that had the greatest economic difficulties, such as

Cleveland and St. Louis, because they tend to have more foreclosures than areas in better economic shape. Even in the second quarter of 2008, in 22.8 percent of 149 metropolitan areas tracked by the NAR home prices were still rising; that is, they were higher than in the second quarter of 2007.

■ Press attention seems to focus on those metropolitan areas with high price run-ups, which overstates the degree to which home prices have fallen in the nation as a whole. This is partly a result of press focus on the Case-Shiller index, which is based on a disproportionate sample of coastal metropolitan areas and areas in California, the Northeast, and the costly West.

■ Metropolitan areas that are experiencing high levels of foreclosures are likely to have larger declines in home prices than those experiencing low levels of foreclosures. That is likely because high levels of foreclosure filings will generate about one-fourth to one-sixth as many foreclosure sales as filings, on average. Those sales will occur at prices that are significantly discounted from the official assessed values of the homes concerned. If those foreclosure sales are included in the set of home sales used to measure overall home price levels (as now occurs), that will cause such measures to fall much more than if only sales of unforeclosed homes were included in that set.

According to RealtyTrac data from the first half of 2008, nine states had year-to-date levels of foreclosures equal to 0.5 percent or more of the state's total 2007 population. Those nine states combined contained 35 percent of the nation's total 2007 population but 64 percent of all foreclosure filings in the first half of 2008. Those states were Nevada, Florida, Arizona, California, Colorado, Michigan, Ohio, Georgia, and Massachusetts (listed in descending order of the incidence of foreclosures in their states). It seems likely that home prices in those states will decline from their peak values more than home prices in states with lesser intensity of foreclosures within their boundaries.

In California, for example, the median price of homes sold in August 2008 was 40.5 percent below the median price of homes sold in August 2007. But that result was heavily influenced by a sharp rise in the sale of distressed or foreclosed homes, compared with one year earlier. In August 2007, 40 percent of all homes sold were valued at less than $500,000, but in August 2008, that figure rose to 72 percent, according to the California Association of Realtors. This increase clearly resulted from more foreclosed or otherwise distressed sales in the mix in that year rather than a true 40.5 percent drop in the prices of homes of the same nature and quality. It is therefore inaccurate to say that the market values of all homes in California fell 40.5 percent from August 2007 to August 2008. Normal homes—those whose owners were not suffering from economic distress and that were also not located in neighborhoods experiencing many foreclosures—surely declined in market value far less than the decline in sales prices derived from actually measured current sales, because those current sales were heavily influenced by high fractions of distressed foreclosure sales.[4]

■ It is likely to take several years for home prices in many metropolitan areas to reach a bottom and start rising again. In areas where foreclosures are numerous, home prices have been falling faster than in other areas. That is true because so many of the homes sold there have been foreclosed and then sold at bargain prices by banks anxious to get rid of them. In areas with fewer foreclosures, prices have been falling much less rapidly—so it may take longer for them to hit bottom.

Possible scenarios for home price declines are as follows:

- Prices keep falling well into 2009 but stop late in 2009.
- Prices fall throughout 2009, then hit bottom in 2010 not far above the 2000 level.
- Prices keep falling well into 2010, then hit bottom near the 2000 level.

However, these projections are based upon price changes measured from actual sales, which are biased downward by the high proportions of foreclosure sales. The market values of the vast majority of U.S. homes—those that will mostly not be sold in the next few years—will not fall nearly as much as the prices of those actually sold.

It should also be emphasized that home prices on a national scale have fallen much less since hitting their peaks—usually in 2006—than have stock market prices. All three major home price indices peaked in 2006 or early 2007. Thus, the Case-Shiller index peaked in July 2006 at 206.52 (if the value in the first quarter of 2000 equals 100 in the index). By December 2008, it had fallen to 150.66, a decline of 27.0 percent from the peak. The Dow Jones Industrial Average hit its highest level since 2000—14,164.03—on October 9, 2007. On December 31 2008, that average closed at 8,776.39, a fall of 38.0 percent from its peak. By mid-March 2009, the Dow Jones average had declined another 15.7 percent to 7,395.7, or 47.7 percent below its peak in October 2007.

The NAR single-family median home price measure peaked at $227,600 in the third quarter of 2005 and had fallen to $170,300 in January 2009, a drop of 25.2 percent. The S&P 500 stock index had a pattern similar to that of the Dow Jones Industrial Average. Thus, investors in stocks measured by those two indices had significantly larger losses in value than investors in homes during the same period, wiping out much longer periods of asset appreciation than has occurred at the national level in U.S. housing markets—at least up until mid-March 2009. Moreover, this difference is heightened by the fact that the majority of homeowners have significant leveraging in the investment in their homes through large home mortgages. So, on the average, owning homes has been much more rewarding than owning stocks in that period—or at least much less unrewarding.

Homebuilding Industry Recovery

After U.S. homebuilders flooded markets for new homes with more than 2.0 million units per year—including manufactured housing—in 2004 and 2005, the industry went into a major slump. New housing starts fell from 2.222 million in 2005 to 1.918 million in 2006 and to 1.451 million in 2007—a fall of 34.7 percent in two years. New starts in 2008 totaled only about 900,500 new housing units. That total would be 21 percent below the total for 2007 and 56.4 percent below the peak in 2005. The 2008 figure would also be the lowest number of new housing units started in any year in the United States since 1949.

Yet that low figure is likely to be followed by an even lower figure for 2009 because of two factors. One is that the number of subprime loans with interest rates being reset upward will be larger in 2009 than in 2008, and that may lead to more foreclosures—hence greater competition for newly built units from the inventory of existing units for sale. The second

EXHIBIT 8-3. Inventory of Existing Homes for Sale, 1982–2008

Source: National Association of Realtors.

reason is that in periods since 1945 when U.S. homebuilders have created 2.0 million or more units in one, two, or three years consecutively, new building has declined significantly for several years thereafter. Since new homebuilding fell to about 900,500 starts for all of 2008, it was far below the point it reached in the other four slumps shown on the chart in the third year after each 2.0-million-plus peak—or even in the fifth and seventh years after those peaks. Thus, it is not likely that the U.S. economy and housing market will get much positive stimulus from increases in new homebuilding in 2009 and perhaps not even in 2010.

Home Inventories

The inventory of existing homes for sale comes into being because

- Homebuilders create new units and do not sell them immediately.
- Owners of existing homes need to move for pressing personal reasons, such as getting a new job in another city, getting divorced, having more children, and having children leave home.
- Owners of existing homes decide that home prices are so high that they want to cash in, even though they do not need to move.
- Homes are foreclosed by lenders and put on the market for sale.
- Speculators trying to flip homes for a profit are unable to sell them at prices they are willing to accept.

Exhibit 8-3 shows how many such homes the NAR believes were for sale in various years. The number rose sharply during a major homebuilding boom in the mid-1980s, then declined to a low point in 1994 after a housing slump in 1991, then took off upward from 2002 through 2008. The last surge resulted from a combination of three developments: another homebuilding boom from 2001 through 2005, many homeowners deciding to cash in on high prices in 2006–07, and rising foreclosures after 2006.

By the end of 2007, most homeowners who did not have to move but were hoping to cash in on high home prices had probably decided that the tactic was not going to work, because prices were falling in most metropolitan areas. Hence, many chose to remove their homes from active marketing until prices improved from their viewpoints. At least that put a floor under the prices they were willing to accept. Moreover, homebuilders drastically reduced the number of new units they were building each year—by 34.7 percent, from a peak of 2.222 million in 2005 to 1.451 million in 2007 and less than one million in 2008. So the main cause of the rapidly rising inventory almost had to be more foreclosures.

By 2008, new foreclosure filings were rising at a rate of about three million per year. But those filings did not all turn into sales, at least not rapidly. In any given year up to 2007, the number of foreclosure sales had been about 25 percent of the number of new foreclosure filings in that year. Yet the inventory for sale reported by the NAR was rising by about 500,000 to 600,000 per year after 2005—far less than 25 percent of the number of foreclosures filed each year. The MBA estimated that the number of foreclosed homes in the inventory actually declined by 43,800 in 2005 because foreclosed homes sold so fast. But that number rose 109,000 in 2006 and 420,700 in 2007, as the number of foreclosures soared and sales slowed. In 2008, the number of foreclosed homes entering the unsold inventory undoubtedly rose to equal almost all the increases in the unsold inventory measured by the NAR's data.

If home foreclosures continue rising in 2009, as many experts forecast, so will the inventory of unsold homes. That will make up for further declines in new home construction, to maintain a rising inventory of unsold units. This means downward pressure on home prices will probably remain in force throughout most or all of 2009, even if homebuilders slow new production in 2009 below their 2008 levels, which I believe they will. As the U.S. recession deepens in 2009, that will worsen the unsold inventory problem for the housing industry.

The pressure of a rising inventory of unsold existing homes will probably prevent the housing market—and housing prices—from recovering significantly until 2010 or later. If the U.S. economy experiences another two-year recession like it did in 1945, 1974, and 1980, that would postpone any recovery in housing markets past 2010. I believe that is quite possible.

One conceivable sequence of events might significantly reduce the number of foreclosure sales in 2009. Commercial banks are still holding many mortgages that are likely to default, especially if the rates on those mortgages will be reset upward in 2009. Many of those banks could decide to sell many of those mortgages at a discount to investors who are willing to work out deals with mortgage holders, or they could accept "haircuts" by adjusting the rates or terms in their shaky mortgages in order to improve the chances that their borrowers will be able to pay without default. If those behaviors occurred at a sufficient scale, the number of additional foreclosures in 2009 might decline well below the three million that occurred in 2008. However, commercial banks are limited in their ability to write off capital because they must meet stringent reserve requirements mandated by law.

Capital Market Stabilization

In the capital markets, the key questions going forward relate to when investors and capital suppliers will regain confidence in the markets and see opportunity to invest again. Markets must bottom out and start to clear at stabilized prices. How and when will this happen? As of early 2009, capital markets were in turmoil and investor confidence was low, and the bottom was not in sight.

Capital Suppliers and Real Estate Asset Values

A fundamental problem that is now causing the unavailability of credit for real estate is that capital suppliers—providers of both equity and debt capital—have lost their confidence that they know, or can readily find out, the true market values of both real estate securities and real estate properties. Many capital suppliers around the world were far removed geographically from the markets where the properties in which they invested were located. Hence they had to rely on others' credit ratings to be sure their investments were worth what they were paying for them.

The three major credit rating agencies—Moody's, Fitch, and Standard & Poor's—did a terrible job of analyzing and rating many of the security issues sent to them for evaluation. Those agencies were under heavy competitive pressure from each other. They were also overwhelmed by massive amounts of new types of securities to rate. So they systematically underrated the riskiness of many such security issues, especially those involving subprime mortgage loans. When many defaults began showing up among those loans, investors around the world lost confidence in the credit ratings of those and other agencies. In a globalized economy, where capital generated all over the world seeks investments in distant lands, having confidence in those who create or rate securities is crucial to maintaining an international flow of investment capital. Once that confidence is lost, how can an investor know whether securities he or she is being offered from some faraway place are really worth buying? Most investors cannot know or find out on their own. Therefore, they stopped investing and put their money into what they regarded as safe havens, like U.S. Treasury securities or money market funds. That is precisely what happened in 2008 to capital suppliers the world over—including within the United States—as a result of their being surprised by the poor performance of mortgage-backed securities issued in the United States.

How can such a loss of confidence be overcome? The first crucial ingredient is the mere passage of time. Capital suppliers must go through a period in which the frequency of write-downs and losses by those who create securities fades away. And that takes time—often years. After the collapse of commercial real property prices in 1990, it took at least four years for investors to start recognizing that owners of commercial property were succeeding in making money in much-improved property markets. In the meantime, out of desperation for capital, many property owners shifted their sources of funds from traditional institutional investors to the stock market by putting their properties into REITs.

But the soaring prices of Internet stocks in the late 1990s persuaded many institutional investors to put most of their available money into tech stocks and ignore real estate, even though real estate was doing well in terms of operating profits. Then came the stock market crash of 2000. Suddenly capital suppliers the world over decided that prospects for real estate—then ten years from its value collapse in 1990—were far better than those for most stocks and bonds, then still sinking in value. That is the second ingredient in overcoming investors' lack of confidence: space market conditions must improve over a long enough period to provide improved profits to property operators.

The third ingredient is that real estate must compare favorably to other asset classes such as stocks and bonds. A means of restoring investor confidence would be to require originators and packagers of securitized investments to retain ownership of at least 10 to 20 percent of their own issues, preferably from the lowest-rated tranche of every issue. This would give them enough skin in the game to assure other investors that the originators will have done enough due diligence to be sure they will not lose their own funds. I believe government regulators should make such retentions compulsory.

Even so, these conditions imply that widespread investor confidence in real estate will not be restored in a short period. Too many commercial and investment banks have gotten into serious financial trouble, or soon will do so, because of real estate loan defaults. I believe investor confidence will only gradually return. One factor encouraging such a return will be that many investors will feel pressure from the very low yields that they earn from parking their funds in Treasuries and money market funds. They will want to get higher yields, so they will start trying real estate securities and properties that are packaged in ways that emphasize their high quality and security. One important factor will be that dividend yields from REITs will rise significantly in percentage terms, as REIT stock prices decline but the underlying real estate markets remain reasonably sound despite the recession. However, this turnaround in the sentiments of capital suppliers will not occur as long as there is a severe financial crisis and great uncertainty about the true value of real estate and other assets on the books of banks, as was the case in early 2009.

Investors will also demand higher yields than they were getting from 2000 to 2006 when intense competition eroded their underwriting, driving property prices up and capitalization rates down. Thus the fourth ingredient in improving investor confidence will be for property prices to adjust downward to reflect the new investment and economic realities. Property owners will need to cut their prices and accept that capitalization rates need to rise to provide higher returns to buyers.

From these observations, I conclude the following:

- The credit crunch will not end quickly but will take at least one more year and perhaps up to three more years to disappear.
- Real estate capital markets will gradually improve as investors become impatient with low yields on other assets and as more property owners accept the need to give investors higher returns.
- The recovery of real estate capital markets will depend in part upon how well the non-REIT part of the broader stock market fares: the better it does, the longer it will take for capital to come back to real estate.

The Gulf between Buyers and Sellers, Lenders and Borrowers

As of late 2008, transaction volumes in commercial real estate markets had fallen to near zero, partly because suppliers of both debt and equity capital could not agree with borrowers or users of capital about the terms on which capital should be supplied. The suppliers want to get higher yields than the ones they received from 2000 to 2006. They have concluded—correctly—that those yields were inadequate to cover the risks they were bearing. That means they want higher interest rates and lower property prices. In contrast, borrowers do not want to pay higher interest rates and property owners do not want cap rates to rise, which would reduce the value of their properties. They want to retain the huge gains they made when prices rose and capitalization rates fell.

It is true, as discussed above, that capital suppliers are also concerned about accepting anyone else's estimates of what real properties or securities are really worth, given the adverse experiences they have had with such estimates in the past few years. Those investors are gripped by a degree of uncertainty that is causing many of them to freeze on any lending, almost regardless of the terms they are offered. But underlying that freeze is another equally fundamental conflict between capital suppliers and capital users: How much should users pay suppliers for access to capital?

This standoff arose in late 2006 and intensified throughout 2007; it was still going strong when this chapter was written in early 2009. Forces on both sides of the standoff are pressing people on each side to give in to some extent. On the capital supplier side, investors are unhappy with both the low yields they received from 2000 through early 2007 and the low yields they were receiving in early 2009 from having parked their money in Treasury securities and money market funds. Ironically, just as the Federal Reserve is trying to reduce mortgage interest rates in housing markets, most investors—especially those in commercial property markets—are seeking higher yields than they obtained from 2000 through 2007. They would much prefer to make commercial deals than buy Treasuries, but not at the prices and interest rates that are presently acceptable to most property owners and other borrowers. Moreover, investors are deterred from making loans on or buying real properties by huge uncertainties about the true values of such properties.

On the other side, property owners are pressured to accept lower prices by two forces. One is their need for additional capital to make capital improvements to keep their properties competitive and to roll over debts against their properties that are coming due. The other force is the fact that all types of asset prices plunged in late 2008, including all the real estate held by REITs as shown by their collapsing stock prices. The FTSE NAREIT index dropped from 8,885 on September 19, 2008 to 3,551 in mid-March 2009—a fall of 60 percent. Even if the stock market overshot the "true" decline in property prices, no reasonable observer could avoid believing that the prices of real estate held outside of REITs had also declined significantly in that period.

So both sides are under some pressure to compromise. Until at least early 2009, the capital suppliers seem to have stronger motives to demand better yields, considering the beating that many have taken from investments made in the recent past at low yields.

As time passes and transactions stay at low levels, people on both sides will make more and more efforts to define terms that will seem reasonable to both them and their counterparties. This will gradually lead to the completion of more transactions. However, experience in the 1990s shows that the time interval required to generate more such compromises can be very long—even several years. That is why I expect that this standoff will not suddenly disappear but will have to be gradually eroded as pressures for action rise on both sides.

Four Scenarios

The analysis above reveals that at least three major influences on the duration of the current financial crisis are likely to prolong it:

- Continued high volumes of home foreclosures in 2008 and throughout 2009 will prevent the inventory of unsold homes from declining significantly until 2010. That factor will also depress the average prices of homes that are sold each year, thereby preventing any notable recovery of home prices until 2010.
- Levels of new homebuilding will remain very low in 2008 and even lower in 2009, and will not begin to recover until 2010, if then. That will keep employment in construction low and weaken any economic forces that would otherwise tend to end the recession in 2009.
- Real estate investors and capital suppliers around the world will not regain strong confidence in real estate for several years. Therefore, they will continue to be reluctant to invest heavily in real properties or real estate securities until significant time has passed, space markets have returned to a balance of supply and demand, and pricing has become attractive in relation to investment alternatives.

There will be no return to the easy availability of financial credit for real estate during most or all of 2009. Only in 2010 and beyond will such a return be possible, though certainly not assured. That situation is consistent with the likelihood of the 2008–09 American recession lasting well into 2010. Four possible scenarios are outlined below for moving beyond the current financial crisis.

Scenario One: Weak U.S. Recession, Speedy Return of Credit Availability by Late 2009

The most optimistic scenario involves a short general recession through most of 2009. It includes a sharp fall-off in foreclosure filings and sales in 2009 compared with 2008, because banks will sell—at a discount—many loans that are likely to default to investors willing to work out payment plans with borrowers. Also, banks will take voluntary haircuts on many other mortgage loans by writing down remaining amounts due and working out deals with the borrowers concerned in order to reduce the incidence of foreclosures. The Federal Reserve Board, having already nationalized both Fannie Mae and Freddie Mac, will provide enough capital to keep them operating as mortgage buyers and securitizers. The Fed's new asset-buying program will remove many of the most toxic assets from banks' books, thereby encouraging private investors to buy newly issued bank stocks that provide banks with more reserves that they can use to support additional lending. The Fed will also directly invest some of its own capital into major banks to increase their equities. And the federal government's program to slow down foreclosures will prove successful.

Investors—both lenders on and buyers of property—concerned about the low yields they were getting in 2008 will start to make loans at higher interest rates or buy properties at higher capitalization rates in 2009. Moreover, property owners will be willing to pay higher interest rates and accept some lower property values. Lenders will therefore become willing to make mortgage loans on good commercial properties sometime late in 2009. Homebuilding will remain depressed in most of 2009 but start to recover late in the year or early in 2010. The economies of nations outside the United States will show surprising strength in 2009, stimulating American exports and reducing their own savings surpluses. Although credit availability and low borrowing costs will not return to their conditions before 2006, they will greatly improve relative to their conditions in mid-2008.

Regarding federal regulations of financial markets, Congress will undoubtedly greatly increase regulation of mortgage lending and federal financing of investment banks and other credit institutions during periods of financial crisis. However, the basic antiregulatory stance of the government toward the financial sector will not be totally abandoned, because the sector's speedy recovery will reduce congressional motivations for such basic changes in viewpoint.

Scenario Two: Strong U.S. Recession in 2009, Continued Lack of Real Estate Credit Availability until 2010

This scenario is much less optimistic than the first one. It involves prolonged suspension of real estate credit availability and a credit freeze throughout 2009 and well into 2010, if not longer. The strong U.S. recession that began in 2008 will last throughout 2009 and perhaps well into 2010. Unemployment will rise to levels not seen for decades. Foreclosure filings will continue at more than three million per year in 2009 and only slightly less in 2010. U.S. banks will be limited in their ability to take writedowns of shaky mortgages or accept haircuts on such mortgages and try to work them out with borrowers, because of their need to maintain legally required capital reserves. Few American or foreign investors will be willing to put up capital to help U.S. banks deleverage. Fannie Mae and Freddie Mac will be operated by the federal government even if they are divided into several smaller institutions with functions similar to those previously carried out by the two government-sponsored enterprises. Levels of commercial real estate transactions will remain very low compared with those in the past. Homebuilding will fall in 2009 below the already low 2008 levels and will not start recovering until after the first half of 2010, if then.

The economies of foreign nations will slip into recession or near-recession levels of activity, causing major declines in world output and trade. American exports will rise but not make up for continued distress in the financial sector. Many more banks will become bankrupt and have to be taken over by the FDIC, which will run short of funds.

The federal government will adopt strong economic stimulus programs in 2009 to slow the recession, aggravating already large federal deficits. It will also have started a new organization along the lines of the Resolution Trust Corporation of the late 1980s and early 1990s to take over defaulting mortgage loans and liquidate them at large losses—financed by taxpayers. The federal government will change its basic stance toward the financial sector from being strongly against regulations to being strongly in favor of much more government influence on how the sector behaves. This change will be motivated in part by the much larger federal costs that will be involved in getting through this period of disarray. Yet recovery from this serious recession will be much slower than in most of the post–World War II period since 1982.

Scenario Three: Serious U.S. Recession, Collapse of the Dollar, Higher Interest Rates, and a Prolonged Recession through 2010

In this scenario, other nations shift their major trading currency away from the U.S. dollar to euro or other currency bundles. That causes a collapse of the dollar that forces the Federal Reserve to sharply raise interest rates, as in 1980–82. This prolongs the U.S. recession through 2010 and beyond and worsens the real estate borrowing situation.

This scenario differs from the second one because the economies of nations outside the United States do not slow down as much, so there is less of a worldwide recession. But the U.S. economy has a serious recession and a large, continued negative balance of payments. As a result, many other nations decide to stop holding all their reserve capital in dollars. They switch to bundles of currency based on the euro and other currencies, start valuing oil in nondollar currencies, and dump many dollar-denominated securities on world markets. The resulting collapse of the U.S. dollar's international trading value forces the Federal Reserve Board to raise U.S. interest rates very high in order to at least partly counteract the flight from the dollar. Those higher interest rates prolong the already serious recession within the U.S. economy. At the same time, the lower trade value of the dollar encourages more foreign nations to import goods and services from the United States. Even so, the U.S. recession lasts through most of 2010, because no other one nation takes over America's longtime role as the basic economic engine driving world trade and production. Eventually the combination of rising exports, federal fiscal stimuli, and renewed lending stimulates an economic recovery after the longest recession since 1945–47, or perhaps even since the 1930s.

Scenario Four: Two- to Three-Year Recession, Massive Federal Spending, Inflationary Pressures, High Interest Rates

This scenario starts like the second scenario, but massive federal spending to get the nation out of recession gradually generates strong upward pressures on price and employment levels throughout the economy. Such spending includes a large-scale infrastructure investment program; creation of new sources of electrical energy such as nuclear plants, natural gas plants, and wind-capturing fields; plus extensive unemployment benefit programs, food stamps, and other benefits for persons without jobs. These spending programs are supported by expanded federal deficits, and the Federal Reserve begins to print money to keep spending flowing—rather than raising taxes, which might slow economic growth, or selling Treasury bonds to foreign investors, who will be reluctant to buy more such securities. As the economy recovers in 2010, upward pressure on prices generates a significant shift into inflationary conditions. These became serious enough within one or two more years to force the Federal Reserve to raise interest rates to levels that are high enough to slow burgeoning economic activity and quell inflation, as in the early 1980s. Thus, the initial recessionary conditions are overcome by spending that generates big federal deficits and inflationary pressures, which in turn require deliberate cultivation of a second recession to prevent runaway inflation. That whole process would take multiple years and might last until close to 2020.

How Likely Are These Scenarios?

Although many economists might roughly agree with the four scenarios I have just laid out, there would be much less agreement about what probabilities to assign to each one. There is no scientific method for arriving at such probabilities; it is a matter of pure subjective judgment. After thinking about this issue for some time, I have tentatively arrived at the following estimated probabilities as of the time of this writing in early January 2009:

- Scenario 1: Weak recession, over quickly—15 percent.
- Scenario 2: Strong recession lasting through 2009 and perhaps into 2010—65 percent.
- Scenario 3: Strong U.S. recession, weaker world recession, and collapse of the U.S. dollar—8 percent.
- Scenario 4: Strong recession overcome through massive federal spending that leads to inflationary pressures that eventually must be halted by the deliberate generation of a second recession—12 percent.

These probability assignments reflect my current subjective judgments. My reasons for arriving at them have been set forth in this chapter. Of course, they are subject to the inherently high degree of uncertainty about any specific future predictions.

NOTES

1. Luke M. Shimek and Li Wen, "Why Do Chinese Households Save So Much?" *International Economic Trends*, August 2008, Federal Reserve Bank of St. Louis, http://research.stlouisfed.org/publications/iet/20080801/cover.pdf.
2. Data from the California Association of Realtors, e-mailed on July 15, 2008.
3. In many cases, the population of each quintile differs notably from those in other quintiles owing to discontinuities that arise because some areas have quite large populations. I tried to select boundaries for the quintiles that come as close as possible to equalizing the populations among them.
4. California Association of Realtors, *Trends in California Real Estate* (Volume 29, No. 9, September 2008), page 1.

Long-Run Consequences of the Financial Crisis

IT MAY SEEM PREMATURE TO DISCUSS THE LONG-RUN consequences of the financial crisis of 2007–09, since it was still going on when this book was written. Yet the financial crisis has affected real estate and financial markets in many ways that will endure long after credit becomes reasonably available again. Therefore, it is important to discuss which of its effects will continue to operate over the long run.

Impacts of Globalization on Capital Markets

The globalization of capital flows around the world, which started long before the current financial crisis, was a major cause of the flood of capital into real estate that eventually generated the 2007–09 financial crisis. Because capital can so easily and so rapidly flow around the globe, governments of individual nations have less power to control what happens to their money supplies than they did in the past. Moreover, they cannot greatly restrict the flow of capital into and out of their nations without making their own economies less competitive. Hence governments must somehow adapt to the reality of big flows of foreign capital into— and out of—their economies.

The impact of the financial crisis on America's financial system illustrates the difficulties that this situation can pose for national governments. Massive inflows of capital into the United States and such nations as Spain and the United Kingdom after the stock market crash of 2000 flooded real estate markets with funds that drove property prices upward. Those flows were abetted by the efforts of U.S. banks, investment banks, and mortgage brokers to sell U.S. mortgage-related securities around the world. So the global capital inflows cannot be blamed mainly on the foreign investors who put up the money.

The globalization of capital flows limits the ability of national central banks and other government agencies to control what happens in their own economy. In fact, attempts by any one nation to influence financial events within its borders through very strict government regulations may make its financial centers less competitive with those of other nations. Thus, imposing heavy regulations on financial behavior in the United States might shift a lot of American financing business from New York to London, Tokyo, Hong Kong, or even the Bahamas or Bermuda. This potential shift and outcome will influence just how far the cyclical swing from a highly deregulated financial system to a far more regulated one goes in the United States in the next few years.

Yet another implication of globalization is that closer coordination should be established among the central banks of the major developed and emerging nations concerning their key policies on the behavior of banking and financial institutions. The financial crisis provides decisive proof that each nation's financial system is heavily influenced by, and in turn influences, what happens in the financial systems of many other nations in the world. It would be very desirable for these systems to avoid serious financial crises that could periodically erupt from their interdependence and from the inherent instability of financial systems everywhere. To achieve that goal, they must work together to establish similar rules and principles across the entire globe. Such coordination has already begun in response to the current credit crisis. But it needs to be carried out to a much greater extent to help prevent similarly serious crises from arising in the future.

Global Policies to Reduce International Financial Crises

Martin Wolf's recent book, *Fixing Global Finance*, argues that major global capital flows since the late 1990s have been caused by, and are in turn contributing to, financial crises. In the 1990s, several Asian countries suffered severe recessions when they were suddenly forced to devalue their currencies. Those governments—and the people and firms within those countries—had been borrowing money from abroad and running up large debts in foreign currencies, mainly U.S. dollars. When their economies slowed down, speculators sold their currencies short. Those nations did not have enough currency reserves to prevent devaluation. That meant their domestic borrowers of dollars—including governments—were suddenly unable to repay foreign debts because of the reduced value in dollars of their own currencies, in which they held their wealth. This led to severe recessions, including large-scale unemployment and lower incomes.

Those governments were determined not to suffer such disasters again. So they decided to build large reserves in foreign currencies by not permitting domestic borrowing in such currencies. They adopted export-led growth approaches but used the profits from such exports to build currency reserves rather than to expand their domestic economies. This behavior contributed to the creation of surplus savings around the globe that was a key element in the flood of financial capital into the United States after the stock market crash of 2000.

However, such behavior also contributed to globally perverse flows of financial capital. The governments of poor nations, especially in Asia, kept their currency values low by preventing those values from rising in international trading, even though they had large export surpluses. For example, China kept its renminbi from rising in exchange value, in order to encourage more exports and thereby employ more of the people flooding into its cities from poor rural areas. To do that, the Chinese government had to pressure firms and households to maintain high savings rates so the nation could build up large foreign currency reserves. Those high savings in turn supported higher levels of American consumption than Americans could finance for themselves.

In China, the national savings rate was just under 60 percent of GDP, even though China still had more than 800 million very poor residents. China should have been spending more of those savings to improve its domestic economy and reduce its poverty.

As a result, though, around the world financial capital was flowing from many poor nations to the richest nation—the United States. Poor residents of the world were supporting unusually high levels of consumption in the richest country. For the long-run benefit of world growth and prosperity, global financial capital flows should be the reverse—from rich nations with high living standards and high savings rates to poor nations with lower savings rates but greater investment needs. But the governments of the poor nations were fearful of financial crises like those they suffered in the 1990s and earlier.

What can be done to change this perverse arrangement? It is a global problem, not just a national one, because it is rooted in international trading relationships between different nations and in international currency speculation. Martin Wolf believes that "the dominant theme remains the need to nurture a wider range of domestic currency markets in emerging countries [the ones now trying to protect themselves by using high savings to build up large foreign currency reserves]."[1] He recommends three fundamental approaches:

- "Countries running huge current account surpluses need to ask themselves whether they could not better use these resources at home. . . .
- The U.S. [trade] deficit should diminish, but not disappear . . . [because] there are [still] a large number of countries with massive surpluses. . . .
- Emerging countries must do more to give themselves the stability they need [rather] than accumulate massive foreign currency reserves."[2]

International movement toward adopting and supporting these approaches should be one of the long-run consequences of the current financial crisis, if the world wants to reduce drastically the possibility of more dire crises in the future. Whether this will happen remains to be seen.

Greater Financial Regulation

I believe a major swing from a highly deregulated U.S. financial sector to a much more intensively regulated one will occur during the next few years. The new president and Congress will inevitably react to the excesses and frauds in the financial sector of the 2000–08 period. They will impose considerably more stringent regulations on the sector, especially concerning lending to households. The specific increases in regulation that I believe will—or at least should—occur are discussed in chapter 6. They can be briefly summarized here as follows:

- Lending to homebuyers will be much more restricted than it has been in the past.
- Organizations owned by bank holding companies but not consolidated onto bank balance sheets will have to change their behavior. They may be required to consolidate their activities onto bank balance sheets and to hold reserves against their activities.
- Investment banks as we have known them in the past will disappear.
- There will be more emphasis on using equity rather than maximizing debt to finance real estate transactions.

- The U.S. financial system's ability to create debt will be severely constrained for the next decade or so, except for federal government borrowing to shore up the financial system. That will reduce the system's ability to support lending in real estate and other markets to a much smaller multiple of the total amount of reserve capital in the system. This will be a direct result of deleveraging the entire financial system by reducing the total amount of debt in relation to the total amount of financial capital available. Another cause of such shrinkage will be the impact of new regulations concerning how the financial system must operate. Hence, the ratio of equity to debt will be increasing in most real estate transactions for the foreseeable future.

- As a result, the private financial sectors of all developed nations and many emerging nations will shrink relative to the overall outputs of their economies, at least during the next half decade or longer. To put it another way, financial activities will constitute a smaller share of each nation's GDP than they have been from 2000 to 2008, except for activities financed by national governments rather than the private financial system. This also means that the volume of lending in real estate and other markets relative to the total amount of property in such markets will be lower than has been the case for the past decade or longer.

- Securitization through pooling loans and issuing loan-backed securities based on such pools will be greatly reduced until better and clearer forms of transparency are developed and new credit rating agencies are created that are capable of earning respect from lenders. The one exception in the United States will be securitization of home mortgage loans by Fannie Mae and Freddie Mac, since both will continue to be owned by the federal government. These changes in other securitizers will not be easy to carry out. Securitization was the primary device that broadened real estate's access to capital markets. For these two reasons, the number of funding sources willing to invest capital in real estate will diminish in the near future until some form of a well-functioning debt securitization market can be restored.

- The role of national governments in the financial sectors of their economies will expand greatly as a means of replacing some, but probably not all, of the capital origination required to keep financial markets working effectively. This expansion will involve a major restructuring of financial markets around the world. National government funding sources will step up to replace the private debt sources that have failed or that must shrink as part of the deleveraging of lending and banking activities. As a result, the importance of national government policies in financial markets will increase significantly.

Impacts on the Residential Housing Sector

Lending practices in residential markets will also be affected by restructuring. This will affect housing prices, affordability, product type, policy, and industry structure. How that will happen is discussed in the following sections.

Impacts on Housing Prices

The nation's press has been highlighting the extent to which home prices have been declining in the United States since their peak in 2006. However, the press has not pointed out that in most parts of the nation, home prices in current dollars rose much more from 1997 to 2006 than they have fallen since then, as shown in chapter 2. In most metropolitan areas, even though home prices have declined from either 2006 or 2007 through 2008 and probably will decline farther through 2009 or even longer, those prices are still much higher than they were in 1997 or 2000. In California, median home sales prices had risen 163 percent from 2000 to the peak in 2006. So even though median prices for single-family homes that were sold in California fell more than 40 percent from their peak in 2006 to September 2008, they were still significantly higher in mid-2008 than in 2000. Moreover, the decline in actual sale prices from 2007 to 2008 was heavily influenced by a sharp rise in the proportion of home sales consisting of foreclosure sales or other sales of distressed homes in 2008 over the proportion in 2007. Hence, in California the decline in normal home prices has been much lower than the decline in overall median sale prices reported by the California Association of Realtors.

True, this situation is somewhat different when home prices are stated in real terms; that is, corrected for inflation. In current dollars, the California median home price soared by 216 percent from 1996 to 2007, then plunged by 38.1 percent from 2006 to 2008. In constant-value dollars, that price rose by 146 percent from 1994 to 2006, then fell 42.1 percent from 2006 to 2008. Thus current dollar prices in California showed much greater percentage increases than constant dollar prices, though the two declines were quite similar. In more than 50 years of experience in all aspects of real estate, I have found that, in analyzing or thinking about home prices, everyone except academic economists uses current dollars, not constant dollars. So I place more weight on current dollar data.

Using an index which sets 1997 median home prices equal to 100, home prices in the nation rose from 100 in 1997 to an index peak of 182.18 in 2006 (that is, they were 82.18 percent higher in 2006 than they were in 1997), and then fell to 166.89 in mid-2008. Thus, they rose 82.18 points in nine years and then fell 15.29 points in one and a half years. In mid-2008, the national median price was still 66.89 percent higher than it was in 1997 and 46.3 percent higher than it was in 2000—despite having declined 18.6 percent from its peak of 182.18.

In California, the median home price rose to an index peak of 300.59 and then declined to an index value of 197.46 in mid-2008. Thus the California price rose 200 percent from 1997 to its 2006 peak and then fell 34.31 percent to its mid-2008 level (the decline of 103.13 index points was 34.31 percent of 300.59). So in mid-2008, California prices were almost double what they had been in 1997 and were still 52.5 percent higher than they had been in the year 2000.

In Florida, the median home price peaked at an index value of 257.93 in 2006 and then dropped to an index value of 214.51 in mid-2008. So Florida prices in mid-2008 were also double what they had been in 1997—and 77.3 percent higher than they were in 2000.

Moreover, even these declines in home prices have been exaggerated by all three major home price indices because they have not distinguished between what has happened to the prices of normal homes in undistressed neighborhoods and what has happened to the prices of foreclosed homes in highly distressed neighborhoods. Hence the three indices have, in effect, overweighted the influence of highly discounted foreclosure sales in describing what has happened to the market values of all 125 million homes in the nation, the vast majority of which have not been involved in foreclosures.

More complete data on changes in home prices in 132 metropolitan areas from 1997 to 2008 are discussed in detail in chapter 2. Those data bear out the conclusion that home prices in current dollars in 2008 were still far higher than they were in either 1997 or 2000, despite the much-commented-on declines since about 2006.

Another impact on housing prices is this: the belief that such prices will inevitably rise each year will not return to prominence for many years. The NAR reported 38 years of continuous increases in the national median price of single-family homes sold from 1968 to 2006. But the assumption that this trend would continue was shattered by the declines in 2007 and 2008. It is quite likely that home prices will keep falling in 2009 and perhaps even after that, especially because the United States will be in a deepening recession.

Impacts on Housing Affordability

When the financial crisis is over, home prices throughout most of the United States in current dollars will still be significantly higher than they were in 2000 or especially in 1997. This is an important outcome to consider because it means that housing will be less affordable to low-income households than it was before the Niagara of capital drove up housing prices, especially after 2000. Even significant declines in high-priced states like California and Florida will not make buying a home as affordable as it was before 2000.

Furthermore, homebuyers will face tougher borrowing terms in the future than they did in the early 2000s. Despite the Federal Reserve's attempts to drive home mortgage rates down, interest rates on home loans will be higher than they were from 2000 to mid-2007 because capital suppliers want to obtain greater yields from lending than they did in that period when capital was plentiful. Larger downpayments will be required, and other lending terms may be more stringent, as noted above.

Impacts on Federal Housing Policy

Not only will home prices remain relatively high, but also consumers' incomes—in both current and real dollars—are likely to remain relatively stagnant or even decline in the near future, especially because the United States will be in a serious recession. This means that the availability and cost of rental housing will remain critically important to the welfare of low-income American households. The next few years would be an excellent time to shift the emphasis of federal housing policy away from an exclusive focus on promoting homeownership to a more balanced approach to both rental and ownership housing.

Unfortunately, this view will probably be undermined by a strong push by homebuilding, real estate, and even local government interests to "save and rebuild" homeownership as a means of coping with the high levels of foreclosures that now dominate housing markets in many areas. Therefore, I expect federal housing policies to remain biased in favor of homeowners—especially wealthier ones—rather than favoring the low-income households that need federal help the most.

Impacts on Housing Size

Another aspect of housing affordability involves the size of new homes to be built in the future, because size has a major influence on housing costs. The average size of new single-family homes built in the United States rose from 1,660 square feet in 1973 to 2,521 square feet in 2007, an increase of 57.5 percent. In that same 34 years, the average household size fell from 3.01 to 2.57 (in 2006), or by 14.6 percent. Clearly, the impetus for larger homes has come from rising incomes, more borrowing, and changes in consumer tastes rather than from larger households. If homebuilders would build smaller units, they could substantially reduce the price of buying a new home. After World War II, thousands of quite small single-family homes containing less than 1,000 square feet of space were built in many small towns and rural areas. Those smaller homes were quite satisfactory for larger households than we have today.

I believe some homebuilders will try to build smaller homes as a tactic to make their products more affordable for people in the middle- and lower-income parts of the social hierarchy. If this happens, it will be a direct result of the financial crisis and the preceding and unsustainable explosion of home prices caused by the Niagara of capital.

Impacts on Housing Density

By reducing the affordability of single-family homes and the ease of financing purchases of them, the Niagara of capital and the ensuing financial crisis have increased the relative demand for rental housing in the United States, compared with what it was from 2000 to 2007. This will create some pressure for builders to construct rental apartments rather than focus on single-family homes. From 1960 through 1989, single-family homes constituted about 54 to 58 percent of all dwelling units built each year. That share rose to 66.8 percent in the 1990s and 74.0 percent in the 2000s. It is time to return to placing greater emphasis on apartment buildings, in order to reduce average home size and unit costs.

This shift is also consistent with the need to increase settlement densities in order to reduce additional vehicle miles driven. Doing so would both reduce our consumption of gasoline and constrain our creation of greenhouse gases. Many urban planners and environmentalists are urging a shift from various forms of sprawl in new suburban growth to much higher densities in growth areas, plus more use of infill sites to raise densities within existing settlements. If such shifts occur, the force of the movement to reduce greenhouse-gas emissions will be more important than the need to cut home costs, but both will be significant.

Disappearance of Home Flipping as an Occupation

In the early 2000s, continuous increases in home prices across the nation generated a new occupation: home flipper. These aggressive speculators put downpayments on new homes in the hopes of quickly selling them to genuine resident buyers at higher prices than the speculators had paid—preferably without having to make many payments on the mortgages. The replacement of ever-rising home prices by mostly declining home prices has ended this occupation, at least for quite a few years. Home flippers came to constitute as high a share as 40 percent of all homebuyers in some markets and even higher shares in some condominium markets such as Miami and Las Vegas. Their abandonment of homes they can no longer sell at higher prices has contributed greatly to the number of home foreclosures in those high-flipping markets. This occupation will not be missed by genuine homebuyers, though many homebuilders profited from it for several years.

Impacts on Residential Mortgage Securitization

During most of the housing boom in the early 2000s, mortgage lending was dominated by the securitization of most residential mortgages, as discussed earlier. But after thousands of subprime home mortgages went into default despite having received high ratings from credit rating agencies, investors the world over lost faith in their ability to tell a sound mortgage security from a toxic one, and residential securitization virtually disappeared. Some securitization was continued by both Fannie Mae and Freddie Mac until defaults among their securities caused their stocks to plummet so much that the federal government nationalized them. The two agencies then resumed buying and securitizing home mortgages, with the help of FHA insurance and the guarantee provided by U.S. government ownership. The federal guarantees underlying the bonds reassured investors that they would not suffer from punishing defaults. As of early 2009, over 90 percent of all new home mortgages being made in the United States were handled by either Fannie Mae or Freddie Mac.

Securitization of home mortgages provides immense benefits to housing markets as long as the issuers of securitized mortgage bonds are trusted by potential investors. Such securitization reduces the risks of buying mortgages in two ways: each bond is backed by dozens or hundreds of individual homes, and investors can diversify their portfolios by buying several such securities backed by different types of homes from different areas. As a result, securitization expands the number of investors who are willing to put money into residential lending. Therefore, American housing markets need a permanent means of carrying out such securitizing.

The only sure way to do so after the collapse of investor trust in American private credit rating agencies is to provide federal guarantees underlying the resulting bonds. That has become the key function carried out by Fannie Mae and Freddie Mac. It will take many years for private agencies to build reputations for backing their bonds that will encourage thousands of investors around the globe to purchase residential mortgage-backed securities without fear of excessive defaults. That is why I believe the federal government will continue to own and operate both Fannie Mae and Freddie Mac rather than privatizing them. Privatization would remove the federal guarantees underlying the bonds that make their operations viable even in today's untrusting investment markets. Perhaps the government might eventually merge the two organizations, but I believe it will keep some form of them in their present business, under government ownership, for as long as the eye can see into the future.

Impacts on the Commercial Property Sector

The commercial property sector has been and will continue to be hard hit by the financial crisis and the shrinkage of overall private lending activity, for reasons explained in the following subsections. The most direct impact will be related to the recession and the overall decline in demand for commercial space that has resulted and will continue. A second impact is the rise in capitalization rates resulting from increased uncertainty and the greatly reduced appetite for risk in financial markets. Higher capitalization rates mean lower commercial property prices, as also reflected by the huge decline in REIT share prices. A third impact is the turmoil and upheaval among traditional real estate financing sources that is still playing out, with no defined outcome in sight, resulting in a severe lack of financing available for real estate transactions. This turmoil is affecting not only the banks, which have been discussed at length elsewhere in this book, but also REITs, pension funds, life insurance companies, private equity firms, and many other financial players. These impacts together have translated directly into steadily falling commercial property prices and a dramatic reduction in transactions. Several other impacts underway are described below, including the decline of housing-financed retail consumption, less speculation generally, and a growing emphasis on prudent asset management. In short, the commercial real estate finance business is in a state of upheaval.

CMBS and Refinancing Problems

As discussed in chapter 4, the financial crisis is undermining the ability of many owners of commercial real estate properties to roll over the debts they created when buying those properties. Many owners financed their purchases of commercial properties in the period from 2000 through 2006 and early 2007 by borrowing heavily against the perceived market values of those properties. Those market values had been driven upward by the flood of capital into real estate markets from 2000 through early 2007. Moreover, the relatively easy availability of debt capital, much of it flowing from the CMBS sector, enabled such property purchasers to benefit from high loan-to-value ratios, low interest rates, and high property values. Many such purchasers chose relatively short-term loans, because the interest rates were lower, with the expectation that the market values of the properties they were buying would rise, enabling them to refinance and withdraw tax-free capital in just a few years.

But the financial crisis has radically altered the terms available to such property buyers for paying off loans as they come due. Instead of rising, commercial property values have declined significantly. Furthermore, capital suppliers are now insisting on much lower loan-to-value ratios and higher interest rates. It has become extremely difficult to borrow money against commercial properties from banks or anyone else, because no one can be certain just how much a given property is worth. Finally, a major source of debt capital—CMBS—has been largely shut down, greatly reducing the supply of capital for mortgage origination or refinancing and increasing its price. The result is a huge financial gap between the amount of equity funding that property buyers were required to put up for their initial purchases and the amount that they are now required to put back when their loans mature (see chapter 4).

How will a property owner come up with huge amounts of equity after owning a property for only a few years? Unless the owner has access to a lot of additional equity capital, which is unlikely, or is loaded with wealth from other sources, he or she probably cannot do so. It is almost impossible to borrow such an amount from other lenders in the currently frozen credit market. Therefore, in many cases, the owner will have to turn the property over to the lender. But most lenders do not want to take over and manage commercial properties.

This is not just a hypothetical example; it describes conditions that prevail for thousands of commercial properties across the United States. The situation is even worse for commercial property loans financed by CMBS issuances. For such issues, capital has been lent by hundreds of suppliers for each property involved. Real estate industry groups have been discussing these problems with representatives of the federal government in the hope of gaining some federal aid for property owners caught in these circumstances. As of early 2009, no concrete solutions had been developed. The possibility that thousands of commercial properties will be turned over to those who made loans on them remains an unresolved issue in the nation's financial and commercial property markets.

Moreover, the CMBS sector in early 2009 was in shambles, and it will take years for the sector to recover. Investor trust in the sector has been severely undermined. When the sector is resurrected, it will likely be transformed, offering simpler products with less tranching and much more transparency. A panel of investors at an early 2009 Commercial Mortgage Securitization Association conference held in Miami Beach proposed numerous changes to revitalize the industry, including the following:

- Require issuers to retain 5 to 10 percent of offerings on their own books,
- Set minimum requirements for debt-service-coverage ratios and maximums for loan-to-value ratios,
- Have issuers pay rating agency fees over time and base them on how a deal performs relative to the ratings,
- Discourage issuers from rate shopping, and
- Require more disclosure of information and data on all loans and properties involved.[3]

Clearly, reforms are essential to bring the CMBS industry back to life. Without such reforms and the revival of the industry, a commercial real estate credit shortage could drag on for years.

Private Equity Funds

During the early 2000s, private equity funds raised huge amounts of money from investors and used that cash to buy out existing managements of many private and public corporations, including public REITS. One of the most notable transactions at the high-water mark of the commercial real estate boom was the acquisition of Equity Office Property Trust by the Blackstone Group in 2007. Most private equity funds were motivated primarily by the desire to make high profits in relatively short time periods. So they tended to restructure the firms and sell off the some of the assets relatively quickly, often breaking up those firms and disposing of their assets to separate buyers. This strategy was made possible by the huge amount of capital that was seeking high-profit returns and was willing to accept major risks to get them. It was also made possible by the cheap and plentiful debt that was available at the time. So these firms used heavy leverage strategies to make these deals work to their advantage.

But the financial crisis of 2007–09 greatly reduced the ease of and increased the cost of raising money for such funds, and the leverage strategies they used were no longer viable. It became more difficult for these firms to borrow money at low enough costs to justify going through the complex process of buying out existing firms and restructuring them. Because of the much higher cost of debt today and in the near future, I believe private equity firms will play a much smaller role in the operation of the U.S. economy than they did from 2000 through 2007. However, they are raising capital for new distressed real estate investments and thus will likely play a major role in clearing these assets into new ownership structures at greatly reduced prices. Many new private equity shops are being created following the decline of larger Wall Street firms and investment banks. All of these firms will need to use more equity and less debt to undertake their investments, which will limit their overall impact on the flow of capital into real estate.

Real Estate Investment Trusts

REIT stocks were severely hammered in the fall of 2008 and into 2009. From January 2 to September 22, 2008, the FTSE NAREIT equity index remained relatively flat at about 8,000. But from September 22, 2008, to March 2, 2009, that index plummeted 62.2 percent, compared with losses of 42.9, 41.0, and 38.6 percent for the Dow Jones Industrials, S&P 500, and NASDAQ, respectively. In the opinion of most experts, as of early March 2009, REIT stock values are well below the net asset values of the properties held by REITs. Therefore, if and when the economy begins to recover, REIT shares may be excellent bargains at their present levels.

However, some REITs with heavy debt rollover schedules in 2009 and even 2010 may have difficulty finding the funds to pay the higher interest rates and achieve the lower loan-to-value ratios that their lenders will be demanding. But in many cases, the lenders will not want to take over the properties themselves, but will provide forbearance as long as REITs pay both interest and dividends.

Over the longer term, REITs will remain viable players in the real estate and financial markets and are in relatively stronger positions than many other real estate players, because most of them have reasonable debt levels and they are strong operators. Some REITs that used too much leverage will suffer and may not survive the crisis. In general, REITs will likely recover sooner than private real estate owners, and REITs will likely be early and aggressive buyers of property once markets stabilize and begin to recover. The lack of new commercial real estate construction is also favorable for an increase in REIT share prices when markets stabilize.

Life Insurance Companies

Most insurance companies have suffered big losses in real estate, especially from declines in asset values. Some were still making a few mortgage loans in the $20 to $70 million range in the latter part of 2008, but at interest rates in the 7 to 8 percent range and with loan-to-value ratios no larger than 60 percent. Those loans will be held on a portfolio basis until each loan is paid off. Insurance companies will make larger loans only if they can syndicate them with a few other insurance companies with which they are familiar. However, insurance companies are no longer in the CMBS markets, which were in effect dead as of early 2009.

Historically, most life insurance companies have allocated relatively small amounts of their capital to real estate. Mortgage loans and real estate holdings constituted only 7.3 percent of the $5.091 trillion in assets held by life companies at the end of 2007, according to the American Council of Life Insurers. Their allocations to real estate lending have been cut back in 2009, in view of the large losses they experienced in 2008 and 2009. So, many may run out of funds to lend in real estate early in 2009. However, they can dictate very favorable spreads and terms for the loans they do make. However, they will not be substantially increasing their real estate lending, and reports in early 2009 suggested that they were reducing their lending, which means life insurance companies will not play a significant role in replacing the debt capital previously supplied through the CMBS sector.[4]

Pension Funds

Pension funds were the largest group of institutional investors in 2006. They held $10.4 trillion, or 38.3 percent, of the total assets of $27.15 trillion held by all institutional investors in that year, according to the Conference Board. The largest group among pension funds consisted of state and local government funds; the second largest group consisted of private corporate pension funds.

According to the Watson Wyatt Worldwide 2009 Global Pension Assets Study, total pension assets in the 11 largest pension areas, which contain 85 percent of world pension savings, shrank by about $5 trillion in 2008, from $25 trillion to $20 trillion, a drop of about 19 percent. At the end of 2008, pension assets amounted to about 61 percent of the average GDP of the nations studied, down from 72 percent ten years ago. The United States contains about 61 percent of all pension fund assets, with Japan next at 13 percent and the United Kingdom third at 9 percent.

Although pension fund holdings grew in 2007, they were reduced by the general financial crisis in 2008. Most pension funds suffered major losses in real estate markets in 2008 and are losing still more in 2009. They have not substantially increased their real estate holdings for over ten years. As of early 2009, many were suffering from the "denominator effect," which means they were overallocated to real estate because the value of their real estate assets did not decrease as much as the value of their stock market assets. Hence many will not have large amounts to invest in real properties in 2009 and even 2010. Vestiges of the paradigm shift toward investments in real estate that took place after the stock market crash in 2000 have now almost disappeared.

Decline of Housing-Financed Consumption

The deleveraging of household finances will have direct impacts on retail real estate. Retail properties will be affected by a decline in consumer spending resulting not only from the recession, but also in part from the inability to borrow against net equity in homes. That tactic was widely used by homeowners when home prices were rising rapidly. As noted earlier, from 1960 through 1999, consumer spending averaged 63 to 67.5 percent of real GDP. Heavily influenced by that borrowed home equity, personal consumption averaged 70.4 percent of real GDP from 2000 to 2006 and rose to 71.7 percent in the second quarter of 2007. Households' net equity in real estate fell from 57 percent of their real estate assets in 2001 to 46.2 percent in the first quarter of 2008, partly as a result of increased home equity borrowing. Mortgage borrowing also increased in the same period, from 43 percent of real estate assets held by households and nonprofits (almost entirely by households) in 2001 to 53.8 percent in the first quarter of 2008. Even after home prices stop falling, they will not rise fast enough in the foreseeable future to permit homeowners to gain ever-increasing amounts of net equity against which to borrow in order to finance more general consumption.[5]

Therefore, personal consumption as a percentage of real GDP ought to decline in the future below the high levels it reached in 2007. This trend will be harmful to firms in the shopping center and retail businesses in particular. However, such a shift in spending will actually benefit the U.S. economy in the long run because American consumers have been outspending their incomes since the mid-1990s. The federal government has been outspending its income, too. The resulting two types of deficits have been the main causes of our massive negative balance of payments with other nations. Reducing consumer spending as a percentage of real GDP would help restore a better balance in U.S. economic performance—but only if the nation compensates for that fall in spending by increasing its savings and its spending on investment. Savings ought to rise both as households reduce their consumption and increase personal savings, and as the federal government cuts some spending and reduces its annual deficits.

This basic long-run shift in the composition of the nation's overall product and its use will be difficult to achieve for two reasons. First, reducing American spending on consumption is the opposite of what the government wants Americans to do in the near future, because more consumption spending will help the nation get out of the current recession. As economist Jim Griffin put it:

> We're in this mess because we borrowed and spent too much, so the way out is to borrow and spend much more. . . . It's a problem akin to one of those Zen puzzlers about holding two opposing thoughts in the mind at the same time; it may be analytically correct but it seems contradictory.[6]

The second reason is that a large part of the nation's population will retire in the next decade and thereby generate rising health care costs. With both Social Security and health care costs going up, the federal government will have difficulty reducing its seemingly chronic deficits. Nevertheless, I believe that trying to make this shift in our long-run economic behavior is an effort well worth pursuing.

Speculation on Rising Asset Prices

During the 2000s, the U.S. economy has gone through two bubble or bubble-like periods in asset markets. Such periods occur when strong market demand for a particular type of asset drives up its price much faster than its actual earning power. Eventually, the price of that type of asset gets so far out of range of its true economic value that the bubble bursts and the prices of that type of asset fall sharply. That happened in the late 1990s with Internet and other tech stocks, leading to the stock market crash of 2000. The same type of behavior then shifted to real estate, especially housing, driving up the prices of homes spectacularly from 2000 to 2006. Now that the financial crisis has blocked the type of borrowing necessary to fuel such a process, it is not likely that heavy speculation in real estate—whether housing or commercial—will soon cause another sharp increase in real property prices.

However, there is still a lot of capital in the world looking for some way to earn high returns over relatively short periods. Unless the general stock market returns to another period of irrational exuberance, that money will not soon generate another asset price bubble in either stocks or real estate. True, the same money may shift to other types of assets, such as gold or commodities or even food production, as has seemed to occur in a mild way in the past two years. However, they will not absorb enough capital to generate significant bubbles comparable with those of 2000 or 2007–09.

As a result, the greater skepticism of investors the world over toward putting funds into assets about which they know little seems likely to dampen any near-future generation of another asset-based bubble like the two described above. Assuming Minsky was correct in his analysis of business-cycle psychology, it will take another relatively long period of continuous prosperity to generate enough optimism about prevailing economic conditions to motivate investors to adopt the herd-like behavior needed to make another asset-pricing boom a reality.

Increased Importance of Asset and Firm Management

Real estate in recent years has been a business heavily influenced by dealmakers and speculators, who focus on relatively short-term transactions that produce quick profits. But in times of restricted credit availability, declining property income, and falling property values, another aspect of real estate activity comes to the fore: skilled management of existing properties and assets, rather than transactions involving property or asset turnovers. When money is scarce, those who know how to use their limited funds to maximum positive effects in their ongoing operations will do better than those looking for another fast deal. The near future appears to be a period when good management of existing assets will be of primary importance to any investor's prosperity.

Financial management will be an especially important aspect of good overall management. Real estate has always been a business in which borrowing and the management of debt are more critical to success than in most businesses. That is mainly because creating real properties is very costly and capital intensive and those properties typically last a long time. Therefore, it is almost always necessary to borrow money to get real estate properties going and to manage the resulting debt over long periods. This current period of credit scarcity certainly emphasizes the need for careful financial planning.

Managing these properties efficiently will be critical in this environment. Doing so will require increased focus on operating cost reduction, energy efficiency, tenant retention, aggressive leasing strategies, effective marketing and promotion, and strategic investments in property improvements and repositioning. In short, asset management will be the name of the game.

Changing Public and Private Roles in the American Economy

The sharp decline in levels of real estate prices and transactions in the nation's markets, plus the financial strains on state and local governments from both lower values and transaction levels and a major recession, plus the very active roles of federal government agencies in trying to overcome both the financial crisis and the recession—all these factors will profoundly affect the future roles played by both government and the private sector in the American economic system. In general, there will be a shift of power and importance from state and local governments and the private sector to various parts of the federal government. This shift will mainly be caused by three factors:

■ State and local governments are finding some of their most important sources of revenue shrinking sharply because of lower transaction levels, lower property values, less consumption spending, and less private investment activity—all caused by a combination of the financial crisis and the recession. Property taxes, sales taxes, state and local income taxes, and transaction taxes are all important sources of funding for state and local government activities. Yet all have been undercut by declining economic activities in state and local jurisdictions. Many local and state governments have large fixed expenses owing to long-term labor contracts and fixed operating costs for schools, transportation systems, regulatory activities, hospitals, medical care programs, and cultural activities. Yet their incomes from the tax sources mentioned above have fallen precipitously, leaving them in precarious financial condition. Many local governments are close to bankruptcy because they cannot reduce their long-term labor contracts and other expenses to match their huge declines in current revenues. Some states, such as California, have annual budget shortfalls for the 2008–09 fiscal year amounting to many billions of dollars, even though their constitutions prohibit them from running current deficits.[7] This situation has arisen at the state level because many states that experienced large increases in revenues during long periods of prosperity mistakenly assumed that those high revenue levels were permanent. Therefore, they used those high revenues as bases for permanent expansions of state spending programs. When the recession occurred and their revenues declined, they had great difficulties cutting back on the new programs they had established. Similar behavior is common among local governments too.

■ The federal government's ability to run large current deficits gives it the ability to create large new spending programs to help stimulate the economy and provide needed funds to state and local governments. This tends to increase the relative power of the federal government during periods of national recession or other emergencies, such as major wars. It is quite likely that such a shift in the relative power of various parts of our governmental structure will occur again over at least the next few years while we are coping with both the financial crisis and the recession. Over the decades, this situation has caused a creeping expansion of both the relative and the absolute power of the federal government and its many agencies into many facets of national economic and social life. This has occurred partly because once the federal government assumes responsibility for some activity, the beneficiaries of that activity develop a vested interest in maintaining federal supports, even after the immediate need for federal participation has passed. Hence, they form a lobbying group to perpetuate that activity at the federal level or at least to perpetuate federal funding of state and local activities.

■ The increase in federal regulation of the financial sector that is sure to take place in the next few years in response to the failings of the private financial sector will shift the balance of power in economic affairs and policies away from the private sector toward the national government. This shift will by no means transform the American economy completely away from its allegiance to a private, free-enterprise orientation toward a more socialized orientation. But it will increase the powers of federal agencies both in influencing fundamental policies of the economy and in funding key aspects of those policies, as compared with similar powers formerly exercised mainly by private organizations. As noted in chapter 5, this shift is part of two long-term movements: a cyclical shift every 15 years or so in policy dominance from conservative interests to more liberal interests, and a slower long-term trend toward increasingly expanded roles of federal agencies in the economic life of the nation. During the next decade, both movements will increase the importance of national government policies and funding in the overall activities of the American economy, especially as compared with the relatively deregulated atmosphere that dominated from about 1980 until 2008.

These changes in the American economy will amount to a significant long-run modification of the entire capitalist system, not only in the United States, but around the globe. National governments have become the major economic forces in most of the world's economies. Those economies now depend upon national government actions to make up for the virtual collapse of activity in financial markets and the underlying economies that support most citizens. The belief that private interests can operate all aspects of a major economy with minimal government support or "interference" has been destroyed by the severity of the global recession we are now experiencing.

Yet it is still true that governments are handicapped by many shortcomings that limit their ability to provide the innovation and experimentation that have historically made capitalism so successful in raising living standards around the world. Governments in most developed nations are dominated by political considerations that limit their ability to initiate major changes in the status quo. Every developed nation and most emerging ones need the inspiration, innovation, initiatives, and creativity that come from private actors pursuing their own interests in a larger context. Politically, the "creative destruction" that Joseph Schumpeter regarded as the great strength of capitalism has always been too change-oriented—and therefore highly upsetting to millions of people—to gain much government support in democracies. The major impetus for the creativity that has raised living standards in modern nations has come from private sector innovations and developments. But the past few years have demonstrated that leaving all markets to be dominated by purely private actors without much government regulation can lead to tremendous disasters over the whole world.

It is not yet clear exactly what type of mixture of strong national governments and strong private actors will emerge from the financial crisis. I believe that both elements are crucial to economic success and freedom in the long run. However, I also believe we are in for a period in which much more power within democracies is shifted to national governments than has been typical of life in the past century, outside of wartime. It will take an immense resurgence of private initiatives and innovations to return the U.S. economy and many others to the appropriate balance of powers among these types of key actors. It will also take a clear recognition by government leaders of the limitations of national government powers to resuscitate a weakened economy and of the need to stimulate a rejuvenation of the private sectors of the world's economies. So we are in for a considerable time of experimentation and innovation by both governments and private actors that will call forth the best efforts and greatest imagination of everyone involved.

A New Financial Era

In my earlier book, *Niagara of Capital*, I pointed out that the huge flow of capital into real estate that pushed real estate prices upward in the early 2000s could not last forever and might not last much longer than late 2007, when the book was published. In fact, the big inflow of capital was beginning to end as I wrote those words. The same message is relevant to how long the current financial crisis will last. It will surely not last forever and might even end soon. But in this chapter I argue that the most probable outcome would be a prolonged financial crisis over at least one more year and perhaps two to three more years.

Even after the financial crisis is over, and borrowing money for real estate becomes possible again on reasonable terms, some of the effects of the current shortage of available funds will remain in force. Therefore, it behooves anyone interested in real estate to be aware of both the current conditions affecting credit availability and the longer-run consequences likely to endure after the financial crisis itself has ended. The era of abundant capital, easy credit, poor underwriting, and rapid real estate gains is long gone and will not return any time soon. For real estate investors, lenders, owners, and developers, a reversion to more conservative and prudent approaches to real estate investment and finance will govern activities going forward. I hope this book has contributed to a better understanding of both the path we have been on and the path we need to be on in this new era.

NOTES

1. Martin Wolf, *Fixing Global Finance* (Baltimore: Johns Hopkins University Press, 2009), page 169
2. Wolf, page 195.
3. "Investors Urge Sweeping Changes in CMBS," *Commercial Mortgage Alert*, January 16, 2009, pages 1-2.
4. "Many Insurers Halt Lending as Crisis Widens," *Commercial Mortgage Alert*, March 6, 2009, pages 1, 6.
5. Data from the Federal Reserve Board *Flow of Funds Accounts of the United States* for June 5, 2008, Balance Sheet of Households and Nonprofit Organizations.
6. James Griffin, "Urgency from the Bully Pulpit Re: Economic Recovery," *ING Investment Weekly*, January 12, 2009, page 4.
7. Evan Halper, "California's Budget Gap at $16 Billion," *Los Angeles Times*, February 21, 2008. On the internet at http://latimes.com/news/local/la-me-budget21feb21,0,6427050.story.